D0753188

2006

APR 1 2 2006

John Soane
Architect

Master
of Space
and Light

Master of Space and Light

Edited by
Margaret
Richardson
and
MaryAnne
Stevens

Royal
Academy
of Arts,
London

John Soane
Architect

Figure 1 (pages 2–3)
Joseph Michael Gandy,
Public and Private
Buildings Executed by
Sir John Soane…, 1818,
detail (cat. 210)

Figure 2 (page 4)
Christopher William
Hunneman, Portrait
of John Soane, 1776,
detail (cat. 1)

First published on the occasion of the exhibition
'John Soane, Architect: Master of Space and Light'

Royal Academy of Arts, London, 11 September – 3 December 1999

Sponsored by

IBSTOCK

The Royal Academy of Arts is grateful to Her Majesty's Government for its help
in agreeing to indemnify the exhibition under the National Heritage Act 1980, and
to the Museums and Galleries Commission for its help in arranging this indemnity.

Any copy of this book issued by the publisher as a paperback is sold subject to
the condition that it shall not by way of trade or otherwise be lent, resold, hired
out or otherwise circulated without the publisher's prior consent in any form of
binding or cover other than that in which it is published and without a similar
condition including these words being imposed on a subsequent purchaser.

All Rights Reserved. No part of this publication may be reproduced or
transmitted in any form or by any means, electronic or mechanical, including
photocopy, recording or any other information storage and retrieval system,
without prior permission in writing from the publisher.

British Library Cataloguing-in-Publication Data
A catalogue record for this book is available from the British Library

Library of Congress Catalog Card Number: 99-66155

Copyright © Royal Academy of Arts, London

ISBN
0-900-94680-6   (Royal Academy paperback)
0-300-01895-2   (Royal Academy hardback distributed by Yale University Press)

Catalogue design by Esterson Lackersteen

Printed in Italy

Editors' Note
All drawings are by the Soane
office, unless otherwise stated.
In many cases it has been
possible to identify Soane's
hand, or the hands of his pupils.

Dimensions are given in
millimetres, height before
width. Model dimensions
are given in millimetres
(or centimetres), height
before width before depth.

A Soane Museum reference
number (e.g. SM Vol. 42, p. 37)
follows each work lent by the
Trustees of Sir John Soane's
Museum.

Authors responsible for the
catalogue entries are indicated
as follows:
DA Daniel Abramson
SA Stephen Astley
BC Barry Clayton
PD Ptolemy Dean
HD Helen Dorey
HE Heather Ewing
JL Jill Lever
SP Susan Palmer
MR Margaret Richardson
NS Nick Savage
SS Sean Sawyer
GW Giles Waterfield
DW David Watkin
JW John Wibberley
CW Christopher Woodward

Contents

Sponsor's Preface

Ibstock Building Products wishes to thank the Royal Academy for the chance to participate in celebrating the work of Sir John Soane. Throughout its hundred-year history, Ibstock has worked closely with architects to produce the materials that incorporate their vision for the built environment.

Soane, the son of a builder and the brother of a journeyman bricklayer, understood the nature of his materials and wanted others to see them as he did. He often created imaginative pathways of natural light into his buildings to reveal the true colours and textures of his surfaces. He incorporated brick in most of his projects, often manufacturing it on site. By using local clays, the brick reflected the colour, tone and quality of its neighbourhood.

Not all of our customers have proved as demanding as Soane must have been, but when their projects have required unusual materials in size, shape, colour or texture, they have often turned to Ibstock as the nation's largest manufacturer of clay brick and terracotta products to supply their needs. The Academy's exhibition helps to remind us that, through the vision of a great architect, humble materials can find triumphant application.

Philip Mengel
Chief Executive
Ibstock Building Products Ltd

President's Foreword

John Soane RA was a person of uncommon distinction, a creator of spaces. Architect, teacher, collector and innovator, he produced over some fifty years of practice a body of work which has continued to inspire leading architects of today, from Philip Johnson and Richard Meier to Arata Isozaki and Tadeo Ando. Schooled in the classical style by George Dance the Younger and inspired by Piranesi's powerful vision of the Antique, Soane extended the range of Neoclassicism. He reinvented the traditional language of the classical orders, radically orchestrated sequences of internal spaces, flexed the rigidity of traditional axial planning, explored the dramatic effects of indirect light, and uncovered through economic necessity the potential of common stock brick to create novel architectural statements. These elements were encapsulated in Soane's outstanding designs, created over more than forty years, for the Bank of England – alas no longer extant – and in two buildings that have survived demolition: Dulwich Picture Gallery and his own house in Lincoln's Inn Fields. As Professor of Architecture at the Royal Academy Schools from 1806 to 1837, Soane both transmitted to his students the essential elements of the European Enlightenment and sought to make relevant to his own age the achievements of classical architecture. As collector he amassed in his home in Lincoln's Inn Fields (now Sir John Soane's Museum) a collection of objects, from sculptures to paintings and architectural fragments, which he displayed with ingenuity and to dramatic effect.

Soane had a long association with the Royal Academy of Arts. He entered the Schools as an architecture student in 1771, obtained a Gold Medal for his design for a Triumphal Bridge in 1776 and won a travelling scholarship in 1777 which permitted him to visit France and Italy, two countries whose architectural heritage was to prove decisive in the formation of his own architectural idiom. He was elected an Associate Member of the Royal Academy in 1795, becoming a full Academician in 1802. He subsequently acted as Professor for thirty-one years. It is therefore fitting that this first major retrospective exhibition of his work should be shown here at the Royal Academy.

This exhibition could not have been realised without the close collaboration established between the Royal Academy and Sir John Soane's Museum. The Museum's trustees have generously allowed us to borrow freely from their remarkable archive of drawings, models and memorabilia. The Museum's staff, notably Margaret Richardson, Helen Dorey and Christopher Woodward, have provided essential curatorial and organisational input into the exhibition and the creation of the accompanying catalogue. They have worked closely with MaryAnne Stevens at the Royal Academy. Other lenders have also been most generous in their willingness to make available crucial works. We are much in their debt.

The Royal Academy seeks to present architecture in an accessible form. To achieve this, inspired exhibition design is required and significant funds needed for its realisation. Piers Gough has undoubtedly provided the former, and our many sponsors and supporters the latter. In particular, we extend our sincere thanks to Ibstock Building Products Ltd for its sponsorship of the exhibition. Our thanks also go to our other supporters, notably Morgan Stanley Dean Witter and the Casson Fund of the American Associates of the Royal Academy Trust, whose involvement is much appreciated. We acknowledge too the ongoing support guaranteed to our architecture programme by the Hon. Mrs Drue Heinz's generous Endowment for Architecture. In addition, through the dedication and commitment of two Academicians, Richard MacCormac and Edward Cullinan, significant funds have been received from a number of architects, many of them Members of the Royal Academy. We thank them all.

Sir Philip Dowson CBE
President, Royal Academy of Arts

ARCHITECTURAL
Visions of Early Fancy
In the gay morning of youth
And dreams in the evening of age

Exhibition Organisation

Figure 3 (pages 10–11)
Architectural Visions of Early Fancy..., drawn by Joseph Michael Gandy, 1820 (detail of cat. 211)

Figure 4 (pages 14–15)
Aerial cutaway view of the Bank of England from the south-east, drawn by Joseph Michael Gandy, 1830 (detail of cat. 119)

Executive Committee
Ptolemy Dean
Helen Dorey
Margaret Richardson
Christopher Woodward
Sir John Soane's Museum

MaryAnne Stevens
Royal Academy of Arts

Advisory Committee
Dr Daniel Abramson
Barry Clayton
Gillian Darley
John Harris
Dr Robin Middleton
Dr Sean Sawyer
Giles Waterfield
Dr David Watkin
John Wibberley

Exhibition Organiser
Annette Bradshaw

Exhibition Design
Piers Gough of CZWG
with Howard Sullivan

Exhibition Installation
Nick Delo

Conservation
Margaret Schuelein
with Jane Bush and Kate Edmundson

Models
Foster and Partners
Andrew Ingham & Associates
Peter Mullan and Thomas Gluck
George Rome Innes and students at the Kent Institute of Art and Design

Plans
Christopher Hawkesworth Woodward

Computer Installation
Professor Robert Tavernor, Bath University, with Henry Choo

Film
Murray Grigor

Special Photography
Paul Barker for *Country Life*
Richard Bryant
Geremy Butler
Martin Charles

Acknowledgements
and Lenders to the Exhibition

Acknowledgements

The Executive Committee extends its thanks to the members of the Advisory Committee for their contributions to the shaping of the exhibition in its initial stages, and to Tom Phillips RA, Chairman of the Exhibitions Committee of the Royal Academy of Arts, and Norman Rosenthal, Exhibitions Secretary, for their enthusiastic and unswerving support for the exhibition. In addition, the Executive Committee would like to acknowledge with thanks the advice and support of Clive Aslet, Alan Borg, Charles Hind, John Keyworth, Phyllis Lambert, Susan Lambert, Jill Lever, Catherine Rickman, Nicholas Savage, Desmond Shawe-Taylor, Michael Snodin, John Studzinski, Adam Waterton and Andrew Wilton. Thanks are due to David Breuer, Sophie Lawrence, Peter Sawbridge and Nick Tite of Royal Academy Publications. The staff of Sir John Soane's Museum have all been engaged in assisting with the preparation of the exhibition, including Stephen Astley, Claire Chalvet, Catherine Draycott, Jean Duffield, Heather Ewing, Judith Maher, Susan Palmer, Lucy Porten and Roderick Smith. Invaluable support for the exhibition has also come from Edward Cullinan RA, Terry Farrell, Lord Foster RA, Nicholas Grimshaw RA, Sir Michael Hopkins RA, Richard MacCormac RA, Michael Manser RA, John Miller, Lord Rogers RA and Michael Wilford.

Lenders to the Exhibition

LONDON
The Governor and Company of the Bank of England
British Architectural Library, Drawings Collection, RIBA
British Architectural Library, Early Imprints Collection, RIBA
Royal Academy of Arts
Commissioners of the Royal Hospital, Chelsea
The Trustees of Sir John Soane's Museum
Tate Gallery
The Victoria and Albert Museum

S. C. Whitbread, Esq.

The Royal Academy of Arts is also grateful to the following for their generous support of the exhibition:

PRINCIPAL SUPPORTER
Morgan Stanley Dean Witter

MAJOR SUPPORTERS
Country Life
Foster and Partners
Michael Hopkins & Partners
Richard and Ruth Rogers
Strutt & Parker

SUPPORTERS
Arup Associates
Aukett Associates
Building Design Partnership
Edward Cullinan Architects
Terry Farrell & Partners
FaulknerBrowns
GMW Partnership
Nicholas Grimshaw & Partners
Robert Holden Ltd
Manser Associates
John Miller & Partners
Richard Murphy Architects
The Ove Arup Foundation
Michael Wilford and Partners Limited

Soane: The Man and His Circle

Figure 5 (opposite)
Nathaniel Dance, Portrait of
Soane at the age of twenty-
one, c. 1774 (SM P317)

Figure 6
Section of All Hallows,
London Wall, by Brinsley
Storace (a pupil of Soane's
1804–07), 1806 (Guildhall
Library, Corporation of
London)

The triumphant transformation of John Soan (*sic*), a country bricklayer's son born in 1753, into Sir John Soane, the senior figure in the architectural profession, knighted by King William IV in 1831, was an arduous journey, despite its great rewards.

Soane (fig. 5), who added the 'e' to his name around his thirtieth birthday and acquired a coat of arms soon after that, saw his humble birth as his greatest disadvantage. Yet even at fifteen, carrying bricks for his elder brother, something marked him out. In 1768 he was introduced, by the surveyor (and sometime author) James Peacock, to the up-and-coming young man in the London architectural world, George Dance the Younger (fig. 94), who had just inherited his father's post as architect to the City. Between them, Dance and Peacock gave Soane, so avid for education and opportunity, the chance to fulfil his signs of promise.

Dance was an original and innovative architect, whose designs, such as those for All Hallows, London Wall (fig. 6), were to be a source of inspiration for Soane. A Founder Member of the Royal Academy of Arts, Dance helped Soane to become a student there in 1771 and the following year encouraged him to move to the office of 'an eminent builder in extensive practice'.[1] Henry Holland was both an architect and a speculative builder and employed Soane as a clerk at £60 per annum, suggesting that he had already learned fast and well under Dance and Peacock's tutelage.

As Soane soon realised, Dance and Holland had both gained their professional status through advantages of birth. Mid-Georgian architecture was peppered with dynasties. Soane not only learned about architectural

FIGURE 6

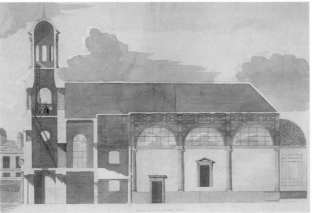

practice from Dance and Holland's offices but also discovered much about the operation of patronage. From now on, his considerable ambition dominated everything; as he later put it, 'My unfortunate attachment to Architecture is as difficult to be extinguished as a passion for play in the mind of a professed gambler!'[2]

At twenty-four, Soane embarked for Rome, then considered the fountainhead of architectural inspiration, with a travelling scholarship from the Royal Academy. His journey to Paris and Rome, and on to Naples and Sicily, between 1778 and 1780, completed his architectural education and set him up for life. Even almost twenty years later his extraordinary success 'much depending upon his own instinctive industry and merit'[3] remained the envy of young architects abroad. In just eighteen months, Soane found the men who would become his patrons, clients and firm friends. He drew and measured the buildings which would serve as a lifetime's architectural source material and achieved a hard-won social and intellectual confidence. In Rome he met the Bishop of Derry (fig. 7), the most famous (even notorious) Grand Tourist of all; soon they were travelling together to Naples and beyond. Soane even learned to relax with his friends as they toured Sicily for, as John Patteson from Norwich wrote to his mother, 'we are never together but we are as merry as it is possible, everyone has his hobby horse and whipping them now and then creates many a good laugh'.[4] Greek temples and plagues of fleas, spectacular Baroque interiors and nights spent in monastic cells were still the subject of happy reminiscence between Soane and Rowland Burdon, another of the party, almost sixty years later.

Yet nothing would ever be effortless for Soane. On the way back to England, he lost the contents of his trunk, and even his precious Gold Medal from the Royal Academy. His laborious self-education and his attempts to become a polished draughtsman and to become socially adept were all time-consuming but remarkably fruitful. Soane's talents lay in his quick absorption of motifs and plan forms, his ability to rework favourite forms into innumerable subtle variants and his willingness doggedly to rework a design until it fell into shape; the results rarely betray the arduous process. Underpinning everything lay his knowledge and understanding of the building process which allowed him, long before he could employ any assistance, to provide detailed specifications and accurate estimates. He was as businesslike on insignificant jobs as he was on the largest

FIGURE 7   FIGURE 8

Figure 7
Hugh Douglas Hamilton,
Portrait of Frederick
Hervey, Bishop of Derry,
with His Grand-daughter,
c. 1790–93, detail (The
National Gallery of Ireland)

Figure 8
Joshua Reynolds, Portrait
of Thomas Pitt, 1764, detail
(Private Collection)

of commissions. He knew the value of a trusted team of skilled tradesmen and of a steady clerk of works, and his professionalism and support of his workforce, in prompt payment as much as in kindly encouragement, kept them utterly loyal. Similarly, his clients often came back. Several of his private jobs stretched over decades and two generations of the same family, while his most stupendous achievement, the Bank of England, was to be a forty-five-year appointment.

Summoned prematurely and peremptorily back from Rome by the new fourth Earl of Bristol, the Bishop of Derry, Soane must have imagined that a commission to work at Downhill in County Derry would launch his architectural career. It was to be a baptism of fire. Soane conscientiously and professionally made the Earl-Bishop face the fact that his rough Irish residence was no 'Tusculanum', Pliny's villa bathed in Mediterranean sunlight, but a bleak house facing due north into the Atlantic gales. Always a demanding patron, the Earl-Bishop surpassed even his own standards of unreasonableness. He appeared to follow the logic of Soane's reasoning one day and the next reverted to notions of his own. The classical dog kennel and elegant summer dining room which they had discussed under happier conditions in Italy were not to be. Soane left Downhill in despair after six weeks, his experiences pitifully recorded in great detail in his notebook;[5] the Earl-Bishop paid no more than a small contribution to his expenses and Soane returned to the mainland, bitterly disappointed and with no prospects.

The foundations of the practice which Soane laboriously built up over the following four years were laid, directly or indirectly, in Italy. Of the five companions who set off with him to Sicily in the spring of 1779, four became clients. He soon had an enviable country-house practice, particularly in Norfolk where he also obtained some public work. At the same time he was building up contacts, and jobs, to the east of London where bankers and City men breathed fresh air, in villages such as Walthamstow and Leyton. Finally, among the aristocratic Grand Tourists he had met, Soane replaced the false promises and fantasies of the Earl-Bishop with the solid patronage of two intelligent and discerning clients, Philip Yorke and Thomas Pitt (fig. 8).

In 1782, the twenty-three-year old William Pitt the Younger, Thomas Pitt's cousin, became Chancellor of the Exchequer. A year later he was First Minister. The timing

suited Soane perfectly; a new generation of the 'cousinage' – as the politically powerful Grenville and Temple families were known – was rising and Soane was perfectly placed to net literally dozens of jobs. His astuteness lay in looking ahead and identifying in whose hands the gifts of patronage were likely to be.

By 1784, Soane already felt secure enough professionally to embark upon the courtship of Elizabeth (Eliza) Smith (fig. 9), the charming and acute niece of George Wyatt, a prosperous City builder, who was also her guardian. In August Soane and Eliza married and by September Soane had taken on his first pupil.

Between 1786 and 1791 Eliza gave birth to four sons, two of whom – John, the first, and George, the third – survived infancy. In 1792, helped by a substantial legacy from George Wyatt, Soane purchased 12 Lincoln's Inn Fields and rebuilt it, to serve as both home and office. In his determinedly professional record, his printed *Memoirs*,[6] hardly a whisper of home life emerges, while his terse notebooks are similarly almost entirely confined to office matters, apart from occasional explosions of anger or self-pity (the latter a strong strand in Soane's character). Eliza Soane's more discursive correspondence and later notebooks reveal a few more glimpses of their lives together.

By 1786, Soane was working as William Pitt's personal architect on his country house, Holwood, near Bromley in Kent. Access to the Prime Minister, a younger man than he, was invaluable to Soane and he paid fifteen visits to Holwood that year, far more than strictly necessary for a modest programme of improvements. That privileged relationship with William Pitt, and encouragement from Lord Camelford (as Thomas Pitt had become), led to Soane's first major public appointment to the prestigious post of Surveyor to the Bank of England in October 1788, on the death of Sir Robert Taylor. Typically, Soane had not relied on just one voice to argue his case at the Bank and already counted several directors among his clients, most importantly Samuel Bosanquet, who became Governor in 1789.

But the greatest prize awaiting an architect at this time remained the rebuilding of the Houses of Parliament, together with the law courts and other departments, then housed in and around Westminster Hall in a shambles of largely medieval structures, some too derelict for use. Wren, Hawksmoor, Kent and Burlington had all designed schemes, but nothing had materialised.

Figure 9
John Flaxman, Sketch
portrait of Eliza Soane,
c. 1800–05 (SM P225)

FIGURE 9

Figure 10
Exterior perspective of
a design by Soane for the
House of Lords, 1794
(SM P273)

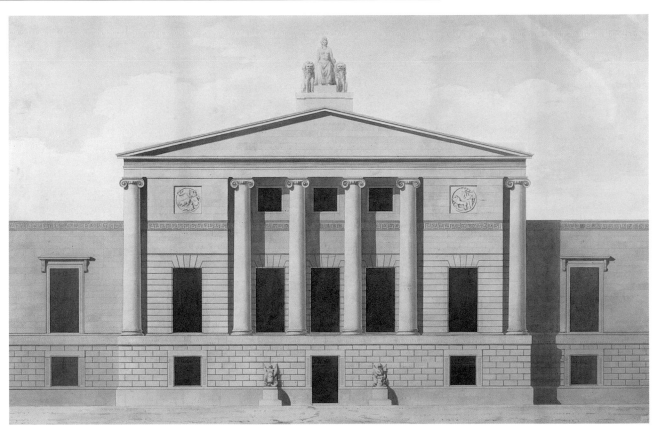

FIGURE 10

Soane had been toying with the idea of a British Senate House even before leaving for Rome, and while there, he had developed the subject as his exhibit for the Royal Academy in 1779. In 1789 Soane, with others, was asked by a House of Commons committee to survey the buildings around Westminster Hall. Soane spotted his chance. In 1790 he became Clerk of Works under Sir William Chambers, the Surveyor-General of the Office of Works, with responsibility for St James's, Whitehall and Westminster.

Meanwhile Soane was building up a useful and impressive list of private clients: in the early 1790s he was working for Joseph Smith, Pitt's private secretary; for George Rose, the key man at the Treasury; and for several of the most influential men in the House of Lords – the Duke of Leeds, the Marquis of Buckingham and the third Earl Hardwicke, the former Philip Yorke. Soane was adeptly manoeuvring himself into pole position.

Despite these preparations, in the autumn of 1793 Soane was mortified to be asked to supply plans of Westminster to thirteen architects – his own role as Clerk of Works

meant that he was excluded. He suddenly became as dilatory in his Office of Works post[7] as he had been conscientious and the enraged Chambers dismissed him. Soane, now unconstrained, reinforced his contacts with important men in both the Treasury and the House of Lords, and was soon asked to carry out much needed improvements to the heating and ventilation there, presenting the scheme in a set of exceptionally elegant sections.[8] So satisfactory was his handling of this small job, which he estimated at a modest £250, that a committee of the Lords, chaired by the Duke of Leeds, commissioned him (in the vaguest of terms) to draw up proposals for a full-scale remodelling.[9]

The designs for a complete rebuilding of the House of Lords in the form of a Roman senate house on the banks of the Thames absorbed Soane and his office for many months (fig. 10). He circulated the finished drawings to anyone with influence, including the King to whom he paid a personal visit at Windsor. Then, without warning, Lord Grenville informed Soane that at this time of war with France the country could not afford his scheme,

Figure 11
Design for the front façade
of Pitzhanger Manor,
Ealing, 1800. Mr and Mrs
Soane and the two boys
are depicted waiting to
greet visitors whose coach
is drawing up before the
house (SM 14/2/3)

FIGURE 11

estimated at £124,600 and represented by 270 plans, elevations and drawings.[10]

The following year, 1795, Soane was invited back to work for Pitt at Holwood. He continued to hope for the best. Encouragingly, in December 1798 Lord Grenville recalled his designs but Soane soon discovered that the King's favourite, the charming but dilatory James Wyatt, had submitted a design in the King's now-preferred style, the Gothic. As Farington, the ubiquitous diarist commented, George III knew Soane's 'peculiarities' well and 'there can be no apprehension of future works being trusted to a bad taste'.[11]

Soane's response to the missed opportunity was to print an aggrieved pamphlet[12] about his rough treatment and year after year to pour out an unrelenting stream of different designs for seats of government on the walls of the Royal Academy. Almost thirty years later, in his capacity as one of three Attached Architects at the Office of Works, again responsible for Whitehall and Westminster, Soane finally built the Scala Regia and Royal Gallery, a Processional Route by which King George IV

could enter the House of Lords: in 1831 he gave evidence to the Select Committee which was considering the rebuilding of the House of Commons and in 1833 he was among those approached to submit designs for a lower house, which he duly did. The fire at the Palace of Westminster soon sealed the fate of both Houses. No single episode in Soane's career illustrates quite as clearly his blend of political skills and tenacity in achieving an objective.

In 1800 Soane embarked upon the most personal of his architectural projects when he bought and rebuilt Pitzhanger Manor in Ealing (fig. 11, cat. 60), then a country village a few miles west of London, the scene of his earliest work with George Dance. His object was to inspire his sons to follow him into architecture. They were, respectively, fourteen and ten years old. Before Pitzhanger was completed Soane employed Joseph Michael Gandy to draw perspectives of the house, inside and out. Gandy's renderings of Soane's work seemed to give him new confidence: the imagery of Soane's architecture was now conveyed through Gandy's eye – much as a modern

Figure 12
William Owen, Portrait of
Soane's two sons, John
(right) and George (left),
1805. John is wearing his
Cambridge University gown
(SM P229)

FIGURE 12

Figure 13
Engraving of Sandycombe
Lodge, Turner's house in
Twickenham, c. 1812
(detail)

Figure 14 (pages 22–23)
J. M. W. Turner, Forum
Romanum, for Mr Soane's
Museum, 1826, detail of
cat. 37 (Tate Gallery,
London. Bequeathed by
the artist, 1856)

architect might work with a trusted photographer. It was also to Gandy's architectural office in Liverpool that Soane later sent young John. As Gandy wrote to Soane, in another context, 'my ready hand and your mind' were a wonderful combination.[13]

At Pitzhanger Soane began to assemble an impressive collection of paintings, including Hogarth's *A Rake's Progress* (formerly in the possession of William Beckford) and to display casts and antique statues, as well as building up an impressive architectural library. Although Pitzhanger was a private house, Soane intended that it should both be known and proclaim his professional standing and social status. Many of Soane's Royal Academy colleagues made their way out to dine at Ealing as did leading figures from the theatrical, musical and literary worlds, such as John Philip Kemble (the great actor-manager of Covent Garden), 'Monk' Lewis (the fashionable young Gothic novelist), the first couple of the musical world, John Braham and Nancy Storace (Mozart's first Susanna), joining men such as John Taylor and John Britton, respectively a newspaper publisher and editor and an antiquarian and topographical writer. Other regular guests included Timothy Tyrrell, from whose father the Soan family had rented a house in Reading, who was now the City Remembrancer, an influential position linking the institutions of the City with those of government, William Praed, the banker for whom Soane had built Tyringham, the most perfect of his country-house schemes, and Samuel Thornton, a leading figure at the Bank of England.

FIGURE 13

John and George Soane (fig. 12), the boys for whom the venture had been ostensibly designed had, respectively in 1805 and 1806, gone up to Cambridge. Their father, unfamiliar with university life, expected them to live economically and was furious to discover their debts, although these were largely incurred for books and medical expenses, the latter for John who was often unwell. George was a lively youth with literary interests and far less biddable than his elder brother. He was no bibliophile and when his father asked him to catalogue his library he did so but then flew into a furious tantrum, throwing the ink-well on the floor. The signs were not promising.

Yet Soane's architectural enthusiasms made him an excellent guide and teacher of others, a receptive and always curious traveller. While continental Europe remained out of bounds (except briefly, during the Peace of Amiens in 1801–02), Soane rarely lost an opportunity to follow the advice of John Britton or Gandy to visit a cathedral, a picturesque scene or an important new building such as Thomas Harrison's Greek Revival *agora* at Chester Castle which Soane continually revisited over a thirty-year period. Soane most admired those architects, notably Vanbrugh, who thought for themselves and followed their own inclinations. John Nash, despite Soane's contempt for speculative builders, earned his admiration for the panache of his urban planning. Nash, for his part, teased Soane about his ambitions and his freemasonry – and got away with it.

Soane's good qualities maintained him a wide circle of friends over many decades, some, such as Richard Holland (Henry's cousin, a builder), from student days at the Royal Academy Schools and others, such as Rowland Burdon, from Italy. But Soane's short temper and extraordinary sensitivity to slights or criticism, which he did nothing to control, were recorded by Farington and others. His mercurial temperament was legendary but old friends were prepared to weather it; Eliza's pleasant and intelligent company was another strong incentive. The baffling contradictions in Soane were all too evident; Humphry Repton, the landscape architect, believed 'he has as much good nature as he has seeming asperity',[14] while the painter Benjamin Robert Haydon, himself a tempestuous man, found him 'crabbedly good-natured'.[15] Soane, like his close friend J. M. W. Turner, was often called a madman. Both reacted with hypersensitivity to the criticism that their

FIGURE 15

Figure 15

George Jones, *The Opening of London Bridge 1st of August 1831*, detail. Soane and his Housekeeper, Mrs Sarah Conduitt, stand facing the Lord Mayor, who holds aloft a sword (SM P247)

work inevitably attracted and were highly competitive with their peers; both had risen strenuously from similar backgrounds and were astute businessmen in their own affairs. A constant visitor to Pitzhanger, often staying overnight, and an equally dedicated fisherman, Turner (Soane's junior by almost twenty years) was elected Professor of Perspective at the Royal Academy soon after Soane became Professor of Architecture. They prepared for their lectures in close consultation. They fell out and were reconciled. Turner's house at Twickenham, Sandycombe Lodge (fig. 13), bears all the hallmarks of a pocket Soane interior.[16]

In 1810, the year in which he finally sold Pitzhanger Manor, Soane broke an unwritten rule by criticising the work of a living architect in a Royal Academy lecture. His contempt for Robert Smirke's design for the rebuilt Covent Garden Theatre led to the suspension of his Royal Academy lecture series. Meanwhile Soane's relationship with his sons had become very poor. John had neither the stamina nor the ability for an architectural career on the model of his father's, while George had embarked, in the teeth of his father's objections, upon a literary career. Both young men married in 1811, John to Maria Preston and George (just twenty-one) to Agnes, the daughter of Soane's theatrical friend James Boaden.

Soane distracted himself from his professional and personal troubles by embarking on the rebuilding of 13 Lincoln's Inn Fields in 1812. In contrast with the meek No. 12, No. 13 was a determined architectural statement and its projecting loggias quickly attracted the attentions of the district surveyor. That autumn, the ensuing legal action combined with his deep disappointment with his sons and a near estrangement from Eliza, caused him to write a convoluted history of his troubles, which he called 'Crude Hints towards an history of my house in L. I. Fields'.[17] Drafted, scored out and redrafted, it offered a desolate picture of a man who had 'raised a nest of wasps about him sufficient to sting the strongest man to death'.

Yet Soane was always, mentally as physically, enormously resilient. Deep depression or serious illness destabilised him but he quickly regained his professional poise. He reassumed his Professorship at the Royal Academy and began work again for a Prime Minister, this time Lord Liverpool, whose wife was Louisa Hervey, the youngest daughter of the Bishop of Derry, whom Soane had known since her childhood in Italy.

In the autumn of 1815, a puerile and vitriolic attack upon the work at Lincoln's Inn Fields, as well as that at Chelsea Hospital (where Soane had become Clerk of Works in 1807) and the Bank, appeared in *The Champion*, a respectable periodical. It quickly became clear that the anonymous author was George Soane, a discovery which sent Eliza, who had been in bad health that summer, into a serious decline. By late November she was dead, in her bereft husband's view, by the hand of her younger son, who had already been imprisoned in the King's Bench prison for debt and fraud. Soane framed the articles, titling them 'Death Blows', Eliza's words when she read them. They were displayed prominently at 13 Lincoln's Inn Fields, where Soane began to convert his faltering aspirations for his sons into the more concrete form of a memorial to his ambitions and an 'academy' for architectural endeavour.

George's misdemeanours convinced Soane that his son was a foundling, substituted by the wet nurse in his early months. This elaborate myth helped him to deal with the worst excesses of George's behaviour. There was no evidence that John would ever sustain an architectural career either, despite his father's gift of a tour to Italy, in search of both health and inspiration. Soon after his return, John died of tuberculosis.

Soane's cycles of depression and his deep mourning for his wife and son were, in 1824, exacerbated by further criticism and by his bad treatment at the hands of a parliamentary Select Committee which ordered him to demolish the classical new law courts next to Westminster Hall and replace them with a castellated Gothic design of the kind he most despised. Yet despite this, in his seventies and with failing sight, Soane continued to handle a prodigious load of public commissions, while elaborating his increasingly individual architectural language.

Soane had always found distraction and intellectual stimulus in travel: he had returned to Paris in 1814 and again in 1819, putting his pupil Henry Parke to work on lecture illustrations, and continually revisited the evocative Yorkshire landscape to which his friend the novelist Barbara Hofland had first guided him in the summer following Eliza's death. Scenes such as the miniaturised sublime of Knaresborough Gorge offered him emotional catharsis.

Soane's major project after John's death was the completion of 13 Lincoln's Inn Fields as a museum, to be endowed and safeguarded for the nation. To celebrate the

1 Soane, *Memoirs*.
2 Bolton 1927, p. 166: letter to Richard Holland, 13 September 1810.
3 *Ibid.*, p. 33: letter from C. H. Tatham to Henry Holland, Rome, 7 June 1795.
4 Norfolk Record Office, Patteson papers, Box 3/12.
5 SM Vol. 80.
6 See Bibliography for full reference.
7 Soane had first tried to obtain an alternative post, outside Westminster, as District Surveyor and argued his case in person with Pitt, see Darley 1999, chapter 7.
8 HLRO MSS E/77.
9 HLRO Committee Book 1794.
10 HLRO Lords Journals vol. 43, 1 April 1801.
11 Farington's Diary, vol. III, p. 1141, 20 January 1799.
12 Soane, *A Statement*.
13 Bolton 1927, p. 229.
14 Humphry Repton, *Memoir*, BL Add Ms 62, 112.
15 See A. Penrose, ed., *The Autobiography and Memoirs of Benjamin Robert Haydon*, London, 1927, p. 328.
16 A. Livermore, 'Sandycombe Lodge: Turner's little house at Twickenham', *Country Life*, 6 July 1951, pp. 40–42.
17 Published in Visions 1999.
18 See SM Priv. Corr. II.K.I (18) in which Thomas Keate, the Chelsea surgeon, regrets he will be unable to accompany Soane to 'more southern climes'. Soane rejected the picture and Turner returned the 500 guineas he had been paid.
19 Bolton 1927, pp. 393–411.
20 Soane could not accept the position because he was a Royal Academician.
21 *The Times*, 5 July 1821.
22 Bolton 1927, p. 531.

FIGURE 16

Figure 16

Sketch by Soane, in one of his copies of Jean-Jacques Rousseau's *Confessions*, of Rousseau's tomb at Ermenonville (SM GL26H)

acquisition of 'Belzoni's' sarcophagus, the alabaster tomb of Sethi I and his most impressive and expensive acquisition yet, Soane gave a three-day party in 1825. Almost nine hundred guests were invited, including the Prime Minister, the Duke of Sussex, J. M. W. Turner and Samuel Taylor Coleridge. The following year Turner painted the *Forum Romanum, for Mr Soane's Museum* (cat. 37, fig. 14), a memorial perhaps to Soane's dashed hopes of returning to Rome and meeting Turner there.[18]

Meanwhile the fear of blindness hung over him. Although a cataract operation saved his sight, the overwhelming dread of losing his most valuable faculty cast a long shadow. A young architect, George Wightwick, became his amanuensis in 1826 and endured the old man's furies and frustration by day while in the evening he heard interminable tales of his thwarted hopes and read to him *Gil Blas*, in French, Soane hidden behind a screen to protect his eyes from the glare of the candles and the fire. Wightwick, later to be one of Soane's most perceptive critics, returned to his lodgings exhausted at the end of each arduous day and left after a few months.[19] With hindsight, Wightwick was fond of him and touched by Soane's remorse for his outbursts. Soane, increasingly irascible, still inspired affection. When, in 1833, 13 Lincoln's Inn Fields was entrusted to the nation (well-endowed, to George Soane's fury) Soane's chosen Curator was George Bailey, who had worked in his office since 1806, and the Inspectress, Sally Conduitt (fig. 15), his kind and loyal companion-housekeeper since the death of Eliza.

Where his family was concerned, Soane was implacable. For some years George Soane was a hard-working and intermittently applauded dramatist, translator and adaptor, based at the Theatre Royal in Drury Lane, but his debts continued to mount, his family life was disastrous and his employment depended on the vicissitudes of shaky theatre managements. Once Soane realised that his own sons had failed to carry on his dynastic project, he subjected the next generation to similar pressures. John junior and Frederick Soane were both educated at their grandfather's expense, but neither fulfilled his hopes. When, in his late seventies, Soane discovered that George had had an illegitimate son by his wife's sister some years before, his anger knew no limits.

By the 1830s Soane had become the father of his profession. He was invited to become President of the new Institute of British Architects on 30 April 1834[20] and was known to be a considerable philanthropist. In addition to the Museum and its collections and library, established for the benefit of future generations of architects, he had long been involved with the Artists' General Benevolent Institution and the Royal Literary Fund. Soane was acutely aware of the vulnerability of artists to circumstance and continually assisted Gandy and his family in their financial difficulties. Yet he could not bring himself to extend the hand of forgiveness to his son George or his distressed family, causing a bitter family backlash after his death.

Soane's reading, which veered between the extremes of the shambling adventures of *Gil Blas* – which he read in Le Sage's original French as well as in Smollett's translation – and the terrible tragedy of *King Lear*, provided him with no insight into his personal difficulties. His literary tastes, like his architecture, were guided by association. Nor could Soane turn to religion and find comfort there; he disliked the church and churchmen intensely. Like his hero, Napoleon Bonaparte, even at the worst periods of his life he was 'not yet so prostrate as to take refuge in spiritual remedies'.[21] The family tomb, where Eliza, then John and finally Soane himself were buried, has not a single Christian emblem on it. George called his father, abusively, a 'son of Voltaire' and indeed it was to Jean-Jacques Rousseau's island tomb at Ermenonville (fig. 16), encircled by poplars, that Soane derived inspiration for his design.

In 1835, near the end of both their lives, Rowland Burdon congratulated his old friend on his 'merited celebrity'. As he wrote warmly: 'Believe me I have not witnessed with indifference the honours which your brother artists and the public have been bestowing upon you … It seldom happens in this life that two friends maintain their regard and attachment to each other for so long a period as we have done … I wish we could be oftener in each other's company…'[22]

By then Soane's clutch of official positions, his letters from emperors and great men and the continuing affection of old friends might have suggested to him that his had been a life well spent, a career triumphantly brought to a close, rewarded with wealth and superb possessions. But complacency was foreign to him. The contradictions which continually surface in Soane's unpredictable behaviour, signal the tensions which gave Soane's architecture its profoundly personal qualities and sustain its subtle, taut beauty.

Soane's Spaces and the Matter of Fragmentation

Robin Middleton

Figure 17 (opposite)
The Breakfast Room ceiling, 13 Lincoln's Inn Fields

In a recent book,[1] Jonathan Crary set forth a case for considering the shift of vision from the classical age to that of the modern era to have occurred in the early years of the nineteenth century. This shift involved the collapse of stable representations of space, which were replaced by visual sensations effectively severed from any fixed points of reference, instead shifting and disjunctive, centred on individual experience. Crary pinpoints these phenomena with reference to Goethe's investigations into colour theory and optics, a range of new viewing gadgets, and to the dazzling studies of lighting effects of J. M. W. Turner. Though the details of his arguments may be contested, many of his descriptions and analyses seem to be illustrated in the architecture of John Soane in an uncanny way which has never been satisfactorily analysed.

I would like to quote Crary's analysis of the stereoscope at some length: 'In the stereoscopic image there is a derangement of the conventional functioning of the optical cues. Certain planes of surfaces, even though composed of indications of light and shade that normally designate volume, are perceived as flat; other planes that normally would be read as two-dimensional, such as a fence in a foreground, seem to occupy space aggressively. Thus stereoscopic relief or depth has no unifying logic or order. If perspective implied a homogeneous and potentially metric space, the stereoscope discloses a fundamental disunified and aggregate field of disjunct elements. Our eyes never traverse the image in a full apprehension of the three-dimensionality of the entire field, but in terms of a localised experience of separate areas. When we look head-on at a photograph or painting our eyes remain at a single angle of convergence, thus endowing the image surface with an optical unity. The reading or scanning of a stereo image, however, is an accumulation of differences in the degree of optical convergence, thereby producing a perceptual effect of a patchwork of different intensities of relief within a single image. Our eyes follow a choppy and erratic path into its depth: it is an assemblage of local zones of three-dimensionality, zones imbued with a hallucinatory clarity, but which when taken together never coalesce into a homogeneous field. It is a world that simply does not communicate with that which produced baroque scenography or the city views of Canaletto and Bellotto.'[2]

This reads curiously like a description of one of Soane's interiors (fig. 17). Elsewhere in the book, Crary's cryptic remarks on Turner's experiments with light strike equivalent chords. Soane's interior spaces were, however, all contrived before the development of the stereoscope in 1832. Though he knew Turner well and set himself up as a patron of British art, Soane cannot really be said to have appreciated his friend; he had only three of Turner's paintings in his collection and the one large canvas he commissioned from Turner, the *Forum Romanum, for Mr Soane's Museum* (1826, cat. 37, fig. 14), he rejected, probably because it was too brightly coloured. Both men would no doubt have been stirred early by the bright light and colour effects of Philippe de Loutherbourg's Eidophusikon, which opened in London in the winter of 1782 with a representation of the raising of Pandemonium, a subject which had already been favoured for fantastic display by Servandoni. Soane had no wish to set himself up as a radical, but despite himself, and no doubt unwittingly, he produced an architecture of explosive portent, one that undoubtedly embodies some of the key elements of Crary's modernity.

Soane wanted desperately to succeed as an architect in the grand, classical manner. Throughout his career he prepared and presented designs for buildings on the largest of scales, beginning with his Triumphal Bridge of 1776 (cats 12–15), which won him a travelling scholarship that took him to Rome, and ending with his designs for the new Houses of Parliament (cats 190–192), reworked more than once in the closing years of his life. There are many more such designs, some no more than academic exercises: the Monument to James King, of 1777; the Pitt Mausoleum of the following year; the castello d'acqua that he began soon after for the Academy at Parma; and the British Senate House, also of 1778 (cat. 25, p. 96). Other designs were quite seriously intended: an Opera House for Leicester Square, London, of 1791 (fig. 18); a design for a museum and Senate House for the University of Cambridge, of the same year; proposals for Caius College, Cambridge, also incorporating a museum, of 1792; a seat for the Bank of Ireland, in Dublin, of 1799, and an Academical Institution for Belfast, of 1807. All are dull, commonplace designs showing scant understanding of the power of classical composition, still less of the progressive spatial arrangements that underpin such compositions and give architectural coherence and significance to the whole. Soane seems not to have grasped the concept of climax in academic planning. However severely one might judge

Figure 18

Design by Soane for a
proposed Opera House,
Leicester Square, 1791
(SM 14/3/1)

FIGURE 18

Figure 19

The interior of the Court of
Chancery, drawn by Joseph
Michael Gandy, c. 1823
(SM P274)

FIGURE 19

these designs, there can be no doubt that they represented Soane's highest aspirations as a professional architect. The eleventh of the twelve lectures that he prepared for the Schools of the Royal Academy is a lament on the poor condition of public architecture in England, as opposed to France, ending with a plea to the authorities, and to the King in particular, to redress the balance and commission a series of great public monuments that would make London a proper metropolis. That Soane considered himself the proper architect of such buildings is hinted at in the lectures, and is made quite overt in the endless variants of the *Brief Statement of the Proceedings respecting the New Law Courts at Westminster...* and the *Designs for Public and Private Buildings* that he composed between 1828 and 1832: there are no less than thirteen distinct compilations under these rubrics. In these he proposed a ceremonial route to be used by the monarch for the state opening of parliament, adorned with buildings of his own design, beginning with a new Royal Palace (two versions were offered) and concluding with his new parliament buildings (see pp. 252–263). Nothing much came of this, for which one might, perhaps, be thankful.

Whatever his professional aspirations, Soane's talents lay elsewhere. He was not an architect of the traditional classical sort. He could compose classical details with a degree of finesse, as in the celebrated Tivoli Corner at the Bank of England (for which he referred to Dance's drawings of the Temple of Vesta at Tivoli), but he could not handle a classical composition entire with any degree of conviction. Soane is not valued for his ability to combine masses. When his name is mentioned, no clear-cut, formal composition is conjured to mind, though discrete parts of

28

FIGURE 20    FIGURE 21

Figure 20
Bird's-eye perspective of
the Bank of England from
the north, 1810 (cat. 120)

Figure 21
Aerial view of the
Monastery of St Catherine,
Mount Sinai, founded
c. 540

buildings or small-scale combinations might indeed be recalled and upheld: the gateway to Tyringham, Buckinghamshire, of 1792; the entrance façade, perhaps, of his own country house, Pitzhanger Manor, of 1800–02; the Governor's Court at the Bank of England, of 1803; the 'loggia' of his town house, 13 Lincoln's Inn Fields, London, of 1812 and onwards, and also the rear wall of this house; the Mausoleum attached to the Picture Gallery at Dulwich; and the centre of the stable block at the Royal Hospital, Chelsea, both of the same period. The gateway apart, none of these offers the impact of a building whole. Soane's real abilities lie in his handling of space: internal space. In this respect he was unique. He had neither peers nor rivals.

His drawings reveal that he resolved his designs with the utmost hesitation and difficulty, but once he came to a solution he implemented it with conviction and firm precision. His control was absolute. Soane's interiors are his great achievement and his claim to fame, beginning with his Bank Stock Office, at the Bank of England, of 1791–92 (cats 123–127), continuing through on that same site to the extraordinary Colonial Office, of 1818 (cats 164–165), ending, Soane by then in his seventies, with the Privy Council Chamber in Whitehall (cats 164–165) and the New Law Courts hard against Westminster Hall (cats 197–209): all sublime creations. None of these survive. They can be recalled only in some few photographs and in the perspective representations of Joseph Michael Gandy (fig. 19). The only surviving interiors to give hard evidence of Soane's achievement are those of his own house at 13 Lincoln's Inn Fields, and these, owing to his foresight, survive intact, much as he left them. It is by that labyrinth of spaces that he must be judged.

Soane, it is clear, aimed to be an architect in the grand, academic manner (one can provide reasons of the social sort for these aspirations), but he was a failure in this respect. However, he transcended his failings. His very weakness set him free to explore new combinations, and his idiosyncratic approach to spatial composition led to altogether unprecedented resulting effects. Soane might be judged to have rejected the classical tradition; absolutely, he subverted it.

The emphasis of classical architecture is on form; Soane stresses space, and this he organises in wholly unclassical ways. In the most personal and intriguing of his works – the Bank of England, where he began building in 1791,

continuing for four decades; the house at 13 Lincoln's Inn Fields, built mostly between 1812 and 1825; and the New Law Courts of 1822 to 1825 – the external forms are entirely subordinate to the interior arrangements and effects. Very different conditions prevailed in the design and construction of each of these buildings. The Bank was erected piecemeal, over a long period of time, with much on the site preceding Soane and much of the ground acquired only gradually, though by no means as gradually as has sometimes been thought. Soane's house was all his own, and, in the main, constructed in a single campaign (though connected to his earlier work at the rear), to be extended and altered over the years. The Law Courts were erected all at once, though the site was severely restricted by Westminster Hall and its buttresses on the one side and by Vardy's Stone Building on the other. The plans of all these buildings nonetheless have a curious resemblance: they look disordered, disordered, that is, in classical terms.

The closest parallel that comes to mind for the bird's-eye view of the Bank of England (fig. 20) is the Monastery of St Catherine at Sinai (fig. 21), where the Emperor Justinian threw a protective wall around the church precinct, which was gradually filled in over the centuries. The plan of the Bank, as completed, reveals that the only elements of conventional ordering are those contrived under equally uncertain and difficult conditions by the architects who preceded Soane, George Sampson and Sir Robert Taylor. Soane was forced to build his great Stock Offices within Taylor's walls. He would willingly have torn down all of Taylor's work on the site. When unconstrained by Taylor's architecture, he composed very differently, in what, at first glance, might seem to be a totally arbitrary manner. The ordering of Soane's building can be understood only if it is analysed as a series of routes giving access to an odd variety of spaces, a task that cannot be undertaken here.

The plan of the house at 13 Lincoln's Inn Fields looks, at first, like an alteration. But Soane completely demolished the existing building when he bought it, though the house was neither old nor ill-built. The spatial arrangements he organised there are highly unusual, with what appear to be simple axial configurations between some rooms, but with dynamic visual connections overlaid. Soane creates what appear to be perfectly regular, symmetrically framed spaces. He then wraps layers of space around these skeletal

Figure 22

The Pasticcio in the
Monument Court,
13 Lincoln's Inn Fields,
19 August 1825
(SM Vol. 82/72)

FIGURE 22

Figure 23

Plan for the Law Courts and
Houses of Parliament by
William Kent, 1730s
(SM 36/2/2)

Figure 24

Plan for the Law Courts
by John Soane, 1821
(SM 53/1/16)

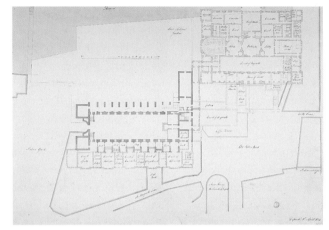

FIGURE 23

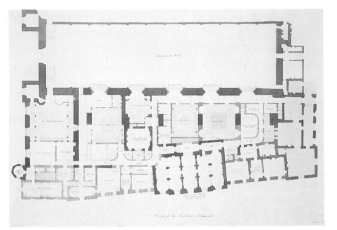

FIGURE 24

frameworks and proceeds to subvert the geometry of these
conglomerate spaces by dematerialising the architecture,
flooding the walls with light from concealed sources, often
streaked with colour and breaking the surfaces with linear
patterns and a mess of accumulated objects. The
accumulation makes more powerful the violation of the
original symmetries. The prime pockets of space are
connected to one another in the most extraordinary ways,
rarely on the main axes, as one would imagine, but
obliquely and tangentially, to the left and to the right,
above and below, so that wholly unexpected views are
opened up both between spaces and from one series of
spaces to another. Nor is there a sequence of views, rather
multivalent views, offered in quite different directions all
at once. Panels can be opened and closed to open and close
vistas. Mirrors create further complications. And lest there
be any doubt that this concatenation of views was
intended, Soane commissioned Gandy to paint
compositions with myriad alternative views jostling
alongside one another. Soane's spaces cannot be
apprehended as a whole. They have to be experienced.
And you can never be sure quite what to expect as you pass
from one to the next, of what will emerge around the
corner. At the house's heart, in the middle of the central
court, stood the Pasticcio (fig. 22), a hybrid confection
composed in 1819, with assorted elements of architecture,
including a capital from an Indian temple, piled high on
the base of Lord Burlington's statue of Apollo from
Chiswick House.

Soane's emphasis on internal architecture is even more
evident in the New Law Courts. The façades were well-
nigh irrelevant (Soane offered them in classical or Gothic
form), though he was greatly angered when he was
required to alter them to conform to the architecture of
Westminster Hall. William Kent, in an earlier proposal for
an arrangement of courts for this site, had provided
something by way of geometric ordering. Soane had Kent's
plans to hand (fig. 23), and no doubt took them as a point
of departure, but the building he created owes nothing,
in its spatial effects, to Kent. Soane could not explore the
spatial connections between the individual court rooms,
as he could in his own house, but he nonetheless contrived
the individual spaces in much the same way as he had in his
Breakfast Room; he used corridors, too, as connectors
with an evident delight in emphasising surprising turns
and lighting effects. The whole (fig. 24), whatever the
judiciary's requirement of independence and separation,
was labyrinthine, and was intended to provoke amazement
in the visitor. In some of the preliminary plans, the
corridors are positively warren-like.

The fact that the visitor has no apprehension of the
overall arrangement of Soane's internal spaces, no sense of
the organisation of the whole, at once suggests that Soane
was influenced by picturesque landscape theory. This was
first formulated in full in 1794 in Uvedale Price's *Essay on
the Picturesque*. Price was concerned to identify a critical
category midway between Edmund Burke's qualities of
beauty and the sublime. The picturesque partook of
neither one nor the other alone, though it might merge
with either. It was to be characterised by 'qualities of
roughness and of sudden variation joined to that of
irregularity'. Contrast and variety were essential to its
enjoyment. Ambivalence was preferred to resolution;
open alternatives were approved above fixed systems and

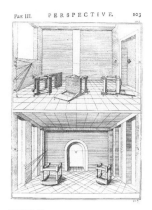

FIGURE 25

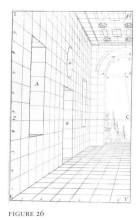

FIGURE 26   FIGURE 27

Figure 25

Demonstrations of
foreshortened objects in a
perpsectival interior, from
Jean Dubreuil's *Perspective
pratique*, Paris, 1642

Figure 26

Plate 86 from Abraham
Bosse, *Manière universelle
de Monsieur Desargues*,
Paris, 1648

Figure 27

Plate 139 from Abraham
Bosse, *Manière universelle
de Monsieur Desargues*,
Paris, 1648

controlled responses. Though geometrical artifice might be integrated into a picturesque composition it was to be combined with irregular and less apparent artifices derived from nature. Sensory stimuli too might be considered a part of a picturesque composition. And temporal effects, including time's accumulations and changes, were to be integral to this new way of framing perception.

Although Price's definitions might be shifting and determinedly imprecise, the taste he sought to describe had became more clearly defined by the time his friend, and enemy, Richard Payne Knight published his sharper and far wittier *Analytical Enquiry into the Principles of Taste* (1805). Though such works were undoubtedly a stimulus (and a vital stimulus one might judge) to Soane's operation as an architect of interior spaces, they served as a reinforcement to notions that he was already exploring, rather than as the catalyst to his experimentation. The movement of the individual through related spaces and the accumulated effect of his responses to them had long intrigued architects. This was yet another aspect, of course, of the realm of sensation that had been opened up by John Locke.

There is not much discussion of planning in English architectural literature of the seventeenth and eighteenth centuries, it must be admitted, and almost nothing on the handling of space. But as the notions of human understanding as propounded by John Locke in the seventeenth century conditioned all radical thinking on the subject for a hundred years and more, it is perhaps sensible to look first to his remarks on the subject in *An Essay concerning Human Understanding*, first published in 1690. In this, his second book, Locke devotes a chapter not only to space, 'Of Space and Its Simple Modes', but also to time, 'Of Duration', followed by 'Of Duration and Expansion Considered Together'. Given his aim to describe the world in terms of human experience it is something of a surprise to find that he defines both space and time in the conventional, arbitrary terms of measurement: space is defined as the repetition of inches, feet, yards, fathoms, miles and even the diameter of the earth, and time as the repetition of minutes, hours, days, months and years.

'In both these, (*viz.*) *Expansion* and *Duration*,' he concludes, 'the Mind has this common *Idea* of continued Lengths, capable of greater, or less quantities: For a Man has as clear an *Idea* of the difference of the length of an

Hour, as a Day, as an Inch and a Foot.' Such notions were quite commonplace. France was the stamping ground for notions of visual perception and methods of representation in the seventeenth century, and French mathematicians and theorists of the seventeenth century, however divergent their views, were in ready agreement that space was to be defined by units of measurement. This is at once in evidence, whether in Jean Dubreuil's *Perspective pratique...* (1642, published in English in 1673, fig. 25), or in the more radical projective geometries of Girard Desargues, beginning in 1636, but takes full form only in the collected edition of his works, *Manière universelle de Monsieur Desargues* (figs 26–27), issued by Abraham Bosse in 1648. This simple, entirely static vision was upheld by most perspective artists in England in the years that followed, and evidently had its effect on the way English architects thought of their internal spaces. Robert Morris, author of *Lectures on Architecture* of 1734 and 1736 and one of the few architects in England even to consider the problems of planning and the relationship of volumes in the architectural literature of the first half of the eighteenth century, conceived his buildings, in particular country houses, as compositions of cubic volumes, all ordered by a simple module arranged in a limited range of proportional relationships. The relationship of the spaces was purely formal; their uses were interchangeable. Even the French, one might note, though they too approved of a simple and formal geometry for the rooms of their houses, had by this time established an organic sequence for the spaces of an apartment, conditioned by social custom and use. They linked these rooms however, in the most elementary way, by an enfilade, a visual axis.

By the middle years of the century, things had changed. Henry Home, Lord Kames, though he based most of his ideas directly on Locke, nonetheless came up with a far more complex understanding of both space and time in his *Elements of Criticism* (1762). He was concerned with the way in which experience might serve to measure time and space. He began with time. This could, as Locke had observed, be measured in terms of hours, days, months and years. But such measures were, to Kames, essentially artificial. They did not relate at all to one's apprehension of time in different emotional states and under different circumstances. Pain could make the passage of time seem endless; happiness could make it pass swiftly. The only natural measure, however imperfect, Kames held, was the

Figure 28

View from the third drawing
room to the Countess of
Derby's dressing room,
Derby House, London.
Engraving by Benedetto
Pastorini in Robert and
James Adam, *The Works in
Architecture*, vol. 2, 1779

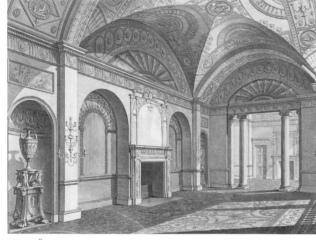

FIGURE 28

intensity of individual perceptions. But even these were
by no means constant, for actual experience might change
greatly in recollection.

The natural measure of space was, for Kames, even more
elusive of definition. He chose the angle of vision, or
rather perception, which provided, as it were, a module to
calculate the extent of space. Kames, unlike Locke, was
concerned with architectural space, with rooms and their
apparent sizes under varying conditions and when viewed
in varying states of emotion. He considers, for example,
the effect of furniture in a room, and likens it to the effect
of elements set in a formal garden. 'Furniture', he writes,
'increases in appearance the size of a small room, for the
same reason that divisions increase in appearance the size
of a garden. The emotion of wonder which is raised by a
very large room without furniture, makes it look larger
than it is. If completely furnished, we view it in parts, and
our wonder is not raised.'[3] Though one might not always
accept Kames's analyses, it is clear that he was thinking of
space in very different terms from his predecessors, in
terms of individual experience and emotion.

Something of this more dynamic approach to internal
spaces suffuses the architecture of Kames's compatriot and
friend Robert Adam (Kames took Adam's advice when
writing the *Elements of Criticism*). Adam composed his
interiors as a succession of related spaces, one
counterpointing the next, together making up an organic
whole. His volumes, though geometrically related, were
designed to be approached from oblique and unusual
angles. The most celebrated example of his diagonal
planning is the relationship between the second and third

drawing rooms on the first floor of Derby House, London,
of 1773 to 1774, which he commissioned Benedetto
Pastorini (fig. 28) to record for the second volume of his
Works in Architecture (1779). This view, showing the
extension of space beyond the third drawing room into
the Countess of Derby's dressing room, is unparalleled in
contemporary architectural publications. The drama of
the view, depicted in all its richness of light and shade, is
new to eighteenth-century conventions of domestic
decorum. Other examples might be adduced, such as the
arrangement of rooms on the first floor of Home House,
20 Portman Square, London, of 1773 to 1776, where the
rooms form a circuit, each, as far as may be, traversed
diagonally. And James Stuart, Adam's rival, attempted
much the same thing, though with the bedroom suite
removed from the circuit, at Montagu House, 22 Portman
Square, of 1775 to 1782. Adam related his concept of
movement in architecture, whether in space or form,
directly to landscape architecture – though it is important
to note that he had already outlined the concept as early
as 1758, long before the appearance in 1770 of Thomas
Whately's *Observations on Modern Gardening*, the pioneering
study on picturesque gardening.

Soane encountered the ideas of Kames early, in the
lectures of Thomas Sandby, which he attended as a student
at the Royal Academy of Arts. Kames's ideas, together
with those of Edmund Burke, also enliven the theoretical
episodes in *A Treatise on the Decorative Part of Civil
Architecture* (1791) by Sir William Chambers, a work much
approved of by Soane. But Soane acquired his copy of
Kames's book only in 1813, when, in the month of March,
he began taking copious notes from it, seventy-two pages
in all, in preparation for his own Academy lectures. Soane
relied on Kames, in particular, in his tenth and eleventh
lectures, when he discussed the relation of architecture
to natural scenery.

Soane, of course, was a great admirer of Adam, whom he
first encountered as a young man, when he was working,
under Holland, at Claremont House, Surrey. In 1833 Soane
purchased the bulk of the drawings from the Adam estate,
almost nine thousand in all, which are still to be viewed
at 13 Lincoln's Inn Fields. He paid only £200 for them.

Soane's knowledge of picturesque theory is less fully
attested. He had only one of William Gilpin's books in
his library. His copy of Uvedale Price's *Essay on the
Picturesque* (1794) was purchased only in August 1827,

Figure 29
Plate X from G. B. Piranesi,
Carceri d'invenzione, **1750**

FIGURE 29

at a sale at Attingham Hall of the effects of the 2nd Baron Berwick, and the annotations it contains are those of Berwick, or more probably those of his cousin Sir Richard Hill of Hawkstone Park, Shropshire. Though no notes by Soane survive, it is clear that he read the *Essay* to good effect when composing the *Description of the House and Museum on the North Side of Lincoln's Inn Fields* in its editions of 1830, 1832 and 1835. But Soane must have read Price's work much earlier, for there is a copy of the second edition (1796) in his library and Price's ideas are in evidence in both the sixth and the ninth of the Academy lectures. Soane's encounter with the ideas of Payne Knight is less problematical. He bought the *Analytical Enquiry into the Principles of Taste* on its first appearance in 1805 and read the book then, though he made his extensive notes and annotations only from March 1813 onwards, when he was preparing his second course of lectures, namely numbers

seven to twelve. Soane agreed with much in Knight on matters of principle such as the fact that Grecian architecture, epitomised in the temple form, was unsuitable as a model for the English country house, but he did not often extract those ideas which one might think pertinent to his own explorations in architecture. Again and again, both in his notes and his lectures, he condemned Knight for combining two styles at Downton Castle, of 1772, the castellated outside, the classical within. And although Soane transcribed Knight's justification that 'variety, and intricacy of form, and light and shadow, may be carried to a degree, which no regular or homogenial building will admit of',[4] he commented sternly: 'Is not this buying the picturesque at too dear a rate?'

One is tempted to pursue further Soane's inspiration from those aesthetic philosophers who followed Kames, such as Priestley, but especially the exponents of the

Figure 30
G. B. Piranesi, Wall elevation of the Caffè degli inglesi, Rome. Plate 45 in his *Diversi manieri*, 1769

Figure 31
Detail from plate VI in Soane's 1835 *Description*, an engraving of the wall of the Library at 13 Lincoln's Inn Fields, showing a crocodile in the same position as in fig. 30

FIGURE 30

FIGURE 31

Common Sense school of philosophers, Thomas Reid and his students Dugald Stewart and Archibald Alison. For whereas with Locke universal understanding emerges as a direct response of the five senses to the phenomena of the universe, with his latter-day followers there is no longer a direct correspondence between matter and the movements of the mind. For them, there is nothing innate in an object that stimulates a specific aesthetic response; this is the result rather of a train of associations, when the faculties of attention and memory combine, a process inevitably different in each individual (though individuals are susceptible to conditioning). This is a phenomenological position, closer, one might judge, to Soane's aesthetic understanding than to that of the earlier theorists. But the influence of the Common Sense philosophers on Soane cannot yet be measured. He owned none of the works of Reid and Stewart, and only a second edition of Alison's *Essay on the Nature of Taste* (1811). The copy remains in mint condition, although it contains, it is important to note, more discussion of architecture than any other of these philosophers' books.

The works perhaps most influential of all on Soane's spatial vision were the etchings of Piranesi. While a student in Rome in 1778, Soane had met Piranesi, just before his death. Soane later bought almost all the drawings for Piranesi's last work, the *Différentes vues de ... Pesto*,[5] on which he was working at the time of his visit. Piranesi gave Soane four of his views of Rome: two arches, the Pantheon and the exterior view of the tomb of Cecilia Metella. However, it was the odd, discordant elements of the *Campo Marzio* and the non-perspectival spaces of the *Carceri* (fig. 29) that must have provided the real stimulus for Soane. There are two sets of Piranesi's works in Sir John Soane's Museum today, one in six volumes, another in twelve. The second set was purchased only on 3 July 1826, for £24.0.0, from Messrs Wood and McCulloch. Both, however, contain the *Carceri* etchings in their second state.

Piranesi's vision emerges, of course, from the tradition of the Baroque theatre and thus, of Baroque architecture. Soane was not responsive to Borromini's architecture, if one is to judge by his academic pronouncements, though it is equally clear, if his lectures are more thoughtfully analysed, that he was more vitally interested in those architects who extended or broke down earlier classical conventions than in those who upheld them. Palladio he considered a bore. He responded rather to Giulio Romano, Bernini and, like Adam, especially to Vanbrugh. Soane looked to Vanbrugh not for spatial intricacies but for liveliness of form. But a case can nonetheless be made for showing that Soane responded to Baroque spatial innovations, in particular as transposed by Piranesi. Piranesi fractured the Baroque vision, adding discord and uncertainty.

In his lectures, though Soane upheld Piranesi as a 'mine of information'[6] on archaeological matters, he castigated him more than once, in the eighth and eleventh lectures, for his 'architectural blasphemy',[7] in rejecting the architecture of Ancient Greece. He also denounced him as an architect, illustrating Piranesi's celebrated demonstration of his abilities as a planner, the plan of a Collegio Romano, without its centre of ever-diminishing spaces. 'Piranesi', Soane proclaimed, 'mistook Confusion for Intricacy, undefined lines and forms for Classical Variety.'[8] And he reverted to this theme again when advising his students that novelty must have its bounds, variety its limits. Borromini and Piranesi, he judged, had overstepped these bounds: 'The works of Borromini and

FIGURE 32

Figure 32
G. B. Piranesi, 'Rovine delle
Terme Antoniniane' (the
Baths of Caracalla). Plate
76 in *Vedute di Roma*, 1760

his followers can only be looked upon as mighty mazes of chaotic confusion, wherein nothing is defined, one form constantly running into another, without taste, use or meaning, works frivolous, and expensive beyond measure.'[9] This was in Soane's eighth lecture, composed after he had built his house at 13 Lincoln's Inn Fields. Despite all disclaimers, one can see the relevance of the work of Borromini and Piranesi to Soane. There are even direct comparisons to be made (figs 30–31).

And in his 'Crude Hints towards an history of my house in L. I. Fields', written in August and September 1812, while the house was still being built. Soane fancifully imagined the house as a ruin, in the process of discovery: some, he suggests, have thought it to have been a heathen temple or a convent of nuns;[10] 'others', he adds, 'have supposed it to have been the residence of some magician'.[11] Inevitably, Piranesi is invoked, the Piranesi of the *Carceri*. Of the empty stairwell Soane writes, 'This very space, if a staircase, would only have been one of those Carcerian dark staircases represented in some of Piranesi's ingenious dreams for prisons.'[12]

Soane, as I have noted, had neither peers nor rivals in his handling of internal space. He had no immediate following, except perhaps Francis Greenway who built a handful of churches of minor interest in Sydney, Australia. Soane's interiors were not much admired, and in fact were actively disliked, by many of his contemporaries. Only towards the end of the century when picturesque theories were integrated into the experience and practice of architecture by the designers of the Arts and Crafts movement is it possible to see something of Soane's spatial contrivance – not in the puritanical works of W. R. Lethaby and C. F. A. Voysey, rather in Philip Webb's Standen or Ernest Gimson's Stoneywell. But these emit no more than the faintest of echoes. Only in the works of Edwin Lutyens is there something more authentic by way of a stirring, and then only in rare, late buildings such as the kitchens at Castle Drogo, of 1910–30. This sort of historical theme-hunting is, however, to trivialise Soane.

I started by suggesting that Crary's notion of a radical change in visual sensibility in the early years of the nineteenth century might be a useful approach to an understanding of Soane's architecture, but there is another, not unrelated and perhaps more appropriate ground for the investigation of Soane's work – the matter of fragmentation and its positive resolution.

Fragments may be construed in both negative and positive ways: as remnants of achievements and a plenitude that is irrevocably lost, or as elements of a restorative power that can provide symbolic and poetic meaning to newly constituted wholes. This ambiguity is all too obvious in the eighteenth-century cult of ruins in which the negative and positive aspects are both strongly in evidence. Even in Soane's work this ambiguity is activated – the bird's-eye view of the Bank of England (cat. 119) looks like a representation of a ruin (in the manner of Piranesi [fig. 32]), but is in fact a depiction of the entire bank being constructed. Soane's house, of course, can be seen as an artificial ruin, a fabrication of bits and pieces from the past, of flotsam and jetsam. Soane was not a serious collector; nor he was a connoisseur. He bought many of his objects in bulk, largely for their associational values and also for their usefulness in composing textures. There is not much that was then considered of real value in the museum; many exhibits would have been thought of as throw-away objects. But the pieces were consciously chosen and painstakingly assembled. I would like to suggest that Soane was stirred by a rebellion against established modes of thinking and making, a rebellion similar to those of artists of the early twentieth century, the Cubists (fig. 33), the Dadaists and the Surrealists, who used the fragments of a world that had become commonplace and devoid of meaning to create new conjunctions and juxtapositions that would articulate their latent meanings once again and provide a new metaphorical and poetic wholeness for the fulfilment of life. Our knowledge and understanding of their culture of fragments might, I think, serve as a lead to the unravelling of Soane's operations.

The configuration of geometrical lines and fragments in the Synthetic-Cubist paintings offers, as in Soane's architecture, a transition to a world in the process of construction, where the resulting configuration remains only a mediating representation. And this representation offers a means of participating in the world afresh; it is not an end in itself. The space of these paintings is not a space that can be understood through geometry or formal structure, but as a living structure in which the metaphorical power of the fragment plays a decisive role.

This new spatial structure was also proclaimed in the art of collage which emerged from Cubism, for example in both Kurt Schwitters's collages and his Merzbau interiors

Figure 33

Pablo Picasso, *The
Architect's Table*, Paris,
1912 (The Museum of
Modern Art, New York. The
William S. Paley Collection)

FIGURE 33

Figure 34

Kurt Schwitters, Merzbau
(Merzbuilding), general
view with *blaues fenster*
(blue window),
photographed *c.* 1930

Figure 35

The roof terrace of Le
Corbusier's Villa Savoye,
Poissy, 1929

(fig. 34), where fragments of familiar reality are set in a radically different framework of space to become part of a new, more complex, articulated world. This is a theme convincingly explored by Dalibor Vesely in a provocative essay in which he outlines a theory of the poetics of displacement.[13]

In modern architecture, the first consistent use of the fragment and the play of displacements to positive effect appears in the works of Le Corbusier. Colin Rowe and Robert Slutzky have analysed the overlapping of elements in Le Corbusier's Villa Savoye at Poissy (1929, fig. 35) and their simultaneous appearance in a variety of spatial locations in terms of both literal and phenomenal transparency.[14] The fragmentation of forms and the fragmentation of space go hand in hand. But such effects should be thought of as no more than a fragment of the history of fragmentation itself. Soane's meandering sequences of spaces can, likewise, be compared to Le Corbusier's 'promenade architecturale'.

More recently, it is possible to make particular reference to the works of Louis Kahn, later in the century, where the fragments are more abstractly configured and transformed by the mediating role of light. I would refer in particular to Kahn's design for a convent for the Dominican Sisters of Pennsylvania, of 1965–68; his Hurva Synagogue, of 1967–69, or his marvellous works in Ahmedabad and Dacca. With the design for Exeter Academy Library (fig. 36), Kahn comes curiously close to Soane: one can compare the detail of the lantern of Soane's Court of Chancery (fig. 37) directly to the central well of Kahn's library, but the similarity is certainly no more than fortuitous. Soane, whatever the revolutionary nature of his achievement, was a man of the early nineteenth century, Kahn a man of the mid-twentieth century. The parallel preoccupations of the twentieth-century artists I have summarily invoked whose works are now beginning to be theorised, might nonetheless provide a critical ground for the decipherment of Soane.[15]

FIGURE 35

FIGURE 34

1 Jonathan Crary, *Techniques of the Observer*, Cambridge, Mass., 1990.

2 *Ibid.*, pp. 125–126.

3 Henry Home, Lord Kames, *Elements of Criticism*, Edinburgh, 1762, vol. 1, p. 126.

4 SM Archives 1/165, pp. 8–9.

5 G. B. Piranesi, *Différentes vues de ... Pesto*, Rome, 1778.

6 Watkin 1996 (1), p. 531.

7 *Ibid.*, p. 641.

8 *Ibid.*, p. 603.

9 *Ibid.*, p. 605.

10 John Soane, 'Crude Hints towards an history of my house in L. I. Fields', August and September 1812, published in Visions 1999, p. 62.

11 *Ibid.*, p. 64.

12 *Ibid.*, p. 63.

13 Dalibor Vesely, 'Architecture and the Ambiguity of Fragment', in Robin Middleton, ed., *Architectural Associations: The Idea of the City*, London, 1996, pp. 109–121.

14 Colin Rowe and Robert Slutzky, 'Transparency: Literal and Phenomenal', *Perspecta*, 8, 1963, pp. 45–54, reprinted in Colin Rowe, *The Mathematics of the Ideal Villa*, Cambridge, Mass., 1976, pp. 159–183.

15 I intend to explore these themes at a later date in a book on Soane's architecture; for those who want to start thinking along these lines themselves, I suggest a reading of Rowe and Slutzky, op. cit., and, by the same authors, 'Transparency: Literal and Phenomenal (part 2)', *Perspecta*, 13/14, 1971, pp. 286–301, reprinted in Joan Ockman and Edward Eigen, *Architecture Culture 1943–1968*, New York, 1993, pp. 206–225. Follow this with Dalibor Vesely, op. cit. Equally useful is the second chapter, 'Fragments', of Charles Rosen, *The Romantic Generation*, Cambridge, Mass., 1995.

Figure 36

Louis I. Kahn, Central Hall of the Library at Phillips Exeter Academy, Exeter, New Hampshire

Figure 37

Interior view of the Court of Chancery, drawn by Joseph Michael Gandy, *c.* 1825 (cat. 201)

FIGURE 37

FIGURE 36

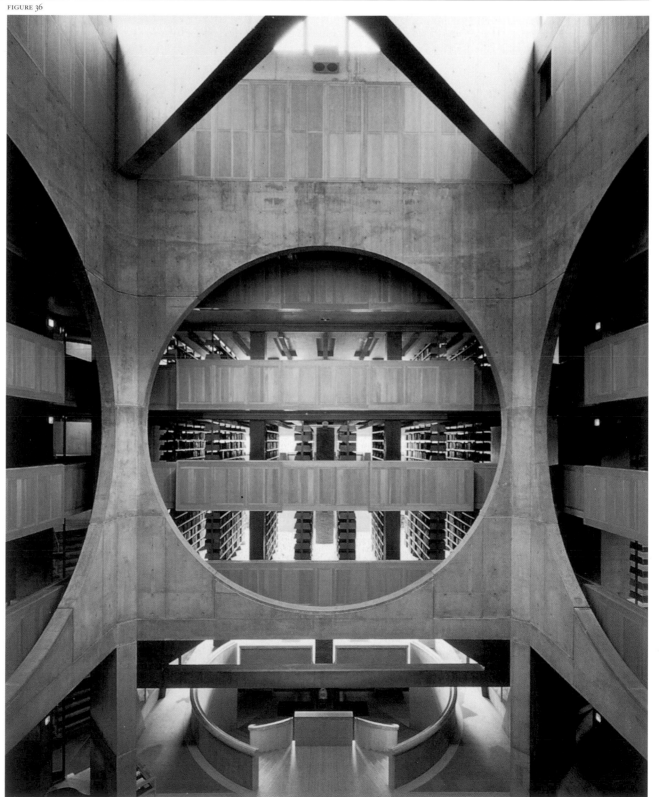

David Watkin

Soane: The Royal Academician and the Public Realm

Figure 38 (opposite)
Design perspective, drawn
by Joseph Michael Gandy,
of Soane's Sepulchral
Church for the Duke of
York, St James's Park,
London, 1827, detail
(cat. 190) (SM P275)

The Royal Academician

We tend to think of Soane as primarily the master of an inward-looking architecture of highly personal interior spaces. However, it seems that what mattered to Soane most was the creation of monumental public buildings in London which would be appropriate to its status as the capital city of a modern world power and as the seat of a historic monarchy. Entranced by the strange, idiosyncratic poetry of interiors such as the Breakfast Room and Picture Room at the Soane Museum, we tend to overlook the fact that the walls of the Museum are hung with images of his own designs for public buildings. Demonstrating his preoccupation with the public realm, these seem to have been dearest to his heart, though they include those least studied today: they include his monumental projects for the Houses of Lords and Commons, his grandiose triumphal arches for Downing Street and for the western approaches to London, his Royal Palace on Constitution Hill, the Pitt Cenotaph, the Sepulchral Chapel for the Duke of York in St James's Park and the prolongation of his Board of Trade and Privy Council Offices in Whitehall, displayed in the Dining Room in an exquisite plaster model, three-and-a-half feet long.

With their grandiose Corinthian colonnades, such projects ought to force us to take seriously the implications of Soane's claim in his Royal Academy lectures that, 'Art cannot go beyond the Corinthian order'.[1] Such a view is entirely in accordance with his acceptance of the *convenance* which operated within the hierarchy of architecture and society in the ancien régime. He would have shared Edmund Burke's view that, 'Nobility is a graceful ornament to the civil order. It is the Corinthian capital of polished society.'[2] Such a view may have been derived from Soane's favourite architectural theorist, the Abbé Laugier, who saw an architectural hierarchy at the summit of which was the Corinthian order, of which he declared, 'architecture has never produced anything greater, more august, or more sublime'.[3]

As a friend of Pitt the Younger, Soane closely identified with the process by which George III had created a new image for the monarchy by attempting to extend its political influence, as well as by rallying the public towards it against the background of defeat in the American war and of the threat of invasion by Napoleon.[4] As one of the three attached architects to the Office of the King's Works, Soane had also, of course, a professional interest in the success of the monarchy.

One institution in which George III took a close personal interest was the Royal Academy of Arts, founded with his support in 1768 as a parallel to the French Académie Royale d'Architecture which had occupied a central role in the French architectural establishment from its foundation by Louis XIV in 1671. It promoted public and royal projects in Paris and the provincial centres of France, while its members were entitled to call themselves 'architectes du Roi', the principal being the 'premier architecte du Roi'. William Chambers, one of the Founder Members of the Royal Academy, had been trained in Paris by J.-F. Blondel, who subsequently taught at the French Academy. A powerful Francophile who shared with the Royal Academy's first President, Sir Joshua Reynolds, a profound admiration for the French Academy, Chambers was a great influence on the young Soane during and after his own years as a student at the Royal Academy in 1771–76. Following the model of the Grand Prix de Rome of the French Academy, Chambers established a competition which enabled the winner to receive funds to cover a period of study in Rome. Soane was an early beneficiary of this institution, winning the Gold Medal in 1776 with his design for a Triumphal Bridge.

For the rest of his life, Soane insisted that the Royal Academy was central to his professional career. Indeed, he considered that he owed everything to it, for it had not only given him his architectural education but had sent him, at its own expense, on his Grand Tour, where he met the patrons who were to shape his future career. In 1795 he was elected one of the twenty Associate Members of the Royal Academy, and immediately began plotting to become a full Academician. The very day after Sir William Chambers died on 8 March 1796, he called on Farington with a view to securing the place vacated by Chambers, though he was not successful in this until 1802. To gain a place at the very centre of the British cultural establishment was no mean achievement, and one which was, potentially, an immense boost to Soane's professional career and social standing.

One of the principal ways in which Soane's ambitious temperament revealed itself was in his intrigues to wrest the Professorship of Architecture out of the hands of his old master, Dance, and into his own. This was not an unreasonable ambition, considering that Dance, who had

Figure 39
**Interior perspective, made
for the Royal Academy
Lectures, of the Pitt
Cenotaph, National Debt
Redemption Office
(SM 14/4/12)**

FIGURE 39

Soane delivered his first lecture on Tuesday 27 March 1809. This was simply to whet the appetite of the public, for he did not begin the first series in full until January 1810. All went well until he reached the fourth lecture of the series on Tuesday 29 January 1810. In this he criticised a number of recent buildings, in particular the Royal College of Surgeons, by George Dance, begun in 1806 but not completed till 1813, and the Royal Opera House, Covent Garden, which had been completed in 1809 from designs by Robert Smirke (1780–1867). To set the criticism in context, it should be pointed out that Soane condemned a wide range of buildings in this lecture, both Antique and modern, for their failure to comply with what he regarded as the first principles of architecture.

The ensuing dispute, during which he refused to lecture, dragged on from 1810–13, but did not in the end sour his relations with the Academy. It was through the annual Academy exhibitions that he chose to publicise his designs: quite remarkably, in the sixty-four years between 1772 and 1836 there were only five, 1778 and 1788–91, in which he did not exhibit drawings. Moreover, in the Act of Parliament which established Sir John Soane's Museum in 1833, he arranged that the President and Council of the Royal Academy would appoint the future Curators of the Museum as well as one of its five Representative Trustees.

been appointed in 1798, managed to hold the office until 1806 without delivering a single lecture. However, even before his appointment to the Professorship in March 1806, Soane was secretly busy translating key works of architectural history and theory by J.-F. Blondel and J.-D. Leroy, both Professors of Architecture at the Académie Royale d'Architecture. This substantial labour must surely have been undertaken in preparation for possible future lectures at the Royal Academy, as was his activity in making a copy of the Professor of Architecture's duties as early as 23 December 1805.[5] By the Instrument of Foundation of the Royal Academy, signed by King George III in December 1768, these duties were, 'to read annually six public Lectures, calculated to form the taste of the Students, to instruct them in the laws and principles of composition, to point out to them the beauties or faults of celebrated productions, to fit them for an unprejudiced study of books, and for a critical examination of structures; his salary shall be thirty pounds a year; and he shall continue in office during the King's pleasure'.

The Realms of Power: Soane's Designs for the Pitt Cenotaph, Westminster and Whitehall

The Pitt Cenotaph

The Pitt Cenotaph (fig. 39) provided Soane with a rare opportunity to design the kind of public monument which he had seen commended in the Enlightenment texts he had studied, such as the Abbé Lubersac's *Discours sur les monumens publics de tous les âges* (Paris, 1775). Soane's Cenotaph was to be installed in the National Debt Redemption Office which had been established in 1694, along with the Bank of England, to handle the life annuities which raised money for the war with France.[6] Its activities had expanded sufficiently by 1818 for Soane to be invited to design new premises for it in Old Jewry. In the meantime, a group of merchants and bankers had opened subscriptions in 1802 for a statue of Pitt the Younger, probably the first raising of public funds for a memorial to an English statesman. They approached Sir William Westmacott RA (1775–1856) for a statue on which he was still working in 1815.[7] In 1818 acceptance was given

Figure 40

Design perspective for the
principal entrance to the
1794 project for the House
of Lords, drawn at a later
date by Joseph Michael
Gandy (SM P277)

FIGURE 40

statue of Pitt dressed in a Roman toga and seated on a
massive Greco-Roman throne.[9]

The House of Lords

In 1794 Soane was invited to consider means of improving
the structure of the House of Lords by a Committee of the
House of Lords which then sat in a medieval, though
Georgianised, room. Soane responded on a grand scale, his
office producing as many as 217 drawings, culminating in
a vast Neoclassical palace for both Houses of Parliament,
ornamented with much symbolical statuary and painting,
'commemorative of public actions and distinguished
talents'.[10] These reflected a growing ambition of the
eighteenth century which had led Sir Joshua Reynolds
to recommend that St Paul's Cathedral should serve as a
mausoleum for the nation's heroes. The provision of a new
House of Lords (fig. 40) was also part of a royal and
aristocratic resurgence in the face of the reaction first to
the American and French Revolutions, and second to the
Revolutionary and Napoleonic Wars.

Soane had been dreaming for years of what he called a
new Senate House, made 'without regard to expense, or
limits as to space, in the gay morning of youthful fancy'.[11]
When he subsequently published details of his designs of
the 1790s for the House of Lords, he always included the
Senate House design of 1778 (cat. 25) which he had made
when he was in Dance's office and had finally drawn up
when in Rome.

The understandable pride he took in the importance of
this commission led him to exhibit drawings associated
with it at the Royal Academy almost annually between
1796 and 1836. His designs, for what was in many ways the
most prestigious commission of his entire career, received
the official approval of King George III and a Committee
of the House of Lords in 1794. The fact that they were
never executed, due solely to a combination of the
Napoleonic Wars and the machinations of James Wyatt,
was the principal misfortune of a career which Soane
regarded as full of misfortunes and constantly thwarted
by persecution.

Soane had taken care to display a ravishing succession of
coloured drawings prepared in such a way as to whet the
imagination of anyone at all sympathetic to grandeur,
colour and display in architecture. He proposed to present
the restored Westminster Hall like a medieval jewel or icon
in a showcase consisting of Neoclassical ranges in the

to their request that the statue should be housed in Soane's
new National Debt Redemption Office in view of Pitt's
close association with its activities.

Soane, who venerated Pitt as 'the saviour of Europe',[8]
created a kind of mythic tomb chamber in which the
brilliantly illuminated cenotaph was visible at the far end
of the entrance hall behind a trio of arches silhouetted
dramatically against light flooding down from the glass
lantern, high above the statue of Pitt. To separate the
public commercial space from the privileged area of the
cenotaph, the central broader arch contained a low
balustrade, reminiscent of altar rails in a church. Soane
created, in effect, a shrine, though there was no reason
why the setting for a statue of a great statesman should
have had any necrological overtones. The idea of calling
it a cenotaph originated with Soane himself.

At the summit of this remarkable tribune was a peristyle
of columns in the Corinthian order, a mark of Soane's
veneration for the greatest political figure of his age and a
fit accompaniment to Westmacott's commanding bronze

FIGURE 41   FIGURE 42

FIGURE 43

manner of Marie-Joseph Peyre, with Corinthian colonnades and pavilions capped with low stone domes. Soane estimated that the scheme would cost £124,600 and take five years to complete.[12]

His design contained a theatrically conceived staircase whose ornament he enriched in subsequent designs, leaving its remarkable disposition unchanged. With its name and its drama inspired by Bernini's celebrated stair for Pope Alexander VII in the Vatican (fig. 41), Soane's Scala Regia would have represented something quite new in England, as well as preceding by nearly a decade Chalgrin's comparable staircase for the French Senate at the Palais du Luxembourg. Rising in three widely separated flights, each of which was marked by a pair of statues of English kings, Soane's Scala Regia (fig. 42, cat. 181) led to a landing lit dramatically by a large lunette window. Soane, who praised Bernini's staircase in his Royal Academy lectures,[13] may have recalled the surprising advice

given by William Chambers to his pupils when visiting Rome to 'Observe well the works of the celebrated Bernini'.[14]

Wyatt's death in 1813, and Soane's appointment in the following year as one of the three 'attached architects' to the Board of Works, brought him into renewed contact with the House of Lords. In February 1822, when George IV approved Soane's designs for the Law Courts, he told the Surveyor General that Soane should prepare designs for a new Royal Entrance to the House of Lords at the south end of Wyatt's new façade.[15] Though conceived as part of the gradual process of improving the surroundings of Westminster Hall, this new entrance undoubtedly owed much to the personal intervention of the King who was always interested in displays of royal magnificence.

As a result, Soane designed and executed a spectacularly theatrical sequence of ceremonial spaces in the remarkably short space of 1822–24. The King was to process to his throne in the House of Lords through the Royal Entrance and up the Scala Regia (see cat. 191) which led via three flights, each of seven steps, to a cross lobby with apsidal ends and into a richly columnar Anteroom. From here, the procession turned at right angles along the Royal Gallery (fig. 43, cat. 192) which consisted of three compartments, each lit with a dome containing stained glass. The panels over the two chimneypieces were to contain paintings of the Battles of Trafalgar and Waterloo.

In this brilliant response to George IV's love of public magnificence, Soane provided the florid splendour required by the King but nonetheless incorporated some of his own personal idiosyncrasies. The whole colourful procession is wonderfully recorded in a succession of watercolours like stills from a film.[16] George IV used these spaces when he opened Parliament in November 1826, a ceremony recorded by Prince Pückler-Muskau who stressed that 'the whole pageant, including the King's costume, reminded me strikingly of one of those historical plays which are here got up so well; nothing was wanting but the "flourish of trumpets" which accompanies the entrance and exit of one of Shakespeare's kings, to make the illusion complete'.[17] Soane, with his own devotion to Shakespeare, would doubtless have been happy with this perception of the historical and theatrical flavour.

The robustly ornamented classicism of Soane's staircase may also reflect that of the work carried out for Napoleon by Percier and Fontaine at the Tuileries Palace in Paris.

Figure 44

The Court of Exchequer, viewed from the entrance from Westmister Hall, drawn by Joseph Michael Gandy, 1826 (cat. 204) (SM Vol. 61, 57)

Figure 45

Interior view of the Court of King's Bench, drawn by Joseph Michael Gandy, 1826 (cat. 203) (SM Vol. 61, 46)

FIGURE 44

FIGURE 45

Soane, who may have seen this on his visit to Paris in 1819, contrasted London royal residences and public buildings unfavourably in his Royal Academy lectures with the splendour of Parisian buildings such as the Louvre and the Tuileries.[18] Certainly, George IV was ever anxious to outdo Napoleon in grandeur.

In his *Description of Three Designs for the Two Houses of Parliament, made in 1779, 1794 and 1796*, Soane made it clear that his house in Lincoln's Inn Fields was a self-portrait where the imposing paintings by Joseph Michael Gandy of his public buildings, which dominated so many of the interiors, formed a speaking repository of his life and ambitions: 'On the walls of this house and in portfolios some hundreds of these designs may be seen – many of them, in their results and associations, the sources to me of infinite delight, and others of bitter mortification.'[19]

The New Law Courts

Soane's commission in 1820 to design new Law Courts presented him with one of his greatest challenges and problems, thanks to the growing appreciation of the medieval buildings at the Palace of Westminster. If Soane's Gothic exterior was unsuccessful (see cat. 208), the complex web of top-lit spaces behind it ranked in architectural importance with his work at the Bank of England and at his own house in Lincoln's Inn Fields. The critic John Britton appreciated Soane's achievement in such interiors, claiming that 'the different modes of lighting the numerous apartments, stair-cases and corridors of these Courts should be studied by every young Architect'.[20]

However, the Law Courts have not received the attention they deserve, partly because they were demolished in the 1880s with no interior photographic record being made, but also because they were delicately downgraded by Sir John Summerson who complained of them that there 'is no new invention here'.[21] Today, we are more struck by the ingenuity and variety of Soane's Law Courts in which he strained to create a language of historical resonance which would be appropriate to the august setting (fig. 44, cat. 210) and the solemn function of the buildings. Rather like Hawksmoor's work at All Souls College, Oxford, this haunting personal language occupied a position halfway between classic and Gothic. It may, indeed, have been a response to the current debate about the relative appropriateness of Greek or Gothic for new

Figure 46

View of the interior of the
Privy Council Chamber,
drawn by Joseph Michael
Gandy, 1827 (cat. 188)
(SM 15/5/1)

FIGURE 46

Figure 47

Model of an early design for
the Privy Council and Board
of Trade Offices, 1824 (cat.
186) (SM MR31)

buildings in this historic setting. The grained oak with
which most of the walls in the lower parts of the courts
were covered had narrow vertical panels almost like an
abstract version of Tudor linenfold panelling. Above, the
elaborate plasterwork ceilings were all white, the only
colour being provided by splashes of red drapery and
carpets, hinting at the rich majesty of the law. The gallery
of the Court of King's Bench (fig. 45, cat. 203), the long
passageways and the side aisles of the Bail Court had
partially concealed top-lighting using a pale amber glass
creating an autumnal glow which we can appreciate in the
Soane Museum now that the coloured glazing has been
restored.

The Privy Council Chamber

The commission to design a new Privy Council Chamber
at the historic heart of Whitehall in 1823, which Soane
received in his capacity as Attached Architect at the Board
of Works, meant much to an architect who shared with
King George IV a veneration for royal ceremony. Though
the Privy Council had already lost much of its power to
cabinet and parliament by Soane's time, it was nonetheless
eloquent of its role as the historic instrument through

which the monarch governed his kingdom from the
medieval period up to the Civil War.[22] The decision to
house it in a splendid new room as late as 1823 (fig. 46,
cat. 188) may have pleased George IV with his love of
ceremony and tradition, but it is hard to imagine that his
Prime Minister, Lord Liverpool, can have welcomed the
expense. Liverpool was, nonetheless, adept at enabling
his sovereign to enjoy the illusion of power. At this time,
the Privy Council was a largely ceremonial body whose
members met in full court dress about half a dozen times
a year, immediately before meetings of the Grand Cabinet,
or Cabinet Council.[23] The sole functions of this latter
body, performed in the presence of the sovereign, were to
approve the King's Speech at the opening and closing of
Parliament, and to advise him on the exercise of the royal
prerogative of mercy on behalf of those capitally convicted
by the City of London and Court of Middlesex Sessions at
the Old Bailey.[24] The ossification and, in purely practical
terms, relative unimportance of the Privy Council and the
Grand Cabinet is suggested by the fact that the *Court
Circular*, contemporary newspapers and even Ministers
were apt to confuse the two bodies.[25]

The Chamber allocated to the Privy Council from the

FIGURE 47

Figure 48

Design perspective of the
portico, with the carriage
entrance on an inclined
plane, for a Royal Palace
on Constitution Hill, drawn
by Joseph Michael Gandy,
1827 (cat. 183)
(SM P260)

FIGURE 48

fire at Whitehall in 1698 until 1811 had formed part of the historic Monmouth Lodgings of the 1660s.[26] The new Chamber which Soane provided on a different site in 1823–27 had a semi-Gothic vault which may have been a response to the medieval origins of the King's Council. The unusual way in which this vault was silhouetted against the light from side windows rising above it was a precise parallel to the vaulting and lighting arrangements in the side aisles of Henry VII's chapel at Westminster Abbey.

The Board of Trade

Soane's Privy Council Chamber was the most interesting part of the large new premises which he built in 1824–26 to house the Board of Trade and the Privy Council (fig. 47, cat. 186). The Board of Trade was established in 1694 as a committee of the King's Privy Council in order to deal with the complaints of merchants and to protect England's trade interests overseas.[27] Re-established by William Pitt the Younger in 1786, it was transformed in the early nineteenth century from an advisory committee of the Privy Council into an administrative department of state.[28]

When the old buildings occupied by the Board of Trade in Whitehall were about to be demolished, Soane's love of historical souvenirs led him to attempt to preserve the seventeenth-century ceiling of the old Board Room, ornamented with the initials of James and Anne, Duke and Duchess of Monmouth and Buccleuch, 'J A M B' beneath a ducal coronet. Soane explained that to 'preserve the recollection of this Room, the new Board Room is decorated in the same character'.[29]

In his final designs for the Board of Trade of June 1824 Soane paid tribute to Inigo Jones's Banqueting House opposite, for he gave it a richly modelled façade,

ornamented with a continuous colonnade of engaged Ionic or Corinthian columns. Soane stressed that his remodelled Whitehall, terminating axially with the north transept entrance of Westminster Abbey, would form 'a great National Work, picturesque and symmetrical in all its parts'.[30]

The Royal Palace

The idea of embellishing the western approach to London, as well as of raising a Royal Palace in Hyde Park, went back to Gwynn's *London and Westminster Improved* (1766). Soane's designs for a new Royal Palace (cat. 183, fig. 48) thus became linked in his mind with the provision of a new western entrance into the metropolis and with an associated ceremonial way which the King would take from Windsor Castle to his throne in the House of Lords.[31] Soane had designed a new Royal Palace to be built in Hyde Park as early as 1779 when he was in Rome.

On George IV's accession Soane remodelled this project, which he now resited in the gardens of Buckingham House since that residence had been in his charge since 1814. He exhibited a succession of striking views of it at the Royal Academy in 1821, 1827 and 1828. As with his scheme for a British Senate House, he chose to illustrate it in its setting at the end of Constitution Hill where it commanded distant prospects of Westminster Abbey, St Paul's Cathedral and the Monument, with 'the ever flowing Thames and its forest of masts and noble bridges, with the undulating hills of Surrey and Kent bounding the horizon, closing the scene and making a superb frame to the picture'. Soane here showed an environmental sensitivity akin to that in contemporary Berlin of Schinkel who had learned much from his early years as a panorama and diorama painter.

Soane regarded his proposal that the palace should be approached through a triumphal arch as one of the utmost novelty. Stressing what he regarded as the uniqueness of his own project, Soane here added a note in his own hand, dated 27 March 1828 that such an arch had never been used 'for the Entrance into a Royal Palace'.[32] However, on his visits to Paris in 1814 and 1819, he must have seen the Arc du Carrousel which had been begun for Napoleon in 1806 from designs by Percier and Fontaine as the entrance to the Tuileries Palace.

Both Soane and Nash showed keen interest in the public buildings and ceremonies created by Percier and Fontaine

1 Watkin 1996 (1), p. 509.
2 E. Burke, *Reflections on the Revolution in France*, London, 1790, in L. G. Mitchell, ed., *The Writings and Speeches of Edmund Burke*, vol. 8, Oxford, 1989, pp. 187–188.
3 M.-A. Laugier, *Essai sur l'architecture*, 2nd ed., Paris, 1755, p. 85.
4 See E. A. Reitan, ed., *George III: Tyrant or Constitutional Monarch?*, Boston, 1964, and L. Colley, 'The Apotheosis of George III: Loyalty, Royalty and the British Nation 1760–1820', *Past and Present*, no. 102, February 1984, pp. 94–129.
5 SM Archives MBi/37/2.
6 *Summary of the Minutes of the Commissioners for the Reduction of the National Debt 1786–1860*, HMSO, London, 1961, M170.
7 M. Busco, *Sir Richard Westmacott: Sculptor*, Cambridge, 1994, pp. 74–75.
8 In a letter to George Canning of 14 April 1820 in which Soane offered him drawings of the Pitt Cenotaph (SM Priv.Corr.IV.P.2.1 no 1).
9 The National Debt Redemption Office was demolished in 1900 but the statue survives at Pembroke College, Cambridge, where Pitt was an undergraduate from 1774–76.
10 Soane, *Brief Statement*, p. 17.
11 Soane, *Description of Three Designs...*, printed privately, 1835, p. 71.
12 Soane, *Statement of Facts*, 1799, p. 31.
13 Watkin 1996 (1), p. 607.
14 From Chambers's letter to Edward Stevens of 5 August 1774, cited in J. Harris, *Sir William Chambers*, London, 1970, p. 21. Soane attached so much significance to this letter that he made a copy of it and eventually acquired the original.
15 SM New Law Courts Correspondence, parcel 2, no. 57 (Stephenson to Soane, 28 February 1822).
16 du Prey 1985, p. 102.
17 E. M. Butler, ed., *A Regency Visitor: The English Tour of Prince Pückler-Muskau, Described in His Letters 1826–28*, London, 1957, pp. 88–89.
18 Watkin 1996 (1), p. 637.
19 Soane, *Description*, 1835–56, pp. 71–74, and in *Description of Three Designs*, 1835, p. 74.
20 Britton and Pugin, 1828, vol. II, p. 261.
21 Summerson 1983, p. 300.
22 See E. R. Turner, *The Privy Council of England in the Seventeenth and Eighteenth Centuries*, 2 vols, Baltimore, 1928.
23 See A. Aspinall, 'The Grand Cabinet, 1800–1837', *Politica*, vol. III, 1938, pp. 324–344.

Figure 49

Claude-Nicolas Ledoux, Barrière de la Villette, Place de Stalingrad, Paris, 1784–87

FIGURE 49

for Napoleon. They both owned copies of Lafitte's *Description de l'Arc de Triomphe de l'Etoile* (Paris, 1810) and of Percier and Fontaine's *Cérémonies et fêtes pour le couronnement de Napoléon et Joséphine* (Paris, 1807).

The National Monument and Processional Route
Soane's Royal Palace was also the product of a new royal iconography of his own invention which was his most remarkable contribution to town planning. This was his unexecuted but imaginative Processional Route first sketched in 1827,[33] linking Windsor Castle to the new public and ceremonial buildings in the heart of the imperial capital. Related to this was his National Monument, dedicated to recent naval and military heroes. One of his designs for this consisted of three single-arch Triumphal Arches, modelled on the Arch of Titus,

dedicated to Wellington and Nelson, and forming entries to Hyde Park and St James's Park.[34] He explained that, 'the entire group forming the great western entrance into the metropolis [was] suggested by the Acropolis in Athens and the magnificent approach into the Piazza del Popolo in Rome', sources chosen to create the 'appropriate character'.[35] In citing the Porta del Popolo, a work of the 1560s then attributed to Michelangelo, he once again returned to papal Rome as a source for modern urban splendour. A related perspective drawn by Joseph Michael Gandy bears an inscription citing as a source 'the magnificent barriers [fig. 49] and other great national Monuments in Paris and ... the Works of Le Peyre, Patte, Baltard, and other eminent architects of the French School'.[36] His Trajanic columns were doubtless influenced by the Colonne Vendôme (1806–10)

24 See V. A. C. Gatrell, *The Hanging Tree: Execution and the English People 1770–1868*, Oxford, 1994, chapter 20, 'The King in His Council'.

25 A. Aspinall, op cit., p. 329.

26 *Survey of London*, 'Parish of St Margaret, Westminster', part III, vol. XIV, London, 1931, p. 78.

27 See H. Llewellyn Smith, *The Board of Trade*, London, 1928.

28 See R. Prouty, *The Transformation of the Board of Trade, 1830–1855: A Study of Administrative Reorganisation in the Heyday of Laissez Faire*, London, 1957.

29 Soane, *Designs for Public and Private Buildings*, p. 8.

30 *Ibid.*, p. 10.

31 See Sawyer 1996.

32 Soane, 'Designs for Public Improvements in London and Westminster', 2nd impression, 1828, p. 3 (unpublished).

33 In a three-page addendum to his *Brief Statement*.

34 SM 15/3/1-2.

35 Soane, *Memoirs*, p. 42.

36 Victoria and Albert Museum, Soane Drawings, no. 2830. The references are to C.-N. Ledoux, M.-J. Peyre, Pierre Patte, and probably to the designs by P.-L. Baltard of the 1820s for enhancing the Panthéon.

37 SM 63/4.

Figure 50

Design perspective, drawn by Joseph Michael Gandy, of Soane's Sepulchral Church for the Duke of York, St James's Park, London, 1827 (cat. 184) (SM P275)

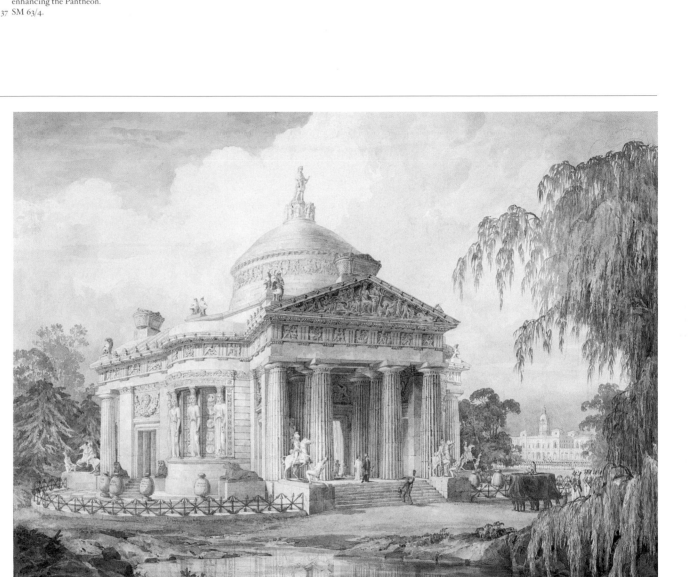

FIGURE 50

which he would have seen on his visits to Paris in 1814 and 1819.

The Processional Route involved a great national monument to the Duke of York, George III's second son, heir-presumptive to the throne, and Commander-in-chief at Waterloo, who had died in 1827[37] (figs 38, 50; cat. 184). The ornamental richness of the interior, with its screens of giant caryatids, echoed the Salle des Maréchaux at the Tuileries, designed by Percier and Fontaine for the Duke of York's arch enemy, Napoleon.

Soane's National Monument and Processional Route came to nothing. A child of his time, he had not imagined that the keynotes of the future development of Whitehall would not be provision for royal display, but government offices on an unprecedented scale. Nor had he ever reconciled himself to the fact that commerce, not the

monarch, was the real king of London, and that trade always came before elegance with the City fathers. In considering the reasons for Soane's failure to erect great public buildings, we should also bear in mind, first, that it was possibly not a field for which his talents naturally fitted him; second, that the opportunities for building of all types were diminished during the Revolutionary and Napoleonic Wars, while government spending in the years immediately following Waterloo was marked by considerable stinginess; and, finally, that, for political and other reasons, Soane may not have endeared himself to George III or George IV. Beyond all these factors, we should not forget the growing belief in early nineteenth-century Britain that Gothic buildings would express the national identity better than Grecian, especially in historic settings such as Westminster and Whitehall.

Soane's Legacy

Figure 51 (opposite)
**Photograph by Frank
Yerbury of the demolition
of the Colonial Office at
the Bank of England,
c. 1925–26**

Soane's idiosyncratic and personal style of architecture had many critics in his lifetime and a small following after his death. In the twentieth century, Soane's stripped or astylar classicism found favour with the protagonists of the Modern movement who re-evaluated his work in different ways: John Summerson, for example, defined the primitivist element in Soane, and Henry-Russell Hitchcock was impressed by his precision in handling materials. In the last thirty years architects have admired Soane's handling of space and light above everything; they find his work relevant and stimulating, and do not dismiss his buildings as they might dismiss the work of Sir William Chambers or Robert Adam. This brief essay attempts to outline the fluctuating reputation of John Soane from his death to the present day.

Soane died on 20 January 1837 at his house in Lincoln's Inn Fields. His funeral service was held privately, and he was buried in St Giles's burial ground in St Pancras, beneath the monument which he had designed for his wife in 1816 (cats 109–111). Shortly thereafter, on Monday 6 February, Thomas Leverton Donaldson, the Honorary Secretary of the newly formed Institute of British Architects, read a paper on Soane and his achievements at a meeting: it was, in effect, a memorial address.[1] The frankness of his homage in such circumstances is strange. He began: 'I stand not here to exaggerate or extenuate his failures nor to be the mere panegyrist of his merits ... I have only to regard him as an Architect, who, as an artist, as a man of science, a munificent lover of his profession, and above all, as a benefactor of this Institute, has just claims to our admiration and respect.'[2] Fairly said, but he went on to be decidedly critical about certain aspects of Soane's architecture. Although he praised the plans of the early buildings illustrated in *Plans ... of Buildings executed in the Counties of Norfolk, Suffolk...*, published in 1788, 'their distribution being simple, convenient, and striking in effect', Donaldson found that the elevations were 'as deficient in taste as the plans are admirable in conception'. The problem was the handling of the orders: 'the entablatures are rarely more than one-sixth the height of the column, the cornices are meagre, and the openings generally without dressings'.[3] For the Bank of England, however, he was full of praise – this was the '*Capo d'opera* of Sir John Soane', principally for the three-dimensional handling of the Tivoli order, although he does refer to the 'many aberrations of genius' in the interior and 'too often

an attempt at effect by ignoble means'.[4] He also admitted that many of the works of Soane's later years, including Chelsea Hospital, the Law Courts, the Board of Trade offices, the Freemasons' Hall and many others, all had the same 'peculiar defects'.[5]

This then was the official summing-up of Soane's career by an arch-establishment member of the profession: Soane was to be praised for his actions as a benefactor, for his work as a Professor of Architecture, for the generosity of his gift to the nation of his house and Museum, with his fine library collected for the benefit of architectural students, but not for his architecture, which was judged to be 'peculiar', personal and given to novelties.

Donaldson was not alone in these opinions, he was simply giving voice to the many criticisms of so-called eccentricities which Soane had borne throughout his career. For example, the reviewer of Soane's *Designs for Public and Private Buildings* (1828), published in the *Athenaeum* in 1829, wrote that Soane in his later works 'struck out into a style peculiarly his own; and faulty and ridiculous as that style undoubtedly deserves to be considered, it still displays so many pleasing inventions, such playfulness of fancy, and so many real master-strokes of genius, that wonder and admiration almost disarm criticism of its just severity. Still, we cannot blind ourselves to the excessive mannerism, to the affectation and quackery which pervade all the works of Mr Soane and are equally recognisable in his designs, his details, his drawings, his lectures, and his letter-press in its every line, to a degree of offensiveness which, if it may be palliated, cannot be excused, by the earnestness and real love for his profession which appear in connexion with them'.[6]

What was the immediate legacy of Soane's work? Very few picked up on the most obvious features of the Soane style although both John Foulston and George Wightwick often adopted the stripped façades, the incised ornament and the domed interior spaces in Plymouth and the West Country. Wightwick, at least, actually understood the nature of Soane's architecture which he describes so perceptively. He had worked briefly for Soane in 1826 as his amanuensis but took umbrage at one of Soane's slighting remarks and walked out. He was later received 'with much kindness' and after his retirement in 1851 contributed an account of his time with Soane to *Bentley's Miscellany*, the most amusing contemporary description of Soane that survives. Wightwick built up a considerable local practice

Figure 52

George Wightwick,
Design for a casino in the
Soanean style from *The
Palace of Architecture*,
1840

FIGURE 52

Figure 53

A. W. N. Pugin's illustration
in *Contrasts* (1836), which
satirised the façade of
Soane's house at
13 Lincoln's Inn Fields

FIGURE 53

in Plymouth as well as becoming what Colvin has called 'the first English architectural journalist'.[7] In *The Palace of Architecture* (1840),[8] he produced an elaborately illustrated survey of the historical styles, devoting a section to the 'Soanean' style which he called 'more than an episode – an essential passage in the progress of Architectural taste. Sir John Soane struck out a style of his own … containing much that is extremely beautiful, and evincing a more playful fancy – if not a more vigorous genius – than had been exhibited for centuries. His reputation as a practiser of Roman and Greco-Roman Architecture is rather supported by his magnificent designs for Royal Palaces, Senate-Houses, etc, than by his buildings: but there is enough in his own peculiar style (as exemplified in the Bank of England) to warrant our deference and high admiration. It seems to have been his aim to unite the classic delicacies of Greek and Roman design with the

playfulness of the Gothic – not by the use of the pointed arch – but by adopting the principle of continuous lines ramifying (without horizontal impediment) from the verticle into the circular'. Wightwick then included an illustration of a small casino in the Soane style (fig. 52) which exemplified Soane's 'peculiar feeling for *linear*, rather than *substantial*, decoration. His surfaces are frequently flat, deriving their character from sunk *frettes* and grooved work.' Wightwick's insight into Soane's work is remarkable for its day and predates any other analysis of the primitive qualities of his style by more than a century.

Several of Soane's pupils, notably John Sanders, Francis Edwards and David Mocatta, continued another aspect of Soane's work: the abstracted brick classicism, which so outraged Soane's contemporaries, of the Norfolk houses, the Chelsea Infirmary and Dulwich Picture Gallery. Sanders's Duke of York's Headquarters and his buildings

Figure 54

An architectural caricature, attributed to A. W. N. Pugin, satirising imaginary schemes for the New Houses of Parliament by Soane, Nash, Smirke and Wilkins, c. 1834–36 (SM 69/3/8)

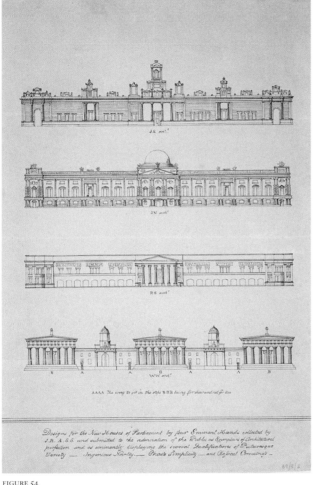

FIGURE 54

at the Royal Military Academy, Sandhurst, Edwards's Lion Breweries and Mocatta's buildings for the London, Brighton and South Coast line were all of stock brick and had the dignified, functional simplicity of early Victorian architecture. Interestingly, Charles Robert Cockerell wrote in a disparaging way about the Sandhurst buildings, mistaking them for Smirke's, and referring to them as 'beautiful architecture finely considered and disposed, but no genius whatever, no character of a College of Military, no vast robust features, nothing to strike or impose, a front much like other fronts whether a library, a Theatre, a conservatory, a mansion, an Hospital – always Temp[l]e of Minerva [i.e. the Parthenon Doric order]'.[9] He is echoing the same criticism made so cruelly by George Soane in 1815 of Soane's Chelsea Infirmary (see p. 188).

After Soane's death, Cockerell stepped neatly into Soane's shoes, both as Professor of Architecture at the Royal Academy and as Architect to the Bank, but had, however, scarcely a kind word to say about his predecessor. He found much to criticise in Soane's Bank and in 1848 destroyed the austere line of Soane's acroteria along the parapets by substituting a massive balustrade. In his *Diaries*, he wrote of the Law Courts in 1826: 'thought them trivial, absurd in their arch[itecture]. Should not expect to hear sense in such foolish Rooms'.[10]

There were a few lone voices in praise of Soane's originality in the 1840s. Richard Brown, an architect, writer and perspectivist who had known Soane, analysed the features of his 'peculiar' style: the continuous lines, the 'linear' rather than 'foliated' decoration, the absence of pediments and simple surfaces.[11] In addition there was John Weale's splendid comment: 'In the midst of all this there was but one man, the late Sir J. Soane, who dared to be positively original. All others were mad in some particular foreign fashion; but he alone was mad in his own way ... there was a method in the old knight's madness.'[12]

Times had changed, however, and originality, and particularly Soane's kind of personal originality, could hardly find favour in the period dominated by the Gothic Revival and Ruskin. His reputation was also especially soured by the biting satire of Pugin's *Contrasts* (1836), where the 'Professor's own house' was placed in comparison with 'similar edifices of more ancient periods' (fig. 53). There was, as David Watkin has pointed out,[13] a deep irony in the fact that both Pugin and Soane hated developers' architecture and the papery meanness of modern Gothic. The very 'papery' quality which Pugin satirised in the façade of Soane's house was later to be praised by Hitchcock for the precision of its finish.[14] Pugin is also thought to be the author of an unidentified architectural caricature satirising imaginary schemes by 'four Eminent hands' for the new Houses of Parliament, datable to 1834–36 (fig. 54). The 'hands' were Soane, Nash, Smirke and Wilkins, and in many ways Wilkins was more severely hit than Soane, whose design is satirised for its picturesque variety. The attribution to Pugin is very likely as he had written in *Contrasts*: 'No one can look on Buckingham Palace, the National Gallery, the Board of Trade, the new buildings at the British Museum, or any of the principal buildings lately erected, but must feel the very existence of such public monuments as a national disgrace.'[15]

Soane's name was kept alive throughout the nineteenth century by references to the Bank of England and to his

Figure 55
The Monk's Parlour,
13 Lincoln's Inn Fields,
as shown in the *Illustrated
London News*, 25 June 1864

FIGURE 55

house and Museum. Most found reason to praise the Bank, which left a legacy of another kind in establishing a grand prototype, not in a specific stylistic sense, but rather for commercial buildings in general. Many banks followed the precedent for single-storey buildings with blind exteriors and interiors lit by skylights set above domes. Soane's 13 Lincoln's Inn Fields was universally liked for its eccentricities, curiosities and picturesque arrangements rather than for its architecture (fig. 55).

Henry James described the Museum in *A London Life* (1889) in a way that is echoed in many descriptions of the period: 'The cab stopped at the Soane Museum which Laura Wing had always wanted to see, a compatriot having once told her that it was one of the most curious things in London and one of the least known ... The heterogeneous objects collected by the late Sir John Soane are arranged in a fine old dwelling house, and the place gives one the impression of a sort of Saturday afternoon of one's youth – a long rummaging visit, under indulgent care, to some

eccentric and rather alarming old travelled person. Our young friends wandered from room to room and thought everything queer and some few objects interesting; Mr Wendover said it would be a very good place to find a thing you couldn't find anywhere else – it illustrated the prudent virtue of keeping.'[16]

Until the 1920s, due to difficulty of access and a reputation for darkness, the Museum had comparatively little architectural influence: it was only open on Wednesdays, Thursdays and Fridays in each week in April, May and June, and on Wednesdays and Thursdays in each week in February, March, July and August. Many heedless visitors came to Lincoln's Inn Fields on the wrong day and went away disappointed.

During the first two decades of the twentieth century a reassessment of Soane was brought about by the revival of classicism and a new public interest in post-Impressionism and modern architecture. Since the 1880s the architects of the Aesthetic and Arts and Crafts movements had taken as much interest in English architecture of the late seventeenth century and the English Baroque as they had in vernacular building. These influences were overlaid around 1910 by an interest in Beaux-Arts classicism led by Sir Reginald Blomfield, which in turn led to such influential books as Albert Richardson's *London Houses from 1660–1820* (1911), and, more importantly, to the same author's *Monumental Classic Architecture in Great Britain and Ireland* (1914).

In *London Houses*, Richardson looked at houses by Adam, Leverton, Taylor, Wyatt and Soane and drew attention to the façade of 21 St James's Square by Soane, praising its 'simplicity' and 'refinement' of detail, which he found 'free from insipidity and mannerisms'.[17] In *Monumental Classic Architecture* he goes much further, devoting considerable attention to Soane's work and illustrating the Bank of England with outstanding black-and-white photographs. His view of Soane was that 'while he kept to the spirit of the Academic Classic he achieved a great deal, but when he attempted to be daringly original he fell into the same pitfall that awaits all who have like desires'; he admired the Roman in Soane and not the 'Bœotian', the name Soane's critics applied to his primitivist style in a supposedly Athenian age.[18] There was nothing very different in this assessment from the criticisms of the 1830s and 1840s, but what was new was the full-blown praise Richardson lavished on the Bank and on Soane: 'The Bank must be regarded as his masterpiece. Sir John Soane was the most original architect of the 18th century. An extremely able Classicist he imparted to his works a rare elegance and finish, the result of care, taste and continual study. From Piranesi's etchings he profited much as portions of the interior of the Bank and the Picture Gallery at Dulwich reveal. Strange as it may seem, his earliest works were his best. The entrance gateway from the Lothbury Courtyard at the Bank is an admirable instance of his monumental work; next in merit ranks the circular end joining the Princes Street and Lothbury façades.'[19]

Richardson had led the way. But it was really in the 1920s that Soane became the generally admired architect that he is today, and it was the somewhat unlikely figure of Roger Fry who first drew public attention to the primitivist qualities in Soane's work in a controversial lecture delivered on 19 May 1921 at the Royal Institute of British Architects. As the organiser of the two pioneering exhibitions in 1910 and 1912 that had brought the new

French art from Manet to Picasso to London, Fry had become the English spokesman for Modernism and abstract form. He also had close links with architects: one of his closest friends was C. R. Ashbee and his aunt was married to Alfred Waterhouse. He had decided views on architecture and design and detested 'the archaeological humbug of the historical-revival styles that typified so much Victorian and Edwardian architecture'.[20] The RIBA wanted a stimulating lecture series and Fry accepted, but with misgivings, writing to Vanessa Bell: 'I'm beginning to be alarmed at my lecture on the 19th to the FRIBA. When I begin to put down what I think of architecture I see I shall be thought a violent and perhaps dangerous lunatic by these practitioners in façades. However, I may as well go through with it.'[21] He called his lecture 'Architectural Heresies of a Painter', and the gist of what he had to say was that 'architects had substituted for the art of architecture the art of dressing buildings according to the fashion; there were two kinds of beauty, the natural and the aesthetic and we had so arranged it that neither of them appeared in our buildings'.[22] Fry did not think that architects ever made much of the possible play of elementary plastic forms and most of his lecture inveighed against useless ornament. As he said, 'To my mind there has been little architecture of outstanding merit in this country since the end of the 18th century. Sir John Soane, who built the Bank of England and the Dulwich Picture Gallery, is, with one or two exceptions, the only architect since then whose work is tolerable. Architects have constantly sacrificed themselves to useless ornament, and within my own time there have been instances in which an architect, after having half erected a building, has been ordered to add a thousand pounds' worth or more ornament!'[23]

Fry's lecture did its job well in stirring up a good deal of controversy. *The Times* covered it extensively on 20, 23 and 24 May 1921, in interviews with John Simpson, Fry and Sir Reginald Blomfield. Blomfield, as one would expect, disagreed strongly with Fry and particularly with Fry's praise of Soane, saying that 'Soane was a man of some ability, with a mischievous passion for original design and for the rehabilitation of some of the ugliest details of the Classic. His façade of the Bank of England, with its blocked windows as a motive of decoration, is hardly a happy illustration of expression of purpose in architecture. If he wanted to denote strength, as it is presumed he did,

Figure 56
A comparison between
Soane's and Herbert
Baker's plans for the Bank
of England, showing the
picturesque quality of
Soane's design contrasted
with the regularity of
Baker's plan of *c.* 1922–23

 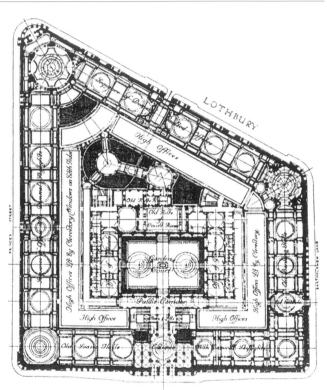

FIGURE 56

it would have been better to make the walls as solid as those of Newgate instead of pretending to have windows and then blocking them in.'[24] Nor did the architectural press have support for Fry's view on Soane. *The Builder* declared: 'How can we agree that Sir John Soane was one of the few tolerable architects since the end of the 18th century?'[25] Fry's lecture had, however, caused a good deal of public discussion and had drawn Soane's name into the arena of Modernism for the first time. He published it later in the year but, strange to say, included no mention of Soane in the final version; perhaps he felt he had gone too far.

During the 1920s Arthur Bolton, who had been appointed Curator of the Soane Museum in 1917, did much to publicise Soane's architecture and the Museum with *The Works of Sir John Soane, F.R.S., F.S.A., R.A. (1753–1837)* (1924), *The Portrait of Sir John Soane, R.A.* (1927) and *Lectures on Architecture...* (1929), as well as numerous articles on Soane and his collections in the architectural press. We owe a lot to Bolton as he was a good historian and an architect: for the first time Soane's work was set in context and his buildings were well illustrated with plans and photographs of many of the drawings in the Museum.

But to some extent, for all his loyalty, Bolton always remained sceptical: Soane never replaced Robert Adam in his admiration. In a lecture on the 'Architecture and Decoration of Robert Adam and Sir John Soane' which he gave at the Royal Society of Arts in May 1920, Bolton described Soane as 'a designer of profoundly original but uncertain quality – a pioneer, pointing towards something which, perhaps, is incapable of being realised, and at the same time hampered himself by difficulties of expression never completely mastered. His buildings are crippled by smallness of scale and means and are inadequate to the real grandeur of the design. He had not, it is clear, Adam's gift of reasonable house design.'[26]

These qualified views, however, did not prevent Bolton from fighting throughout the 1920s to prevent the destruction of Soane's greatest work, the Bank of England. It is ironic that this tragedy, which Pevsner called 'the worst individual loss suffered by London architecture in the first half of the twentieth century',[27] should have happened at the very time when architects were turning to neo-Georgian styles, to the Regency, to Scandinavian Neoclassicism, to Modernism, and to Soane. The great interior banking halls could have been saved as there was

FIGURE 57

Figure 57

Giles Gilbert Scott.
K2 telephone box,
1924–26, influenced
by Soanean forms

growing support for Soane, but there was virtually no lobby at the time in favour of the conservation of buildings that were not 'ancient monuments', and there was still some time to go before the foundation of the Georgian Group in 1937. The Bank needed to expand its accommodation and the chosen architect, Herbert Baker, handled the whole affair with great diplomacy. Soane's supporters were initially mollified by Baker's formal statement in 1922 that the 'proposal under consideration by the Directors includes the retention in its entirety of the outside blank wall with such of Soane's rooms as lie behind it and the construction of a sequence of similar rooms behind the old wall right round the perimeter of the site'[28] (fig. 56). The general consensus at the time was that Soane's plan was chaotic, but few realised at first that it was Baker's intention to sweep away all the interior banking halls, which he then re-created, surprisingly, in a Soanean style.

Ironically, the demolition of the Bank did have the effect of publicising Soane's architecture, as well as his reputation. The splendid black-and-white photographs, taken by Frank Yerbury, of the Bank before its destruction were published widely in the national and architectural press and also served as the plates for a new book on Soane in 1925 by an architect of the younger generation, Harry Birnstingl. Birnstingl, born in 1890, had been trained at the Architectural Association as well as working as a journalist for the *Architects' Journal*. He was, therefore, aware of contemporary thinking in architecture and approached Soane in a different way. He was the first to see Soane as 'the first modern English architect'. 'For', as he said, 'that which distinguishes modern architecture arises from enhanced self-consciousness, from the powers of adaptation and of reasoning; powers acting as often to its detriment as to its good. And these qualities Soane possessed.'[29] Henry-Russell Hitchcock also included Soane as a precursor in his early *Modern Architecture* (1929), recognising him as 'unquestionably the greatest architect of the beginning of the nineteenth century' and as an architect 'working with space, and even with light, for effects of abstract form'.[30]

Consequently, by the time of the centenary of Soane's death in 1937, he was firmly established as one of the greatest of English architects. *The Times* accorded him a third leader and a piece by the young John Summerson, his first on Soane: 'In John Soane British architecture can claim a man of very great imaginative power, whose work has a value of a kind which opinion ascribes readily enough to the English poets, but less readily to the architects.'[31]

During the second half of the twentieth century Soane's architecture slowly came to have a greater influence on the work of contemporary architects. Before World War II this influence was comparatively small, although the work of Raymond Erith in the 1930s is much indebted to Soane's Norfolk and Suffolk houses, and there is, of course, the famous example of the K2 telephone box designed by Sir Giles Gilbert Scott in 1924–26 (fig. 57). In the 1960s, however, architecture began to move away from the orthodox handling of form dictated by the Modern movement in the 1930s towards a more complex manipulation of space and light. This tendency and the reflections of this decade are well represented by Robert Venturi's *Complexity and Contradiction in Architecture* (1966). Venturi took the well-known Miesian jingle 'Less is more' and replaced it with 'Less is a bore', and looked for ambiguities and complexities in the architecture of the past and present that would reinforce an architecture of richness and meaning. The book echoed contemporary thinking and had a considerable influence. Venturi drew attention to many of these qualities in Soane's work: the complex combinations of shapes in his ceilings, the partition of spaces in rooms in the form of suspended arches, the intricacies of planning and of spaces within spaces, and the layering of canopies and domes.

From the 1960s onwards Soane's architecture has been used for inspiration rather than direct imitation, although many architects have acknowledged both the No. 13 Breakfast Room and Dulwich Picture Gallery as direct sources for their designs. Philip Johnson is an early example of an architect experimenting with Soanean 'ambiguities', both in the canopy inside his Guest House at New Canaan (1953, fig. 58), and in the Kneses Tifereth Israel Synagogue at Port Chester, New York (1956, fig. 59), to which Summerson referred in a letter to Dorothy Stroud in 1968: 'Last night I did my "Soanean space" stuff and it went rather well because everybody recognised without being told that Philip Johnsonian space is the same as Soanean space and that in fact his synagogue is some sort of paraphrase of the Court of Chancery'[32] (cat. 201). As Franz Schulze wrote in his biography of Johnson: 'A generation younger than Ledoux and a generation older than Schinkel, Soane was another of the great eighteenth-

FIGURE 59

Figure 58 (opposite)
Philip Johnson,
The Guest House at the
Philip Johnson Residence,
New Canaan, 1953

Figure 59
Philip Johnson, The Kneses
Tifereth Israel Synagogue,
Port Chester, New York,
1956

FIGURE 60

Figure 60
Michael Graves, The
circular entrance lobby
of The Warehouse,
Princeton, 1977–92

FIGURE 63

FIGURE 64

FIGURE 61

FIGURE 62

to nineteenth-century classicists Philip had made a special point of admiring. He was also the most idiosyncratic of the three. In the past, Philip had preferred the soberer formality of Ledoux and Schinkel, but now, perhaps in consequence of his search for new forms, he found Soane's eccentricity especially appropriate to the faintly decadent mood he wished to evoke in the Guest House bedroom. Yet what made that remodeled space appear most radical by the standards of 1953 was Philip's candid use of arch and dome, historical forms that had been universally discarded by the modernists, especially by those close to the International Style.'[33]

During the Postmodern era of the late 1970s and 1980s there have been many reflections of Soanean themes amongst a generation of architects encouraged once more in their architectural schools to seek out imaginative historical references. The Soane Museum became from the 1970s a teaching resource for architectural tutors from all over the world, a place where their students were encouraged to study the handling of light, the canopy and

starfish ceilings, and the vertical and horizontal extensions of space. Michael Graves's house, The Warehouse, at Princeton (1977–92), has several acknowledged references to the Museum, of which the most interesting is a circular entrance lobby, top-lit by a glazed oculus with views down into it from a first-floor gallery (fig. 60). The pleasure Graves takes in the manipulation of light is a link with Soane, although the architectural forms are Graves's own. Arata Isozaki is also interested in Soane. He wrote a book about the Museum in 1989, and his Vories Hall, Ochanomisu Square, Tokyo (1987, fig. 61), uses the classical reference of Soane's Breakfast Room at 13 Lincoln's Inn Fields as an isolated 'quotation', 'to emphasise the strange meeting of East and West in the late twentieth century'.[34]

Oswald Mathias Ungers adapted the theme of buildings within buildings in his design for the Architecture Museum in Frankfurt (1983), where the temple form at the top of the museum (fig. 62) has been likened to the free-standing Students' Room at the Soane Museum.

The work of several architects inspired by Soane was included in an exhibition entitled 'Soane and After' organised by Giles Waterfield at the Dulwich Picture Gallery in 1987.[35] Included were Henry Cobb's Portland Museum of Art at Portland, Maine (1978–82); Jeremy and Fenella Dixon's Tate Gallery Coffee Shop (1983), which is indebted to the Breakfast Room at 13 Lincoln's Inn Fields; James Gowan's swimming pool at the Schreiber House, West Heath Road, Hampstead (1968), and Robert Venturi's and Denise Scott Brown's National Gallery extension (1985–91). In this latter building both Venturi and Scott Brown openly admit their debt to Dulwich Picture Gallery, particularly to its lighting system and to the enfilade of arches (figs 63, 64). Its canted, rather picturesque, plan also has similarities with Soane's plans for the Law Courts and the Bank of England.

As Venturi and Scott Brown wrote in 1986: 'Why do we love the Dulwich Picture Gallery and learn so much from it? We think, because its Classicism is both conventional and deviant:

– Its easy abstraction of the Classical system sets up a tense but subtle balance between Classical form and Classical symbol. The simplification and stylisation of its form and detail achieve a sense of the elemental in architecture, which suggests both Classicism and Modernity and conveys the essence of shelter.

FIGURE 66

FIGURE 65

Figure 65
Juan Navarro Baldeweg,
Congress Hall in
Salamanca, Spain,
1985–92

Figure 66
Juan Navarro Baldeweg,
Top-lit auditorium in the
basement of the Cultural
Centre, Murcia, Spain,
c. 1990

1 Donaldson 1837.
2 *Ibid.*, pp. 7–8.
3 *Ibid.*, p. 14.
4 *Ibid.*, pp. 14–15.
5 *Ibid.*, p. 22.
6 *Athenaeum*, 1829.
7 H. M. Colvin, *A Biographical Dictionary of British Architects, 1600–1840*, London, 1995, p. 1050.
8 G. Wightwick, *The Palace of Architecture*, London, 1840, pp. 191–192.
9 Quoted in D. Watkin, *The Life and Work of C. R. Cockerell RA*, London, 1974, p. 76.
10 *Ibid.*, p. 67.
11 R. Brown, *Domestic Architecture*, London, 1841, p. 289 ff.
12 J. Weale, 'On the Present Condition and Prospects of Architecture in England', *Weale's Quarterly Papers on Architecture*, ii, 1844, pp. 5–6.

13 Watkin 1996 (1), pp. 438–439.
14 Stroud 1961, p. 12.
15 A.W. N. Pugin, *Contrasts*, Salisbury, 1836, p. 31.
16 H. James, *A London Life*, London and New York, 1889, p. 149–151.
17 A. Richardson, *London Houses from 1660–1820*, London, 1911, chapter 6.
18 O. Medley and R. Holyoake, 'On the Sixth, or Bœotian, Order of Architecture' in *Knight's Quarterly Magazine*, vol. II, January–April 1824, pp. 446–463.
19 A. Richardson, *Monumental Classic Architecture in Great Britain and Ireland*, London, 1914, pp. 39–41.
20 Quoted in C. Reed, *A Roger Fry Reader*, Chicago, 1996
21 D. Sutton, *Letters of Roger Fry*, vol. 2, 12 May 1921, London, 1972.
22 'Architectural Snobbery', *The Times*, 20 May 1921.

23 'Mr Fry on Useless Ornament', *The Times*, 23 May 1921.
24 'Sir R. Blomfield and Mr Fry', *The Times*, 24 May 1921.
25 *The Builder*, 27 May 1921, p. 672.
26 *Architectural Review*, January–June 1921, pp. 24–26.
27 N. Pevsner, *London, I: Cities of London and Westminster*, Harmondsworth, 1973, p. 182.
28 *The Builder*, 28 July 1922.
29 Birnstingl 1925, p. 30.
30 Henry-Russell Hitchcock, *Modern Architecture*, New York, 1929, pp. 19–20.
31 *The Times*, 20 January 1937.
32 SM Stroud Bequest, letter from John Summerson, 9 March 1968.
33 F. Schulze, *Philip Johnson: Life and Work*, New York, 1994, p. 238.
34 A. Isozaki in *Apollo*, April 1990, p. 227.
35 Waterfield 1987.

36 *Ibid.*, p. 96.
37 Conversation with Christopher Woodward, October 1998.
38 Conversation with Christopher Woodward, September 1998.
39 Talk delivered at Sir John Soane's Museum, 3 June 1999. MacCormac had earlier written about Soane in the *Architects' Journal*, 1986, 24 April, pp. 40–41.

Figure 67
Rafael Moneo, Atocha Station, Madrid

Figure 68
Rafael Moneo, Library in the Cultural Centre, Don Benito, Badajoz, Spain, 1998–99

Figure 69
Richard MacCormac, Dining Room, St John's College, Oxford

FIGURE 67

FIGURE 68

– It is a small building with generous scale, an architectural oxymoron. The plays of scale between its delicate detail and bold form result in a tempered monumentality, the monumentality most worth having...'[36]

Two Spanish architects have also employed Soanean forms for powerfully simple effects. Juan Navarro Baldewcg's Congress Hall in Salamanca (1985–92, fig. 65), and his Murcia Cultural Centre and Museum (*c.* 1990, fig. 66), use Soane's hanging domes in an imaginative and creative way. Navarro is also a distinguished painter who sees Soane as the 'Turner of Architecture', using coloured light to dissolve walls and solidity. He also describes him as a 'body artist', manipulating visitors' physical sense of their own gravity and weight, and enjoys the way in which Soane sets up points of view on the edge of a room, looking from a doorway or through a niche, and allowing the viewer to stand and appreciate the entire space. The suspended dome of the auditorium at Murcia was in a sense a 'trial run' for the Congress Hall at Salamanca, where the dome weighs 1,500 tons and has the same dimensions as that of the Pantheon in Rome.[37]

Rafael Moneo is also an admirer of Soane and evokes Soanean forms in the Atocha Station, Madrid (fig. 67), and in his Library in the Cultural Centre, Don Benito, Badajoz, 1998–99 (fig. 68). When lecturing at Harvard, he was captivated by the book of Yerbury's photographs of the Bank of England which he found in the university library.[38]

In a recent talk at the Soane Museum, Richard MacCormac defined qualities in Soane's architecture which inspire his own work.[39] The theme of spaces within spaces is present in the Ruskin Library at the University of

Lancaster (1998), where the Archive sits in the middle of the interior as an object inside a building. He also admires the way Soane condenses English landscape ideas in his plans, creating intricate, picturesque journeys; MacCormac has created a similar series of sequential surprises in his student accommodation for Fitzwilliam College, Cambridge. Soane's handling of light also influenced MacCormac's designs for the chapel at Fitzwilliam College and the Dining Room at St John's College, Oxford (fig. 69).

All of these architects openly acknowledge their debt to Soane, but others are inspired by his buildings simply as architecture which they find stimulating and relevant. Soane's ability to continue to engage the attention of architects working at the end of the twentieth century, without inhibiting their powers of invention, is possibly his greatest legacy.

FIGURE 69

'Wall, ceiling, enclosure and light': Soane's Designs for Domes

Figure 70 (opposite)
The Breakfast Room at 13 Lincoln's Inn Fields

Figure 71
The Common Council Chamber in the City of London Guildhall, designed by George Dance the Younger in 1777–78, from an engraving of 1808 by Rowlandson and Pugin. The paintings in the pendentives were added by J. Rigaud in 1794

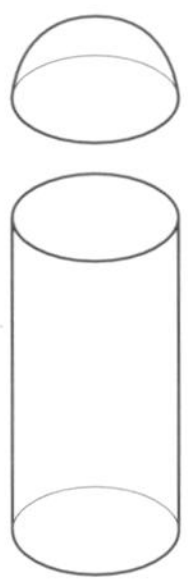

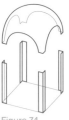

Figure 72
Diagram of a simple dome

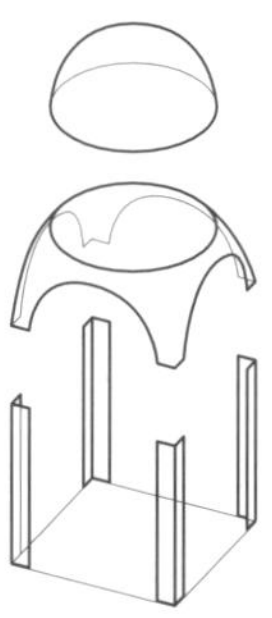

Figure 73
Diagram of the dome of St Paul's Cathedral

Figure 74
Diagram of the Yellow Drawing Room, Wimpole Hall

FIGURE 71

It was Philip Johnson who declared that John Soane was 'really a ceiling architect. That's not trying to make him look small. When you think of one's actual experience of ceilings, you mean wall, ceiling, enclosure and light. I copied Soane's Breakfast Room twice in two different places where I live, and it's the most cuddly, marvellous feeling.'[1]

In his 1835 *Description* of the Museum, Soane described his Breakfast Room at 13 Lincoln's Inn Fields (fig. 70) thus: 'In the centre rises a spherical ceiling, springing from four segmental arches, supported by the same number of pilasters, forming a rich canopy.' The various coloured lights cast by concealed skylights, the mirrors, the views into the Dome and Monument Court are, he continued 'a succession of those fanciful effects which constitute the poetry of Architecture'. This small room is a crystallisation of a type of vaulted space distinctive to Soane. Its 'canopy' dome was the leitmotif of his style, a theme endlessly varied over fifty years of his career. His canopies can be as open to the sky as the ceiling of the Court of Chancery (cat. 201) or as oppressive as the monolith of stone protecting his wife's grave (cat. 109). They can be one or

two storeys high, and square, rectangular or circular in plan. At the Bank of England they can be reduced to the size of a skylight in a corridor (fig. 170), or achieve the grandiloquence of the Consols Transfer Office (cat. 147). As external features, Soane employed them for the lid of a clock (cat. 78), the finial of a gate-pier at Pitzhanger Manor (cat. 64) and the pinnacle of the Mausoleum at Dulwich (cat. 97).

Once again, Soane was indebted in this respect to the boundless genius of George Dance the Younger who had introduced the idea of the 'canopy' dome in an astonishing Council Chamber, now demolished, at the London Guildhall in 1777–78 (fig. 71). Council members sat under a top-lit canopy, while the dais for the Mayor and Aldermen was illuminated by a concealed and elevated skylight – the *lumière mystérieuse* of Soane's Breakfast Room. Members of the public stood in the lobby at the opposite end and viewed the scene through an arch, presaging the position of spectators strolling through Soane's Law Courts (cat. 202). Although Dance established the theme, the pupil, as ever, was determined to move a step ahead of his teacher.[2]

Soane's vaulted interiors synthesise ancient Roman and medieval Gothic architecture. Perhaps his greatest stimulus was the desire for verticality, which he achieved by removing the horizontal subdivisions conventional in domed spaces since the Renaissance. In Britain the proudest example of this traditional type of dome is at Wren's St Paul's Cathedral (fig. 73), and the domed centrepiece to the Triumphal Bridge which Soane designed as a student is a typical imitation (cat. 14).

At its simplest, a Renaissance dome is a hemisphere placed on a cylinder (fig. 72). There are two modifications, however. If the cylinder is pierced by openings at ground-floor level – as any room is likely to be – the weight of the dome must be transferred to structural piers by arches in the upper storey of the cylinder, dividing that cylinder into an upper and lower storey. And if the room is square, this upper storey must also handle the transition in shape to the circular dome by the use of pendentives, the triangular elements of wall set between the arches (fig. 73).

The Drawing Room at Wimpole Hall (1791, figs 74, 119) is the first realisation of Soane's transformation of this traditional type of dome into a 'canopy', and is deeply indebted to Dance's Chamber at the Guildhall.[3] Soane removes the intermediate storey formed by the arches and pendentives so that the dome springs directly from the

Figure 75

Engraving by G. B. Piranesi
of the umbrella-like vault of
The Temple of Canopus at
Hadrian's Villa, Tivoli, near
Rome, now thought to be
a Scenic Triclinium

FIGURE 75

walls of the room. The arches are still necessary to the structure and are therefore sliced out of its spherical surface. Two adjacent interiors at the Bank of England, the New Four Per Cent Office (1818, cat. 165) and the Old Four Per Cent Office (1821), represent the ultimate in Soane's exploration of this theme. In the central area of each, Soane has all but removed the walls, placing the dome on the floor, as it were, so that the hemispherical space becomes the room. At Wimpole, the pendentives are still delineated in the plasterwork decoration; in these later Bank interiors they have disappeared completely.

In his Royal Academy lectures Soane did not explain his own motivation but criticised the Renaissance and Baroque approach of treating the dome as a cupola, a lid capping a high, cylindrical drum: 'In many modern structures domes seem to be placed on the roofs without

any visible support, and without any apparent connection with the other parts of the edifices, as at St Peter's in Rome, St Paul's in London, and the church of Les Invalides in Paris.' In contrast, he continued, 'The domes of the ancients seem always to grow out of the substructure and to harmonise with it in the most gradual and pleasing manner, forming as it were a canopy to the entire edifice.'[4]

Soane might have been describing the Scenic Triclinium of Hadrian's Villa, a semicircular exedra then thought to be a Temple of Canopus or Serapis[5] (fig. 75). The vast ruin of Hadrian's Villa (*c.* AD 118–130) at Tivoli, near Rome, displayed Roman architects' handling of domes and groin-vaulting (fig. 76, cat. 18) at its most varied and inventive. These bare, luminous spaces were to have a far more profound influence on Soane than the splendid porticoes

Figure 76
Engraving by G. B. Piranesi
of the ruins of a Sculpture
Gallery at Hadrian's Villa,
Tivoli, near Rome, 1770
(cat. 18)

FIGURE 76

of the Roman Forum. In plan the villa has an irregular perimeter containing three axial sequences of monumental structures, and the oblique intersections between these axes are concealed by circular rooms; it is hard to believe that Soane was not reminded of this plan when completing the Bank of England, particularly when he was presented with Gandy's bird's-eye cutaway view (cat. 119). The Scenic Triclinium also has the exceptional feature of a surface scalloped with concavities to form an umbrella-like vault. It is a likely inspiration for Soane's decoration of the dome at Wimpole Hall, as noted, and many other interiors such as the Princes Street Vestibule of the Bank (cats 155–158).

'Canopy' not 'dome' was Soane's favoured word. He was trying to give a ceiling the lightness of a piece of fabric stretched over the room. At Wimpole the covering floats as lightly as a silk parachute, while the ceiling of the

Breakfast Room at 13 Lincoln's Inn Fields has been admired by modern architects as 'a weightless billowy sail, a sail-vault'[6] or a 'handkerchief dome'.[7] It is appropriate that the guest room (fig. 58) which Philip Johnson designed at New Canaan is of canvas, while in Spain Juan Navarro Baldeweg has reinterpreted the room as a suspended ceiling in reinforced concrete in his new auditorium in Murcia (fig. 66). Soane's vaults were of wood or brick, not canvas or concrete, so he relied upon surface decoration to complete the effect of a tensile surface. In the Drawing Room at Wimpole the plaster surfaces of the central dome and the semi-domes to the apses are scalloped with concavities to create an umbrella-like vault.

Elsewhere at Hadrian's Villa, in an external niche of the Fountain Court, there is a simple semi-dome whose plaster surface has been patterned to suggest, in abstract form,

Figure 77

Niche in the exterior of the Fountain Court, Hadrian's Villa, Tivoli, near Rome, showing the decorative pattern incised into its plaster surface

FIGURE 77

monk's choir which adjoins the Church of the Holy Sepulchre in Jerusalem, illustrated by Lebrun in his *Voyage au Levant* (1714).[10] More convincing, however, is Daniel Abramson's argument that the innovative form of the Stock Office was generated by the restrictions of the site at the Bank, the precedents set by Taylor, and discussions with Dance. Such on-the-spot considerations were more stimulating than an image from a book.[11] Soane did illustrate the Holy Sepulchre in his lectures but only to criticise its 'dreadfully degraded' architecture.[12] He did, however, admire the 'lightness of appearance and boldness of construction' of the dome of Santa Sophia in Constantinople: 'the entire dome seems rather suspended in the air than supported by the piers'.[13] As his lecture illustration showed, the arches and pendentives are contained within the spherical surface of the dome (fig. 78). But Soane never stood inside Santa Sophia and I suspect that for him to find its 'suspended' dome in a published illustration was a retrospective justification for a type of interior he had already created.

Other types of medieval architecture did have a direct influence. In Italy numerous Romanesque churches were decorated in the Renaissance or Baroque periods with plaster applied to smooth their groin-vaulted ceilings into a spherical profile. The results are identical in shape to Soane's canopies, with the structural arches of the old vaults sliced out of the new plaster surface of the ceiling. Soane's first dated drawing to survive from his study in Rome is a measured survey of the seventh-century basilica Sant'Agnese fuori le Mura, where the groin-vaulted chapels in the side aisles were redecorated in exactly this way in the seventeenth century. Soane's drawing picks away the plaster skin to expose the groin-vault; even at this early stage in his development the similarity of the two forms was apparent to his eye.[14] He was later to juxtapose both forms in didactic scale models (cats 197, 198), and in the adjacent Breakfast Room and Library at Pitzhanger Manor (cats 61, 62).

A further similarity to medieval architecture lies in the treatment of ornamental mouldings. Essentially, Gothic mouldings are vertical and classical mouldings horizontal. The former originated as ornamentation to upright piers and arches, and the latter as decorations to the horizontal entablatures of Grecian temples. In a Renaissance dome, classical mouldings underline its division into three storeys. As seen in Parke's internal view of the Panthéon in

the ribs of an umbrella-like vault; touchingly, the painter Hubert Robert scratched his name in the plaster while a student at the French Academy in Rome in the 1750s[8] (fig. 77). The pattern is startlingly close to that scored into the ceiling of the Breakfast Room and the Rotunda of the Bank (cats 130–134), evidence that Soane was able to find sources within the tradition of Roman architecture to encourage his tendency towards the abstract, linear decoration which seems so refreshingly modern to us.

This concern to express lines of structural tension on the surface contrasts with the Renaissance approach, as at St Paul's in London or the Panthéon in Paris (cat. 16), in which a restful, almost static, poise is achieved by concealing the structural skeleton behind an inner dome. Soane's approach has more in common with Gothic or Romanesque vaults where the surface is divided into the structural 'ribs' and the filling between them (fig. 80). In structural terms, Soane's canopies are neither challenging nor innovative; it is their dissembling of structure which is so imaginative.

In the Breakfast Room at 13 Lincoln's Inn Fields the structural piers are faced with mirrors, as if to dissolve the appearance of support.[9] Perhaps most daring is the central canopy in the Coucil Chamber of the Freemasons' Hall (cat. 195), where the piers have vanished completely and the canopy is actually suspended from the ceiling. The bronze chandeliers hanging from its four corners further invert the visitor's expectation of how a dome should support itself.

Summerson suggested Byzantine architecture as a possible influence upon Soane's vaulting, noting a similarity between the Stock Office at the Bank and the

1 In interview with Shery Weinstock, 1986, in Waterfield 1987.
2 The relationship between the two architects' interiors was first discussed in Middleton and Watkin 1980, p. 201.
3 See Woodward 1999, pp. 8–13. Soane's first experiment with a 'canopy' dome was at Fonthill Splendens in 1786 and unexecuted: see C. Woodward, 'William Beckford and Fonthill Splendens', *Apollo*, February 1998, pp. 31–40.
4 In lecture six. See Watkin 1996 (1), p. 569.

5 See W. MacDonald's and A. Pinto's magnificent *Hadrian's Villa and Its Legacy*, New Haven and London, 1995, pp. 108–14. See also Woodward 1999, for a more detailed comment on Soane's response to this structure.
6 Buzas 1994, p. 15.
7 Eric Kuhne describing his designs for Bluewater, Kent, interviewed by Ralph Rugoff in the *Financial Times*, 6 March 1999.
8 MacDonald and Pinto, op. cit., p. 157, for the decoration of this niche.
9 As pointed out to the author by Michael Brawne in conversation.
10 Summerson 1984.

11 D. Abramson, 'Catalogue of the Bank of England Stock Office Drawings', 1997, manuscript in SM, p. 11.
12 In lecture five, quoted in Watkin 1996 (1), p. 324.
13 In lecture six, quoted in Watkin 1996 (1), p. 569.
14 The drawing (SM 45/3/3) was made on 21 May 1778 and is reproduced in du Prey 1982, p. 130.
15 G. Wightwick, *The Palace of Architecture*, London, 1840, pp. 192–193.
16 D. Watkin, *Thomas Hope*, London, 1968, p. 132.
17 See McCarthy 1985.

Figure 78
Royal Academy lecture drawing of the interior of Santa Sophia, Constantinople (SM 27/4/6)

Figure 79
Fan-vaulted aisles in Henry VII's Chapel, Westminster Abbey, 1503

Figure 80
Diagram of a groin-vault

FIGURE 78

FIGURE 79

Paris (cat. 16), there are two projecting rims: the cornice to the dome, and the entablature which divides the pendentive storey from the ground floor with its giant Corinthian order. As Soane's style developed, these horizontal elements disappeared: in the Breakfast Room at 13 Lincoln's Inn Fields the only vestige of the capital and cornice of the classical entablature is an incised line and ball-moulding, while in the New Four Per Cent Office of the Bank the vertical mouldings curve upwards without any interruption. This again was an innovation pioneered by George Dance the Younger, in his sketch for semicircular arches in the Bank Stock Office of 1791 (cat. 123).

Soane's synthesis of styles was recognised by his assistant George Wightwick: 'It seems to have been his aim to unite the classic delicacies of Greek and Roman design, with the playfulness of the Gothic – not by the use of the pointed arch – but by adopting the principle of continuous lines ramifying (without horizontal impediment) from the vertical into the circular … and continuing vertical mouldings of piers, uninterruptedly, along the curves of the arches above them.'[15]

A final comparison which might be made with medieval architecture is between the Breakfast Room at 13 Lincoln's Inn Fields and the fan-vaulted aisles of the Perpendicular chapel which Henry VII began at Westminster Abbey in 1503 (fig. 79). In each there is no horizontal feature to interrupt the eye's movement from the base of the pier to the apex of the shallow vault; in each the ceiling does not meet the high windows in the outer wall and the light falling through the resultant gap emphasises the ceiling's 'floating' quality. David Watkin has shown how these Gothic fan-vaults also have an empathy with the suspended ceiling which Soane designed for the Privy Council Chamber (cat. 188).[16] We know that Soane examined the architecture of these aisles when designing the Gothic Library in the basement of Stowe House for the Marquess of Buckingham, who had chosen the decoration of the chapel as his model.[17] At Stowe, in 1805, Soane was commissioned to execute a literal copy of the chapel's decoration but was restricted to a flat ceiling; the result, though charming, is more an expression of Buckingham's taste than Soane's. In his own Breakfast Room and in the Privy Council Chamber, however, it is the *spirit* of the Gothic space which we enjoy.

Soane: The Pragmatic Architect

Figure 81

The garden façade, Saxlingham Rectory, Norfolk, 1784

Figure 82 (opposite)

Arches at the stables, Royal Hospital, Chelsea, 1814, showing layers of brickwork casting shadows

FIGURE 81

Soane might have longed to build his Triumphal Bridge over the Thames, or a vast Royal Palace on Constitution Hill, but in practice he found himself confronted with two major constraints: the need to build within a tight economic budget and the client's requirement to incorporate existing buildings rather than building anew. In addressing budgetary concerns, Soane developed an architectural language of remarkable simplicity and versatility which exploited materials to their maximum effect. And when dealing with existing buildings, Soane's approach allowed his internal planning to be determined by them, giving rise to some of his most dramatic interior spaces. Soane became so adept at working in difficult circumstances that his best work seems to occur where the potential of serious compromise loomed at its greatest.

Soane sought to achieve a basic architectural agenda in all his commissions, irrespective of economic or physical constraint, and a number of repeated themes can be identified which extend throughout his work. The first is symmetry, which, when combined with axis, created vistas through buildings and determined internal planning. Coupled with symmetry was Soane's deeply felt conviction about light and shade. His Grand Tour experience had shown him how lighting effects were fundamental to an understanding of Greek and Roman architecture. Soane's Rectory at Saxlingham, Norfolk (1784) demonstrates how he used bow windows to cast shadows across an otherwise plain box of a house (fig. 81). Although Saxlingham was a cheap house for a country parson where extravagance was neither appropriate nor affordable, Soane realised that the

Figure 83
West elevation of the
stables, offices and house,
Shotesham Hall, Norfolk,
1785

Figure 84
The entrance to the walled
garden at Letton Hall,
Norfolk, 1783

FIGURE 83

FIGURE 84

Figure 85
The modillion cornice of
the offices at Letton Hall,
Norfolk, 1783

FIGURE 85

success of his practice depended on such buildings being able to convey sufficient architectural presence for them to be published and exhibited.[1]

Utilitarian country-estate outbuildings, which formed the bulk of Soane's work in the 1780s, were used to develop a low-cost language of live and blind arches cut into the masonry elevations that could accommodate an uneven rhythm of door and window openings and yet give the buildings the appearance of symmetricality. A layered façade created an even pattern of shadows and definition while permitting infinite flexibility in the arrangement and layout of the building (fig. 83).[2]

Such effects required high-quality construction, and from the outset Soane had an instinctive capacity to achieve the most from whatever building materials were available locally. In southern England, where much of his early work was located, this meant using brick. Stone, which had to be brought from afar and was therefore more expensive, was introduced only where structurally required, such as under a gate pin or catch (fig. 84), or as

a lintel over an opening. Unique brick details were devised, such as a 'standard' cornice pattern set on three separate plains that created dramatic shadow effects but avoided the heavy appearance of a traditional applied modillion cornice (fig. 85). Although these details were initially developed to avoid extravagance, Soane made a virtue of them, and they were later applied in buildings where costs were less tightly controlled, such as his own house at 12 Lincoln's Inn Fields (1792). Simple details also demonstrated a sense of hierarchy, such as on the gateway and bridge at Tyringham, Buckinghamshire (1792–99) where mouldings were abstracted to simple slots and grooves in contrast to the elaborate decoration applied to the house itself (figs 122, 124). Local materials were combined to create a picturesque or colourful effect, such as the mix of flint, brick and stone used on the stables at Betchworth (fig. 86) and the entrance arch to Soane's own country house, Pitzhanger Manor (fig. 127).

Soane's versatility with simple detail meant that important buildings constructed at low cost could still

Figure 86

Presentation design for stables, front elevation and section of the stables at Betchworth Castle, near Dorking, Surrey, 1799, detail (cat. 45). The drawing shows knapped flints set in black mortar to form dark pilasters, unknapped flints set in cream mortar for the walls, with bands of red brick for stability and a Portland stone plinth for solidity. The roof is of graded green Westmoreland slate

FIGURE 86

convey a degree of articulation appropriate to their stature, while avoiding the expense of elaborate applied decoration. One response was to focus the decorative element on a small part of the building, such as the founders' Mausoleum at the Dulwich Picture Gallery (1811, cat. 97).[3] Soane recognised the value of silhouette, and consequently only the intricate roof-lantern of the Mausoleum was constructed wholly of stone. The incised Greek-key pattern was simple, and therefore cheap to cut, and effective as decoration in the crisp and easily worked Portland stone. The rest of the building was constructed of London stock brick, whose quality is exceptional. The piers of the Mausoleum rest on thin shadow gaps achieved by simply raking out a course of mortar, an effect which gives them that same sense of 'floating' that is achieved by a traditional classical roll mould.[4] Vertically, thin shafts of space are formed in between the piers creating a rich visual effect of light and shade from an assembly of essentially very basic elements (fig. 87). On the rest of the building, arched brick openings accommodate doors and windows

in the same system which had been originally devised by Soane for country-estate outbuildings.

A different challenge was posed in the design of the Royal Hospital Stables in Chelsea (1814, fig. 88), which faced the wide green in front of the earlier buildings by Sir Christopher Wren. The difficulty here was to create an elevation with sufficient architectural stature, without recourse to applied decoration which would be costly as well as inappropriate to the building's mundane function. Soane's three giant-arched openings are of a triumphant scale, although, as at Dulwich, they are constructed only of London stock brick. The central arch leads into the courtyard beyond, while those on either side diminish in circumference as if in perspective, each one containing only a small window opening. A layered effect of shadow is achieved on four plains. In contrast, the obliquely seen side elevation along Royal Hospital Road consists of twenty narrow blind arches, which appear compressed from afar and consequently exaggerate the length of the building.[5]

FIGURE 87

Figure 87
The Mausoleum, Dulwich
Picture Gallery

Figure 88

East elevation of the
stables at the Royal
Hospital, Chelsea, 1814,
facing Wren's lawn

FIGURE 88

The simplicity of these elevations is now much admired, but when budgetary restrictions were lifted, and circumstances dictated, Soane returned to the literal use of the full classical orders. His strong views about the appropriate use of decoration dominate his Royal Academy lectures.[6] Classical decoration was appropriate for public buildings, whereas private buildings required a degree of restraint appropriate to their stature. Consequently Soane's screen wall to the Bank of England was massive in scale, befitting the institution that processed the considerable funding required for the Napoleonic Wars. With its strong cornice, rustication and plinth, it humbled Taylor's existing Bank screen wall, which it steadily replaced over a thirty-year period (cat. 167). The quality of Soane's masonry in a variety of smooth and tooled textures conveys an absolute appreciation of both material and light, and accords with the Bank's own requirements for security and strength. Soane's later public works in Westminster such as the Board of Trade and Privy Council Offices in Whitehall (1823) or those proposed for the Processional Route were more elaborate still. Soane did not abstract his details unless it was necessary to do so.

Soane's other major constraint, the need to work around existing buildings, was also often the result of economy. But again, Soane was dogged and determined in his application of his favoured axial and symmetrical approach, demonstrated in houses such as Tendring Hall, Tyringham and Pell Wall, and inspired by French Grand Prix and Roman planning. Wimpole Hall (remodelled 1790–94) demonstrates how Soane was able to restrict himself to resolving the symmetries, axes and lighting of only small areas of a much larger building. The Yellow Drawing Room (fig. 119) was inserted into the core of the house, but anchored into the principal enfilade, along the north front of the house; it replaced a secondary stair and closets. A new Book Room (see p. 122) was inserted into part of an existing orangery to form the western termination of this enfilade. A minute 'lozenge'-shaped lobby was formed in an existing thick wall, while a sequence of book stacks was set within arched partitions containing an existing section of ceiling and concealing the existing uneven window-bay sizes. Looking down the enfilade, they appear to diminish in perspective (fig. 120). Such a room would never have occurred in a purely new-build project.

Soane's other major insertion at Wimpole, the Plunge Pool (fig. 118), replaced a former lightwell. In its use of inventive roof lighting, curved-wall and ceiling planes, and apsidal ends, it conveys a spatial intensity without recourse to intensive decoration, the latter a luxury which could not be justified in a bathroom. Interior decoration was reduced to a minimum of flush-reeded mouldings that acted as plaster stops, dado rails, skirtings and door architraves, and denoted the pattern of panelling on windows and doors. This system dealt with every joinery detail in one single, practical and satisfactory way. Linking the bathroom to the rest of the house was a square lobby, with live- and blind-arched openings that accommodated the irregular door openings in a symmetrical pattern, and again drew on Soane's early experience of country-estate outbuildings.

Soane's ability successfully to stitch his new spaces into pre-existing fabric while keeping his basic architectural 'themes' intact would prove invaluable. The reconstruction of the Bank of England involved building within the shell of Taylor's original Banking Halls, and then adding new accommodation beyond them. In each of the new halls, Soane was rigorous in his use of symmetry and top-lighting. But he was particularly skilful in manipulating the form of each of the connecting spaces to achieve changes in route and orientation which could accommodate any pre-existing building's plan or orientation. Typical of his skill was his treatment of the insertion of the new Lothbury Court (1797–1800, cat. 138), where the skew axes of the existing Bullion Court, Bank Stock Office and Accountants' Office were reconciled with the medieval

Figure 89

12, 13 and 14 Lincoln's Inn
Fields in 1810. Soane's first
house at No. 12 was built in
1793. The skew party wall
with neighbouring No. 13
can be clearly seen. Soane
laid out the house axially
with a narrow funnelling
space to accommodate the
skew axis of the rear room.
The Dome section replaced
the stables of No. 13 in
1808. It takes its axial cue
from neighbouring No. 12

Figure 90

12, 13 and 14 Lincoln's Inn
Fields in 1822. This shows
the plan of No. 13 as rebuilt
by Soane in 1813. The
central axis of the 1808
Dome (see fig. 89)
determined the western
edge of the Breakfast
Room and staircase
beyond, while the Dome
arcade determined the
eastern edge of the
Breakfast Room and the
placing of the drawing
rooms beyond. The plan of
No. 13 was therefore
treated as a sequence of
interconnected spaces that
were entirely determined
by the layout of the earlier
buildings

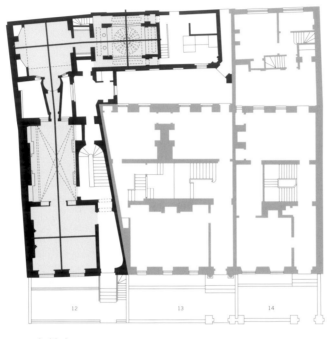

FIGURE 89 (1810)

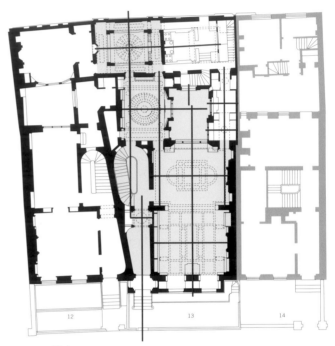

FIGURE 90 (1822)

alignment of the Lothbury Street frontage by using
apsidal-ended spaces to turn the symmetrical axes.

Even the plan of Soane's own house at 13 Lincoln's Inn
Fields was developed directly from the existing distorted
geometry of the original plot and from the section of the
Museum that Soane had already constructed in 1808 at the
back of the site (fig. 89). An axis through the Dome
located the centre of the new staircase and the western
edge of the celebrated Breakfast Room, while the eastern
edge of this room was defined by a parallel axis which ran
from an old blocked back door along the edge of the Dome
and in turn fixed the width of the new Dining Room. By
linking the new rooms so strongly to those that existed,
Soane achieved a continuity of space and sensation which
were intensified by predetermined geometries (fig. 90).

However, perhaps the greatest example of Soane's
ingenuity is revealed in his planning of the new Law
Courts by Westminster Hall. The plan of the building
before he began shows how awkward and cramped the
small site was, with poky left-over spaces between the
ancient buttresses and the rear of Vardy's partially
completed Stone Building. Soane's response was indeed
pragmatic: he completed Vardy's elevation[7] and resolved
the plan on a room-by-room basis, rather as he had done in
his own house (figs 91, 92). The largest volumes, the court

rooms, were placed in between the buttresses and were
served by a spine passageway alongside Westminster Hall
itself, which was where the public gathered. The left-over
space was divided into judges' and lawyers' robing rooms
and chambers, with all the complicated and separate
circulation patterns that these required. Soane's
experience of top-lighting, developed when working
within the shells of other existing buildings such as
Wimpole Hall and the Bank, ensured that natural daylight
was provided throughout. Such a concentration of
complex effects, captured in Gandy's watercolours, could
never have been justified in a new-build project.

The positive influence that existing buildings exerted
on Soane's internal planning contrasts with the monotony
which sets in when such constraints are absent. This is
nowhere better demonstrated than in his designs for the
Processional Route whose buildings have lost their taut
and considered poise, becoming instead ponderous in their
extent and indulgent in their elevational treatment. All
vitality has gone. In the same way that economic control
drove Soane to develop innovative detail, existing
buildings prompted planning ingenuity. At a time when
architects are increasingly required to work with existing
buildings, or to create meaningful new ones cheaply,
Soane's example is of particular relevance.

1 Saxlingham was included in Soane's *Plans ... of Buildings executed in the Counties of Norfolk, Suffolk...*, London, 1788.

2 Soane's country-house projects are described in Dean 1999.

3 This was constructed for just £9,788 14s 11d; see Bolton 1924, p. 82.

4 Soane used and exaggerated this roll-mould detail in his elevations to the Bank of England.

5 He had used a similar trick on the back wall of his Museum (1808), which faces a narrow mews called Whetstone Park, and for a little-known coach house at Moggerhanger Park, Bedfordshire (1812).

6 This is described at length in Watkin 1996 (1).

7 This was demolished in 1824, and replaced with a Gothic design which Soane later disowned. The Law Courts were demolished in the late nineteenth century; see Bolton 1924, pp. 95–101.

Figure 91
Westminster Hall and Vardy's partially completed Stone Building, before Soane's work began

Figure 92
Westminster Hall and Soane's completed Law Courts. Soane's design axes are shown, with the principal spaces shaded. The main courtrooms were ingeniously inserted between the medieval hall buttresses, while the elevation of Vardy's Stone Building was completed to the south

Figure 93 (pages 76–77)
View of the Consols Transfer Office showing the walls unplastered and the dome constructed up to the base of the lantern, drawn by Joseph Michael Gandy, 1799, detail (cat. 144)

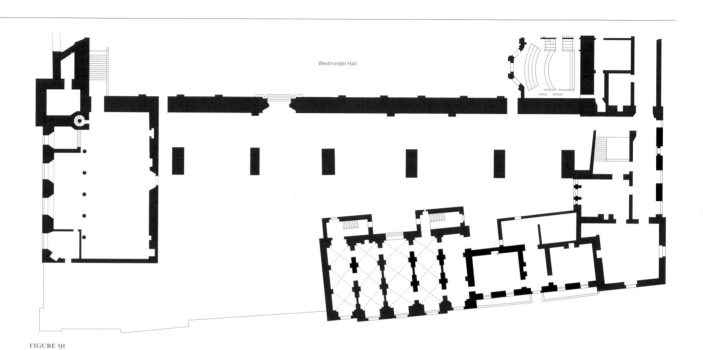

FIGURE 91

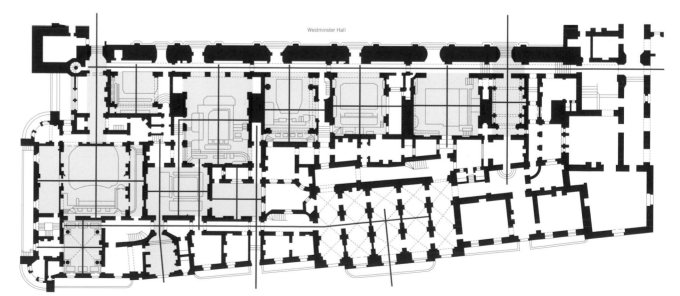

FIGURE 92

Beginnings and Early Training

Figure 94

William Daniell, Engraving of George Dance the Younger, 1825, after Nathaniel Dance's portrait, *c.* 1780–90 (National Portrait Gallery, London)

Figure 95 (opposite)

Christopher William Hunneman, Portrait of John Soane, 1776, detail (cat. 1)

John Soane was always deliberately obscure about his childhood, only writing in his privately printed *Memoirs of the Professional Life of an Architect...* (1835) that he was 'led by a natural inclination to study architecture'.

John Soan, his father, was a bricklayer, an imprecise term which could equally describe a labourer on piecework or, at the opposite extreme, a master mason. The building world has always been one of uncertainty and mobility, in both directions; men could rise within their trade but the failure of an employer or an injury might see a skilled man descend rapidly into poverty. John and his siblings were educated, suggesting that Soan was probably a skilled tradesman.

The Soan family came from Goring-on-Thames, a few miles upstream from Reading, the county town and a centre of brick- and tile-making. In his early years John Soane (he added the 'e' later) lived among both 'polite' and vernacular buildings of ingeniously varied brickwork, often ornamented by flints from the chalk downland nearby; these were the buildings which launched his architectural education.

FIGURE 94

Martha Marcy, Soane's mother, had five surviving children. John, the younger of two sons twelve years apart, was born in Reading and educated at a small school in that town run by William Baker, a bookish man whose school, to judge by a later description, was a cheerful family establishment. By the time Soane was fourteen, his father had died. By then his formal education had ended: perhaps his father had fallen ill or a financial misfortune had overtaken the family.

Soane's elder brother William worked as a labourer. On their father's death, the family joined William in Chertsey, where Soane was remembered, deeply engrossed in a book at the foot of his bricklayer brother's ladder. Martha Soan must have vested all her hopes in her youngest son.

Soane did not remain a hod-carrier for long. Through 'a near relative' he met James Peacock, a surveyor with Chertsey connections who was working with George Dance the Younger. By 1768, aged fifteen, Soane had moved to the Dance household in Chiswell Street in the City of London, working for his keep as an office boy or messenger and gaining invaluable experience in an architectural office. That year George Dance the Elder had died and his son, only twelve years older than Soane, inherited his father's position as Clerk to the City Works. Dance had spotted Soane's aptitude and realised that Soane's family could not afford to pay for his pupillage. Dance and Peacock became Soane's mentors.

In October 1771, aged eighteen, Soane gained entry to the recently formed Royal Academy Schools (see pp. 86–95), where young architects could attend evening lectures and use the library out of office hours. Dance had been one of only four architect founder members of the Royal Academy in 1768. Soane could not have found a more liberal or encouraging master in Dance, a man of wide interests and a musician and portraitist of some ability (see fig. 94).

Soane had been translated at one bound from the narrow confines of the provincial building trades to the office of one of the most progressive architects in London. Dance was involved in housing developments on the fringes of the City, as well as in the latest City church, All Hallows, London Wall (see fig. 6, cat. 98), a courageous departure from the classical norm. He was also preparing designs for Newgate Gaol. In the Dance household, Soane found himself in the midst of a sophisticated family engaged in the theatre, music and the arts.

Figure 96
George Dance the Younger,
Sketch of a design for a
Magnifica Galleria,
illustrating Dance's unusual
interest in the concept of
the interior enfilade
(CCA, Montreal)

FIGURE 96

Figure 97
J. M. W. Turner, Oil sketch
of Goring-on-Thames, 1805
(Tate Gallery, London)

Figure 98 (opposite)
Detail of the barrel vault,
the windows and the frieze
inside George Dance's
All Hallows, London Wall,
showing the reduced
detailing of the frieze which
initially shocked Soane as a
young man (see cat. 7)

FIGURE 97

There is little hard evidence of Soane's time with Dance beyond Soane's own reminiscences and the strength of the relationship between the two men which, despite difficulties, endured to the end of Dance's life. When Soane bought Pitzhanger Manor, Ealing, many years later and made alterations, he retained the south wing as a reminder of Dance's first country-house commission and one of his own first architectural exercises (see p. 142).

After four years with George Dance, Soane moved, at Dance's suggestion, to the office of Henry Holland, where he was to gain entirely different, but complementary, experience. Holland was an architect-builder whose speculative development of Hans Town was just beginning as Soane joined his office as an assistant at £60 per annum. Holland's practice was wide-ranging and Soane worked both on Sloane Street and on several country houses (see cat. 7), including Lord Clive's Claremont House in Surrey, chiefly on measuring and estimating completed work. Soane carefully preserved a number of documents from Holland's office, which suggests that they provided the model for his own exemplary professional arrangements. However, his time with Holland may also have sowed the seeds of Soane's deep distrust of architects doubling as speculative builders.

1 Christopher William
Hunneman (*d.* 1793)
Portrait of John Soane, 1776
Oil on canvas:
59 × 48 cm, framed
SM P400

C. W. Hunneman was a fellow
student of Soane's at the Royal
Academy and probably painted
this small portrait of Soane in
honour of his winning the
Royal Academy Gold Medal in
1776 (see cats 12–15). It was later
erroneously stated to have
been painted in Rome in 1779
but there seems no reason to
disbelieve Soane's own words
in his 1830 *Description* where
he refers to it as 'Portrait of a
young artist painted in 1776'.

The portrait shows Soane
as an eager and earnest young
architect, holding a pair of
proportional dividers. At the
time of Soane's death it hung
in his attic bedroom at
13 Lincoln's Inn Fields –
a reminder of his youthful
triumph. HD

Books from Soane's youth

2 *The Testament of the Twelve
Patriarchs, the Sons of Jacob*
London, 1706
SM GL BR3D

3 William Alingham, *An Epitome
of Geometry...*
London, 1714
SM AL35i

4 John Robertson, *A Compleat
Treatise of Mensuration in all
it's Branches...*
London, 1739
SM AL34i

Soane showed a great
predilection for books from
his early boyhood. His copy
of *The Testament of the Twelve
Patriarchs, the Sons of Jacob* is
inscribed on the reverse of the
title page, 'John Soan His Book
July/23 1762...', one of many
inscriptions scribbled
throughout the book. The
eight-year-old Soane did not
perhaps treat the subject

matter with the reverence
it deserved since, at the
bottom of page 44, he wrote
'John Soan is a/Nody for
Scibbling/His Book &/ought to
have his licking/Bought'. From
the evidence of other
inscriptions, the book had
been passed down to him by his
elder brother, William, who,
although never rising above a
lowly position in the building
trade, was clearly literate and
wrote a good hand. William
also encouraged his young
sibling by passing on to him his
copy of Robertson's *A Compleat
Treatise of Mensuration...* in 1765
when Soane was twelve. By
1767, Soane was signing himself
'Philom[ath]' in a copy of
Everard's *Stereometry...*
(London, 1721, SM AL34i), and,
in 1769, just after he became a
pupil of George Dance the
Younger, he acquired a copy
of Alingham's *An Epitome of
Geometry...* and inscribed the
flyleaf with a flourish in a very
neat hand, 'John Soan/Nomen
hic pono/Quia librum perdere
Nolo' (I inscribe my name here
because I do not wish to lose
the book). SP

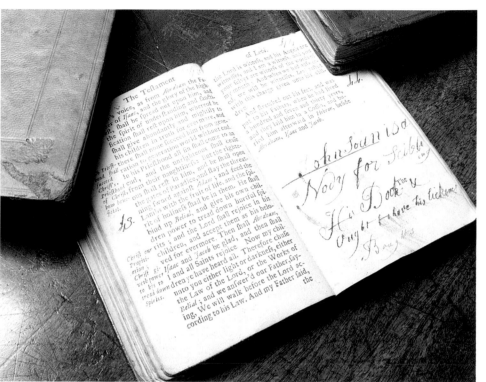

CATALOGUE 2

5 George Dance the Younger
(1741–1825)
Preliminary design for a public
gallery for painting and sculpture
awarded the gold medal of the
Parma Academy of Arts on the
reverse of a letter sent to
George Dance the Elder
Inscr. *Rome June the 7th 1763*
Black and brown pen, sepia,
raw umber and blue washes,
pencil: 415×310 mm
SM D4/11/1

The climax of George Dance
the Younger's six years of
architectural education abroad,
mostly spent in Rome, was the
winning of a competition
organised annually by the
Parma Academy. Dance wrote
to his father in London on the
back of a reduced copy of his
design (cat. 5): 'I beg you will
excuse the/incorrectness of it,
as I had scarce time to finish it
for the Post ... This work Dear
Sir/has been my occupation
for these 8 months pass'd ...
my mind has been in such
agitation/that I confess that
I have pass'd whole nights
without sleeping...'

Since no public art galleries
had been built at this date,
Dance relied on the stimulus of
contemporary Franco-Italian
academic projects as well as the
inspiration of Classical
architecture. In particular,
he drew upon Roman baths,
especially the Baths of
Caracalla with their
symmetrical planning,
courtyards lined with columns,
sequences of rooms with
varying plan shapes, coffered
ceilings and top-lighting; the
Pantheon with its single dome
lit by a central oculus was
another source. Though Dance
exploited Antique precedents,
he did so in a way that was new:
composing his building from
a series of simple geometric
forms so as to stress the ends
rather than the middle,
emphasising a post-and-lintel
system (while retaining domes
and vaults) and using a

multitude of columns in a way
prophetic of their use in many
Neoclassical designs of the
early nineteenth century.
Particularly successful was the
varied handling of spaces and
natural lighting so that a
circular room lit by a wide
oculus was reached from a hall
lit by a clerestory via a lower
and darker vestibule, the
transition between rooms
being subtly modelled by
columnar screens and engaged
columns.

In his Royal Academy
lectures, Soane praised Dance's
design for its 'successful variety
in outline, largeness of parts,
and uniform simplicity ... in
the transition from room to
room, the uninterrupted
succession of new ideas keeps
the attention alive, and
increases the interest first
excited' (Watkin 1996 [1],
p. 604). What would have
impressed Soane most was the
masterly way in which Dance
solved the problem of an
entirely new building type.
On a monumental scale, this
design, with generous
entrances, a legible plan,
windowless walls and top-lit,
single-storey interiors
combining galleries of different
forms appropriately enriched,
incorporated ideas that Soane
applied to his great unrealised
public projects (see pp.
252–263) as well as to those,
such as the Bank of England
(see pp. 208–251), that were
built. JL

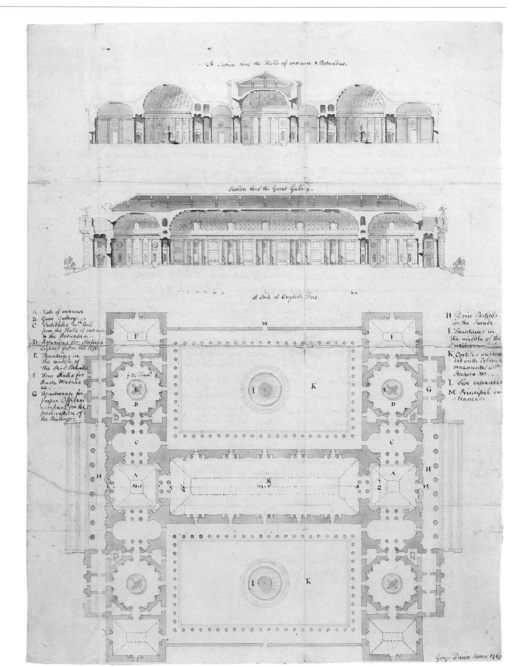

CATALOGUE 5

CATALOGUE 6

6 Royal Academy lecture drawing showing the interior of All Hallows Church, London Wall, City of London, 1816
Pen, pencil and coloured washes, shaded: 980×725 mm
SM 18/7/7

All Hallows Church was George Dance's first commission in 1765 after his return from Rome at the age of just twenty-four. Won in competition, Dance's church (replacing a medieval one that had become seriously decrepit) was built on a small site with a budget of only £3,000. The solution was a single-cell structure of London stock brick and Portland stone dressings with a simple exterior and an exquisite interior.

The inspiration for the barrel-vaulted ceiling, pierced in each bay by cross-vaults above lunette windows set high in the walls, came from the Basilica of Maxentius in Rome. The diagonally coffered half-dome of the windowless east apse was derived from the Temple of Venus in Rome.

The much-discussed and most distinctive element of the church is the frieze above the engaged, fluted Ionic columns and around the apse. Conventionally, a frieze is part of an entablature that also includes an architrave and a cornice. Functionally, a cornice sheds rain and is thus not needed inside a building, while an architrave, a load-bearing lintel, is unnecessary when columns are attached to a wall. Soane said that as 'a young man [he] supposed it defective' but understood the logic of Dance's elision when Greek and Roman precedents for the 'suppression of those parts of the entablature which can only apply to external decoration' (Watkin 1996 [1], p. 527) were considered. As Summerson wrote, 'here, indeed, is the beginning, in England, of that process of omission which

Soane ... was to carry to such extremes' (Summerson 1951, p. 84). Another lesson learnt by Soane at All Hallows was that even a small building can be a masterpiece.

This perspective of the interior emphasises the light cast through the lunette windows that are Dance's modification of the heavier, twin-mullioned windows of the Baths of Diocletian. Prompted by Dance, Soane used them for the Bank Stock Office in the Bank of England, 1791–92 (see cats 123–127). JL

7 George Garrard ARA (1760–1826)
Topographical view of Southill, Bedfordshire, showing Holland's remodelling of the south front in progress, 1797
Oil on canvas: 131 × 186.5 cm, framed
Samuel Whitbread, Esq.

Soane moved from Dance's office in 1772 to work for Henry Holland so as to acquire more practical and constructional experience. In his *Memoirs*, Soane recalled that he was 'placed in the office of an eminent builder in extensive practice where I had every opportunity of surveying the progress of building in all its different varieties, and of attaining the knowledge of measuring and valuing artificers' work' (p. 12).

This view of Southill may well have been commissioned by Holland, who may in turn have inspired Soane to instruct his pupils to make drawings of work in progress so as to learn the practical techniques of building construction. Southill was one of Holland's finest works, and George Garrard, painter and sculptor, was a protégé of Samuel Whitbread, Holland's client. MR

CATALOGUE 7

A Royal Academy Student in Architecture

Figure 99

Edward Francis Burney,
*The Plaister Academy in the
Royal Academy of Arts, Old
Somerset House*, 1779
(Royal Academy of Arts,
London)

Figure 100 (opposite)

Entrance (end) elevation
of Soane's design for a
Triumphal Bridge, 1776
(detail of cat. 13)

On 25 October 1771, just six weeks after his eighteenth
birthday, 'John Soan' was admitted as a student in
architecture at the Royal Academy of Arts in London.
Founded less than three years earlier, the Royal Academy
offered the first and only opportunity at that time in
England to study architecture as a fine art within a
formally constituted 'public' (i.e. free) school of art.
In spite (or perhaps because) of this unprecedented
opportunity, there was no initial rush of architectural
students – Soane was still only the twelfth architect to
enrol out of a total student body of 140. Since the
architectural curriculum was designed to complement
rather than to provide a substitute for what could only
be learnt in the office of a successful architect, it was
presumed, perhaps rather over-optimistically, that busy
architects would be prepared to allow their pupils and
office assistants time off to attend the Academy. This
meant (at the very least) turning up for an annual course
of six illustrated lectures delivered on Monday evenings by
the Professor of Architecture, Thomas Sandby; deriving
what benefit they could from a similar course of more
technical lectures given by the Professor of Perspective,
Samuel Wale; and 'regularly' consulting books in the
Academy's library, which was open to students in term
time on Wednesdays from 9 a.m. to 3 p.m. (changed to
Mondays after October 1773). In return, architecture

FIGURE 99

students were entitled to compete for the Academy's
prizes or 'premiums', namely one or more silver medals
awarded annually for a measured, pen-and-wash drawing
of a notable building within a ten-mile radius of London;
and a gold medal 'for the best Composition in
Architecture, consisting of a Plan, Elevation and Section'
(offered annually until 1772, thereafter biennially). All
gold medal winners, whether they were painters, sculptors
or architects, were entitled in turn to compete together
for the Academy's highest accolade, a single three-year
Travelling Scholarship funded by a royal pension of £60
per annum plus £30 travelling expenses each way.

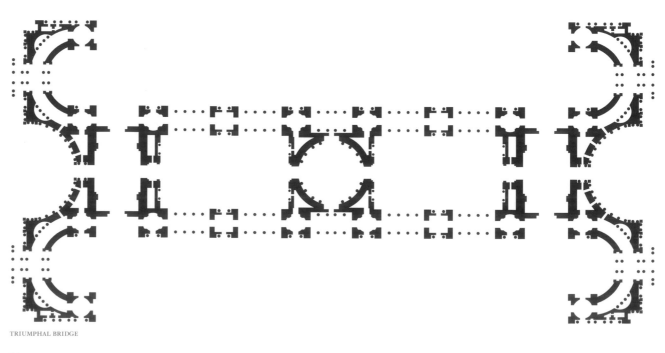

TRIUMPHAL BRIDGE

FIGURE 101

FIGURE 102

These incentives for architectural study were intended to benefit students who had reached the point in their training where they needed to develop their own design skills by producing 'compositions' (i.e. theoretical projects) of their invention, something which it was not generally possible for assistants or pupils to do on their own account within an architect's office at this date. In order to guide this process of self-discovery, the Academy aimed, through its public lectures and its library, to provide its architecture students with the means to mature their taste and hone their powers of discrimination, inculcating an understanding of 'the laws and principles of composition', an appreciation of 'the beauties and faults of celebrated productions ... an unprejudiced study of books ... and a critical examination of structures' ('Royal Academy Instrument of Foundation', 1768, section XI). For students in painting and sculpture, life at the Academy centred on drawing the human figure, either from plaster casts (mainly of Antique sculpture) or from the 'living model', the former being performed under the eye of the Keeper in the 'Plaister Academy' (fig. 99), and the latter (when they were deemed ready for it) in the 'Model Academy' under the guidance of nine academician 'Visitors' (at this date elected annually from the painter and sculptor members only). By contrast, nearly all the work undertaken by the architecture students was extra-mural. Indeed, it was only necessary for Soane to draw (rather than read or listen) within the Academy's walls on two occasions: once, at the beginning of his student career, when he had to produce an architectural design of his own choice for submission to the Council to gain his student's ticket, and again, much later, when as a competitor for the gold medal, he had to undergo the ordeal of producing a timed sketch design (the equivalent to the French academic *esquisse* and Italian *prova*), the subject of which he did not know in advance.

Sir William Chambers, the founding spirit of the Academy, was quite certain that 'the first requisite towards forming a great architect is genius' (Chambers, BAL MSS CHA 1–3, viii, 8, verso). Meagre though its provision for architecture students may seem when compared with the comprehensive courses available at the Académie Royale in Paris under Chambers's old teacher J.-F. Blondel, the Academy in London, through its prizes and its annual exhibition, gave the aspiring English architect a new arena in which genius might discover its own powers of invention and soar within the sphere of an ideal architecture, far beyond the stifling influence of a particular master and without heed to any particular site or client. It was a vision of the dawn of youth's true creativity to which Soane was to return again and again, in the training he gave to pupils within his own office, in the elaborate exposition of architecture as a fine art within his house and Museum, and in his lectures at the Academy, where he was to serve as Professor of Architecture for over thirty years from 1806 until his death in 1837.

FIGURE 103

8 Manuscript notebook
Inscr. in ink on upper cover
*Extracts from/various authors
on/Architecture/J. Soane/abt 1776*
18.4 × 24.7 cm open
SM Soane Case 140

This notebook, the only one to
survive from Soane's student
days, reveals his eagerness to
soak up received wisdom on
the theory and practice of
architectural design. The first
forty-one pages consist of
paraphrases of passages from
two standard eighteenth-
century English textbooks on
the subject, Robert Morris's
Lectures on Architecture (part I,
second edition, 1759) and
Sir William Chambers's *Treatise
on Civil Architecture* (1759).
Although these passages were
almost certainly written out by
Soane while he was a student in
the Royal Academy library,
subsequent pages record facts
and opinions extracted from
Stephen Riou's *The Grecian
Orders of Architecture* (1768) and
Stuart and Revett's *Antiquities
of Athens* (1762), neither of
which were on the Academy's
shelves during Soane's time
(these recent books on ancient
Greek architecture were
probably lent to him by his
new employer, Henry Holland,
sometime after March 1772).
The remainder of the
notebook contains
miscellaneous definitions of
terms and comments on the
faults and beauties of existing
buildings, some apparently
deriving from Sandby's and
Wale's Academy lectures,
others picked up directly or
indirectly by word of mouth
from Chambers, Robert or
James Adam, George Dance
and Henry Holland. NS

9 Roland Fréart, Sieur de
Chambrai (1606–1676)
*A Parallel of the Antient
Architecture with the Modern,
in a Collection of Ten Principal
Authors who have written upon
the Five Orders ... made English
for the benefit of Builders ... by
John Evelyn ... Second Edition,*
London, printed for D. Brown,
J. Walthoe, B. Took, and
D. Midwinter, 1707
Early Imprints Collection,
British Architectural Library,
Royal Institute of British
Architects, London

This is the first known
architectural book owned by
Soane, who not only recorded
on the title page the precise
date of his acquisition (8 July
1771) but also added
retrospectively '– 1776' in
recognition of its trusty
companionship during his
studies at the Academy.
Although archaeologically
inaccurate by the standards of
the second half of the
eighteenth century, its detailed
engravings of authorised
variations on the Greek and
Roman orders provided the
novice architect with a sound
introduction to the core of
Classical architecture. Soane
filled his copy with doodles,
annotations and sketches,
some serious, some facetious,
reflecting the love–hate
relationship commonly felt by
students for their textbooks.
The usefulness of Fréart's
Parallel in training his hand and
eye was never forgotten by
Soane; he went on to acquire at
least six other copies or
versions of the book for the use
of pupils in his office. NS

10 Thomas Sandby (1723–1798)
Design for an idealised bridge,
'A Bridge of Magnificence',
intended to span the Thames
between Somerset House and
Lambeth, ?1776
Elevation and section through
basement of domed terminal
blocks, with scale
Pen with blue and ochre
washes: 650 × 5230 mm
Drawings Collection, British
Architectural Library, Royal
Institute of British Architects,
London

As early as the mid-1750s,
Sandby had fantasised about
urban improvements along the
Thames, producing a series of
imaginary views of Inigo
Jones's unbuilt Whitehall
Palace and publishing a
perspective of a group of
idealised public buildings on an
engraved subscription receipt
dated '175-'. But it was probably
Chambers's official commission
to rebuild Somerset House in
October 1775 (and the selection
of a Triumphal Bridge as the
subject for the Academy's 1776
gold medal competition) that
first inspired Sandby to
illustrate architectural
'magnificence' in his sixth
lecture by unrolling this
drawing of a monumental
Palladian structure which was
designed, he claimed, to 'in
some measure, assimilate and
unite with the new and elegant
pile of building now carrying
on at Somerset House'.
Although Soane was to recall
'the powerful impression the
sight of that beautiful work
produced on myself and on
many of the young Artists of
those days' (Watkin 1996 [1],
p. 564), he may not have seen
Sandby's drawing before
handing in his own on
4 November 1776. If this was
the case, it might explain his
decision to produce an
additional drawing (cat. 15),
though this was not a
requirement of the travelling
scholarship the next year. NS

CATALOGUE 10 (DETAIL)

11 Marie-Joseph Peyre (1730–1788)
'Projet réunir les Académies des
Sciences, des Belles-Lettres, de
Peinture, de Sculpture &
d'Architecture': section and
elevation
Engraving by Michel Loyer
published as plate 4 in *Oeuvres
d'Architecture de Marie-Joseph
Peyre, Architecte, ancien
Pensionnaire du Roi à Rome,
Inspecteur des Bâtimens de sa
Majesté*, Paris, Prault &
Jombert, 1765
SM AL15

It is possible that Soane
originally came across this
design when preparing his
more modest ideal project for
an academy of arts exhibited at
the Royal Academy in May
1776 (no. 289). It was almost
certainly lent to him by
Chambers since there was no
copy of Peyre's book in the
Royal Academy library.
Although it had no influence
upon Soane's academy scheme
it was clearly the source for
the novel idea of curved
colonnades at each end of his
Triumphal Bridge design (see
cat. 13 and plan on p. 86).
Soane's attachment to Peyre's
volume can be gauged from the
fact that it was one of the first
architectural books that he
bought for his personal library
in 1780. NS

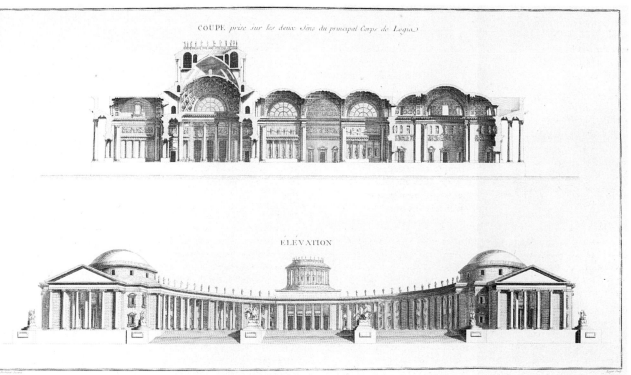

COUPE *prise sur les deux Sens du principal Corps de Logis*

ÉLÉVATION

CATALOGUE 11

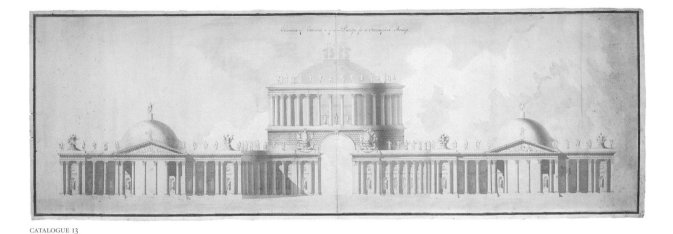

CATALOGUE 13

Designs for the Royal Academy's gold medal competition for a Triumphal Bridge, 1776

12 Plan, in Soane's hand
Inscr. *Plan of the Superstructure of a Design for a Triumphal Bridge. November 4th 1776*
Pen and wash: 669 × 1252 mm
SM 12/5/1

13 Entrance (end) elevation set against a blue sky with clouds in Soane's hand
Inscr. *Elevation of Entrance &c, of a Design for a Triumphal Bridge*
Pencil, pen and watercolour: 478 × 1376 mm
SM 12/5/2

14 Section through the central dome of the bridge, set against a blue sky with clouds and water, in Soane's hand
Inscr. *Section through the Center Building*
Pencil, pen and watercolour: 612 × 864 mm
SM 12/5/3

Together with his five-hour sketch design for the entrance of a church dedicated to the Evangelists, these drawings constitute Soane's winning entry in the Academy's 1776 gold medal competition for the best design for a Triumphal Bridge. The choice of this unusual subject (the first and only time it was set in the Academy's history) was almost certainly made by Chambers on his return from a brief but intensive study trip to Paris in May 1774. It had been the subject of the Prix d'émulation at the Académie Royale d'Architecture in February that year and, as a favourite project amongst the brilliant *pensionnaires* of the Académie Française in Rome in the late 1740s and early 1750s, must have struck a chord with Chambers as a reminder of his own heady student days in the Eternal City. There can be little doubt therefore that

Chambers would have been happy to lend Soane books and prints by his old *pensionnaire* friends, such as E. A. Petitot's 'Projet d'un pont triomphal' (fig. 102), Piranesi's 'Ponte magnifico' (fig. 103) and, in particular, Peyre's *Oeuvres d'Architecture* (cat. 11), from which Soane clearly derived some of the most distinctive colonnaded and domed features of his design. Stirred by the unusualness of the subject, non-architect members of the Academy may also have come to Soane's assistance. The engraver Thomas Major, for instance, who had strong connections with the Parisian art world, may well have lent Soane his copy of N. H. Jardin's *Plans ... de l'Eglise royale de Frédéric V* (Copenhagen, 1765) containing a fine triumphal bridge design etched in Rome in 1748 (fig. 101), which the author had presented to him in 1770, and which Soane was to buy at the sale of Major's library in 1799. NS

15 Elevation of the winning competition design for a Triumphal Bridge, in Soane's hand, 1777
Inscr. *The Elevation to the River of a Design for a Triumphal Bridge*
Signed and dated: *Jn. Soan Archt. 1777*
Pencil, pen and watercolour: 545 × 2410 mm
SM 12/5/4

This drawing dates from after Soane's gold medal competition success but before he was elected to the Academy's Travelling Scholarship at the General Assembly of Academicians on 10 December 1777. It may have been intended specifically to impress King George III, to whom Chambers had submitted Soane's drawings with the idea of gaining direct royal approval for sending him abroad. Ironically, when compared with Sandby's great lecture drawing (cat. 10), which it was doubtless intended to emulate, it reveals more of the principal weakness of Soane's design than his competition drawings had done, namely the unhappy positioning of the terminal pavilions over the first and seventh arches, where they emphasise the disjunction of the bridge in relation to the riverbank rather than helping to anchor it on terra firma. NS

Section through the Center Building.

CATALOGUE 14

The Grand Tour

Figure 104 (opposite)
A student on a ladder measuring a Corinthian capital at the Temple of Jupiter Stator (Castor and Pollux), Rome (detail of cat. 22)

Soane's moment of departure for Italy was one which he marked for the rest of his life. At 5.30 a.m. on 18 March 1778 he and his fellow architect and friend, Robert Brettingham, left London.

Paris, where the two young men spent a few days, was a city in the midst of a building boom. At its heart was the Place Louis XV (later the Place de la Concorde). Paris was being transformed from a medieval huddle on the banks of the Seine into a model of Neoclassical urbanity, the strongest possible contrast to London. Soane and Brettingham met the distinguished elderly architect-engineer Jean-Rodolphe Perronet, director of the Ponts et Chaussées, and admired the engineering of his radical new bridge, the almost flat Pont de Neuilly which linked the country west of Paris to the city. There is otherwise little record of what they saw or the route which they followed to Italy, where they arrived in early May.

Soane wrote of his excitement at seeing Roman antiquity for the first time in a letter to the carver Henry Wood (Bolton 1927, p. 16). He was soon measuring and sketching (cat. 22), choosing the great monuments such as the Pantheon (cat. 23), the Colosseum and the Forum Romanum (fig. 107) – half obscured by mounds of soil and saplings – as well as several early Christian basilicas. Soane was in a small minority of architects among the many artists and Grand Tourists in Rome. His choice of buildings and destinations was guided by a letter written by Sir William Chambers to a previous visitor, Edward Stevens, while George Dance the Younger, who had spent almost six years in Italy, must have provided much additional advice. Soane quickly became part of the expatriate society in the city; Grand Tourists, as Chambers and Dance could have told him, were the men who might lay the foundations of an architectural clientele on his return. Soane met the Bishop of Derry (see fig. 7), Thomas Pitt (see fig. 8) and Philip Yorke; the three became, respectively, the 4th Earl of Bristol (the Earl-Bishop), Lord Camelford and the 3rd Earl of Hardwicke.

At the end of the year, Soane travelled to Naples as the chosen companion of the Bishop, lunching on Christmas Day among the ruins of the Villa of Lucullus and discussing work for Downhill, his patron's house in Ireland, including a classical dog kennel (cat. 26) and a summer dining room with strongly Antique antecedents. While south of Rome, Soane visited Caserta, Capua, Pompeii (cat. 29), Vesuvius, Baia and Paestum (fig. 105, cats 30–34), as well as lesser-known destinations inland and further south, such as the Certosa at Padula and the cathedral and Roman arch at Benevento. Under the Bishop's tuition on these expeditions, Soane learned about Classical antiquity and its architecture, as well as the geology, agriculture and engineering feats of the area. His notebooks brim over with his discoveries while his Italian rapidly improved.

Soane returned to Rome only to go south again in April, with a group of young men who had invited him to travel at their expense as their draughtsman on a tour to Sicily and Malta. The party consisted of John Patteson and Thomas Bowdler, respectively a woolstapler and a doctor from Norwich, Rowland Burdon and John Stuart, north-country landowners, and Henry Greswold Lewis, also a landowner, from Solihull. Soane with Patteson, Burdon and Greswold Lewis traversed Sicily, from Palermo to Segesta, from Agrigento to Etna. Paestum and the Sicilian temples were potent introductions to ancient Greek architecture, and Soane never forgot the ingenious Baroque effects achieved with mirror glass and hidden light sources at the Villa Palagonia at Bagheria and at the Palazzo Biscari near Catania.

Back in Rome again, Soane planned a number of visits to the centres of Mannerism and Palladianism, the northern

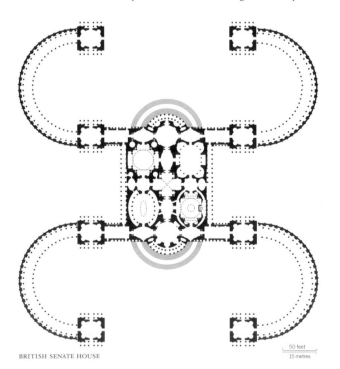

BRITISH SENATE HOUSE

50 feet
15 metres

Figure 105

View showing the setting of the three Greek Doric temples at Paestum and their relationship to one another within the walls of the city. Watercolour (SM Vol. 27,1) from which the engraving in Thomas Major's *The Ruins of Paestum*, 1768, was taken

FIGURE 105

Italian cities of Mantua, Vicenza, Padua, Parma (where he hoped to gain a Diploma, as had Dance before him), Bologna and Venice. His investigations closely followed Chambers's recommendations, and began to extend into the modern period.

By the spring of 1780 Soane had extracted enormous benefit from his time in Italy. No longer a hesitant youth, he had become a confident young man, often seen in theatres and opera houses dressed to catch the eye. He had befriended two remarkable girls, Anna (Nancy) Storace, who was to be Mozart's first Susanna, and the painter Maria Hadfield, later Cosway. A summons had come from the new Earl of Bristol, the Bishop of Derry, and the prospect of such a substantial commission proved too tempting to refuse. Returning via Florence, Genoa and then back over the Alps, Soane paused only to study the same Swiss wooden bridges that his patron had visited

some years earlier. The route, which he was advised to take at the last moment because of the political situation, denied Soane a glimpse of Roman Provence and along the way he lost much of his luggage, including the accumulated record of his Continental sojourn. Soane's return to England was clouded by this accident but the prospect of becoming the chosen architect of the now enormously wealthy Earl, with his estates in Suffolk and Derry and his passion for building, was exciting. Soane's optimism caused him to forget what he must have known about his patron: that he was mercurial, unreliable and rarely paid his debts.

For the rest of his life Soane longed to return to Italy. In 1819 he considered extending a visit to Paris further south, perhaps to meet J. M. W. Turner in Rome, but the harsh journey and the pressure of work in London prevented this; he was never to see Rome, or Mediterranean light, again.

FIGURE 106

Figure 106
Thomas Hearne, *The Ruins of the Great Temple at Selinunte*, watercolour, 1777. Soane visited Selinunte during his Sicilian trip in the summer of 1779 (Department of Prints and Drawings, British Museum, London)

Figure 107
Louis-François Cassas, View of the Forum with (from left) the Temple of Vespasian, the Arch of Septimus Severus and the Temple of Concord, drawn in 1779 while Soane was in Rome. The topographical artist Cassas shows two figures, perhaps architectural students, measuring the Temple of Vespasian (The National Trust, Ickworth)

FIGURE 107

16 View of interior of Sainte-Geneviève (Panthéon), drawn by Soane's pupils, 1820
Dated (in pen): *29th: Feby: 1820.*
Pencil, pen and watercolour:
1112 × 724 mm
SM 22/5/11

Paris was the first city that Soane visited in 1778 on his Grand Tour. Although the records from this part of his journey are slight, it seems likely that he set out to inspect many of the examples of new civic architecture, including Jacques-Germain Soufflot's Sainte-Geneviève, probably at the recommendation of Chambers, who had been there only four years earlier. Chambers, architect to Somerset House, London's only equivalent Neoclassical civic project, was a member of the Académie Royale d'Architecture and the English architect most knowledgeable about, and connected to, matters of French architecture.

Sainte-Geneviève, the largest religious architectural project of the century in France, was still under construction in 1778. Soufflot (1713–1780) had been commissioned to design the church in 1754. The building was the first to be seen as an expression of the Abbé Laugier's rationalist Neoclassical ideal; in 1765, he called the building 'the first example of a perfect architecture'.

This perspective drawing was executed by Soane's pupils following his third trip to Paris, taken in 1819 with one of his pupils, Henry Parke. In 1792–93, during the French Revolution, Sainte-Geneviève had been designated the Panthéon, a temple to the nation. Consequently a number of alterations – such as the removal of the two apsidal bell towers and the addition of many windows which flooded the interior with light – were undertaken to make the

building a suitable resting place for 'the ashes of distinguished men'. In making lecture drawings such as this, Soane's pupils worked from engravings of the building as originally designed. Soane used the building in his lectures to illustrate the concept of *lumière mystérieuse*, 'a most powerful agent in the hands of a man of genius, and its power cannot be too fully understood, nor too highly appreciated. It is however little attended to in our Architecture, and for this obvious reason, that we do not sufficiently feel the importance of Character in our buildings, to which the mode of admitting light contributes in no small degree' (Watkin 1996 [1], p. 598).

In the Royal Academy lectures, the Panthéon represented the finest example of Paris's architectural success as a capital city. Soane dramatically contrasted the situation in Paris with the state of London's public architecture: 'No longer let foreigners reproach us with the total want of great national monuments; let us, in this respect, imitate our Gallic neighbours, let us look at their Pantheon, an edifice dedicated exclusively to the honour of great men. This superb fane [temple], calculated to immortalise the memory of its architect, Soufflot, will ever be ranked amongst the finest specimens of modern art that Europe can boast' (Watkin 1996 [1], p. 591). HE

17 Giovanni Battista Piranesi (1720–1778)
Interior view of the Tempio della Tosse, near Rome, 1764
Engraving: 550 × 625 mm
Early Imprints Collection, British Architectural Library, Royal Institute of British Architects, London

The Tempio della Tosse stands a mile from Tivoli, and is now thought to be the tomb of the Turcia family. The memory of domed, top-lit Roman ruins resonates in many of Soane's interiors, such as the Rotunda of the Bank of England (cats 130–133). His taste for austere, luminous surfaces may also have been inspired by Antique ruins whose marble and plaster decorations have been shed, exposing a bare shell of brick or stone, pitted by patterns of light and shadow.

Piranesi arrived in Rome from his native Venice in 1740. His dramatic images of ruins were the most influential in eighteenth-century Europe, combining archaeological accuracy with a set-designer's eye for a dramatic perspective and an architect's appreciation of the tectonic qualities of Roman masonry. Soane met Piranesi in Rome in 1778, a few months before the Italian's death, and his influence is seen at its most potent in the Dome of the Museum (see fig. 138). CW

CATALOGUE 17

18 Giovanni Battista Piranesi
Ruins of a Sculpture Gallery at
Hadrian's Villa, Tivoli, near
Rome, 1770
Engraving: 455×580 mm
Early Imprints Collection,
British Architectural Library,
Royal Institute of British
Architects, London

Exploring the vast ruins of the
luxurious palace erected by the
Emperor Hadrian at Tivoli,
near Rome, was an essential
element of the Grand Tour.
While the temples of the
Forum presented the
vocabulary of the Classical
orders, Hadrian's Villa revealed
a startling variety of domed
and groin-vaulted spaces and a
ground-plan as complex as any
of modern times. Its ruins were
to have a far more profound
influence upon Soane than
those of the Forum.

The fact that the Villa was
vast, abandoned and
overgrown added to the drama
of discovering such spaces.
Piranesi and his assistants were
obliged to cut their way
through the undergrowth with
hatchets and then to set fire to
the area cleared so as to burn
out the snakes and scorpions,
according to J. G. Legrand's
1799 biography of the artist.
This interior is now identified
as the central hall of the large
baths complex. cw

19 Giovanni Altieri, model-maker
(fl. 1767–1790)
Model of the Temple of Vesta
at Tivoli, near Rome
Inscr. *IOA . ALTIERI / NEAP .
F . 177-*
Cork: 395×523 × 515 mm
SM MR2

The Temple of Vesta, dating
from the early first century BC
and set dramatically on the
edge of a precipice at Tivoli,
was Soane's favourite Antique
building. He sketched and took
careful measurements of it as a
student in 1778–79, and the
temple was a powerful source
of inspiration throughout his
career (see cats 160–162). He
even created a 'Tivoli Recess'
in his home at Lincoln's Inn
Fields in tribute to the
monument's enduring appeal.
In two spectacular views of
Soane's Museum as it appeared
in 1811 this model is shown
perched on a pile of
architectural fragments (see
cats 68–69) balanced, Piranesi-
fashion, on the edge of the
parapet beneath the dome.

Giovanni Altieri was one of
the leading cork model-makers
of the late eighteenth century.
He made a number of models
of the Temple of Vesta of which
two, including this one, were
based on measurements taken
by Giovanni Stern (1734–1794),
an Italian architect who seems
to have surveyed the temple in
collaboration with George
Dance the Younger. The cork is
beautifully used in this model
to convey the building's
travertine structure and its use
of *opus reticulatum*. HD

20 Royal Academy lecture drawing
of the Temple of Vesta at Tivoli
Pencil, ink and watercolour:
692×1112 mm
SM 19/7/3

This view, in which the temple
is shown bathed in a romantic
golden light, is testament to
the building's enduring appeal
to Soane's imagination. The
drawing is annotated in his
hand on the verso as being
intended to accompany lecture
three, perhaps to illustrate the
passage in which Soane praises
circular temples, noting that:
'no composition can be more
attractive and pleasing than the
circular peripetal temple. The
variety and smooth gradation
in the perspective, the
different quantity of air which
surrounds each column, the
change produced by the
foreshortening of the capitals
and the ornaments of the
frieze, together with the
accidental play of light and
shadow, make the effect of the
whole composition irresistible.'
Elsewhere in his lectures,
Soane praises the Tivoli order
for the 'singularity and
charming effect of most of its
parts' and its 'beautiful
lightness' and points out the
unusual slenderness and height
of the columns, concluding
that 'the uncommon taste,
lightness and elegance of every
part of this beautiful
composition has never been
surpassed, nor can be
sufficiently admired' (Watkin
1996 [1], pp. 500–532). The
temple is quoted throughout
Soane's work: the bull's head
and garland motif of its frieze
was used at Tendring Hall and
on the porches at Malvern Hall
and Burn Hall, whilst the
whole order was 'faithfully
copied' for the exteriors of the
Bank of England. HD

21 Model of the Temple of Jupiter
Stator (Castor and Pollux) in
the Forum Romanum, Rome
Cork: 515×330 × 170 mm
SM MR 14

In Soane's day the three 47ft-
high columns of the Temple of
Castor and Pollux (dating from
a restoration of the temple by
Augustus, 7 BC–AD 6) rose out
of the largely unexcavated
Forum. The high double
podium of the temple was
completely buried and is
therefore not shown in this
model, probably made in the
late eighteenth century. As a
student, Soane would have
heard the temple cited by
Sandby in his Royal Academy
lectures as the greatest example
of the Corinthian order. He
would also have admired the
plaster casts made by George
Dance the Younger in 1760 of
what he called 'the finest
example of the Corinthian
order perhaps in the whole
world' (Dance letter book,
RIBA, BAL MS DA1/1). On his
arrival in Rome, Soane made
careful sketches of the temple
and in his own Royal Academy
lecture two noted that of all
the examples of this order now
remaining, that 'of the three
columns in the Campo
Vaccino, supposed to have
been a Temple to Jupiter Stator,
is the most sublime and
awefully grand and impressive'
(Watkin 1996 [1], p. 511). HD

CATALOGUE 18

CATALOGUE 19

CATALOGUE 22

22 Royal Academy lecture drawing showing a student on a ladder, with a rod, measuring the Corinthian order of the Temple of Jupiter Stator (Castor and Pollux), Rome, drawn by Henry Parke
Pencil, pen and watercolour: 940×634 mm
SM 23/9/3

This lecture drawing, which formed part of a discussion of the Corinthian order, provided its Royal Academy audiences with a dramatic representation of the activities typically undertaken by architectural students on the Grand Tour.

As Soane wrote to a friend Mr Wood, from Rome during his Grand Tour (on 1 August 1778): 'I need not tell you my attention is entirely taken up in the seeing and examining the numerous and inestimable remains of Antiquity, as you are no stranger to the zeal and attachment I have for them and with what impatience I have waited for the scenes I now enjoy...' (Bolton 1927, p. 16).

Soane's pupils were often instructed to make drawings of the full-size cast of the capital (M47, purchased by Soane in 1801) in the Museum. Soane himself used the order from this temple in his revised design for the exterior of the Board of Trade Offices, Whitehall (cat. 186). HE

23 Elevation of the Pantheon, Rome, in Soane's hand, 1778
Inscr. (in pen, in Soane's hand) *LA.FACCIATA.DELLA. ROTONDA.A.ROMA.OGGI. CHIESA.DI.SANTA. MARIA.AD.MARTYRES.* Signed and dated (in pen, in Soane's hand): *I.SOANE* [e added] *.fecit.in.Romae.1778.* Pencil, pen, monochrome and coloured washes: 632×991 mm
SM 45/3/54

The Pantheon in Rome, a building of the early second century AD, was one of the major monuments of Roman architecture admired and studied by students on the Grand Tour. In his Royal Academy lectures Soane praised the Pantheon as 'the glory of the ancient and the admiration of the modern world' (Watkin 1996 [1], p. 653). Significantly, Soane's response is both analytical and evocative; the watercolour combines accurate measuring and romantic representation.

Soane was a great authority on the building; while on his Grand Tour he corrected Anna Miller's guidebook in the margins where it stated that the church was stripped of its gilt-bronze decorative elements, writing that 'The cornice round the aperture [oculus] is all of Bronze part of the gilding rem[ain]s' (du Prey 1972 [1], p. 119). He revealed his expertise as well in his 1826 interview with George Wightwick, when he interrogated the young man about the interspaces between the columns (Bolton 1927, p. 398). HE

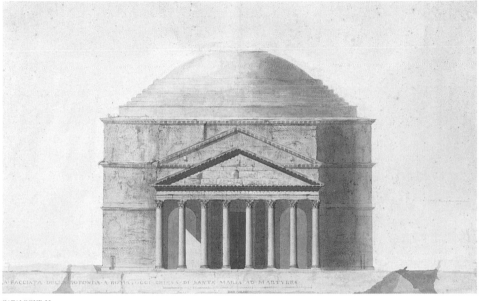

CATALOGUE 23

CATALOGUE 26

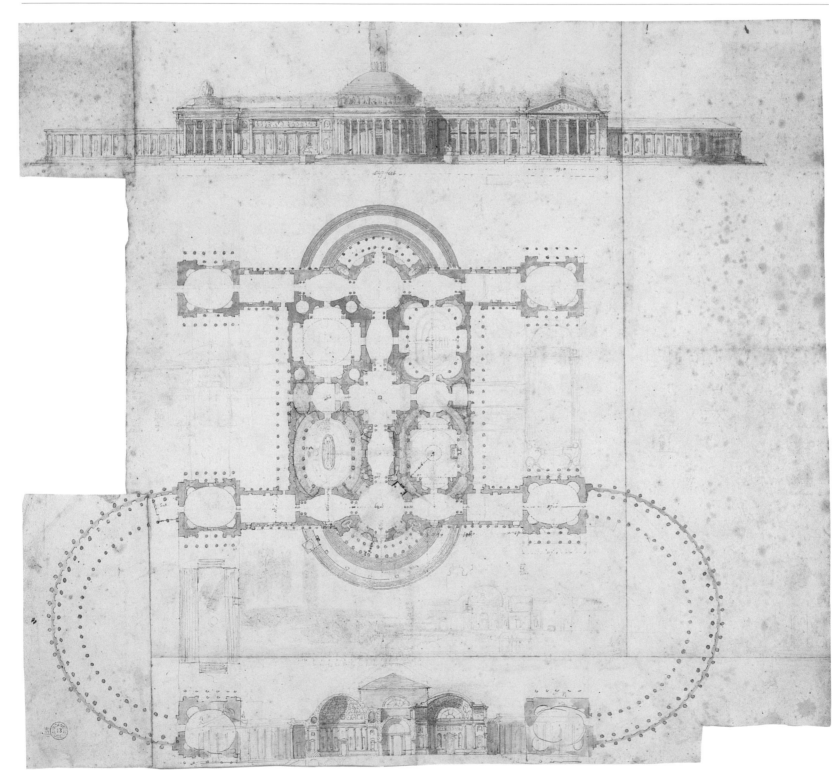

CATALOGUE 25

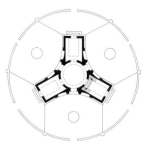

DOG KENNEL

CASTELLO D'ACQUA

24 François Fouquet,
model-maker (*fl.* 1792–1835)
Model of the Pantheon, Rome
Plaster: 240 × 318 × 390 mm
SM MR3

This model was among twenty
'restorations' of ancient Greek
and Roman buildings made by
the Parisian model-maker
François Fouquet and
purchased by Soane from the
architect Edward Cresy in 1834.
Fouquet worked with his
father Jean-Pierre Fouquet
(1752–1829), making models for
architects and collectors,
including Louis-François
Cassas who opened a gallery of
models in Paris in 1806 which
Soane may have visited on one
of his two later visits to that
city in 1814 and 1819. The
models were produced by
hand, the plaster being built up
over a framework of internal
metal armatures with moulds
used for the fine miniature
capitals, entablatures and other
details. HD

25 Design for a British Senate
House, in Soane's hand, 1778
Dated (bottom left, in pen,
in Soane's hand): *Aug. 10. 1778*
Pencil, pen and monochrome
wash: 563 × 610 mm
SM 45/1/13

One of the requirements of
Soane's Royal Academy
travelling scholarship was to
send a submission to each
Royal Academy annual
exhibition. This drawing,
which Soane completed a few
months into his stay in Rome,
features his preliminary
scheme for his first submission:
a British Senate House. It is a
design which already reveals
the inspiration Soane had
discovered in Rome, while also
evincing the continued
influence of French
Neoclassical printed sources
such as Peyre's *Oeuvres
d'Architecture* (see cat. 11).
In the lectures, Soane
employed the British Senate
House design as an example of
the soaring imagination of
youth, 'unshackled and
unsicklied with the frequent
disappointments of a
professional life ... only
occupied in the contemplation
of magnificent remains of
palaces, temples, baths,
triumphal arches, and other
objects interesting to the artist
and firing his imagination'
(Watkin 1996 [1], p. 576). HE

26 Copy of Soane's design for a dog
kennel, drawn by Soane's pupil
C. J. Richardson (1809–1872),
c. 1835
Dated (in pen, lower RH
corner): *Romae*. 1779.
Pencil, pen and ink, and
watercolour: 707 × 1272 mm
SM 14/4/2

This extravagant Antique-
inspired design for a dog
kennel was produced for the
Bishop of Derry, with whom
Soane had travelled south of
Rome to examine
archaeological sites. As Soane
recalled in his *Memoirs*, the
Bishop had exclaimed while
the two were exploring the
ruins of the Villa of Lucullus
(near Terracina): 'Where is the
canile and *tugurium*? I should
like to form some idea of a
classical dog kennel, as I intend
to build one at the Downhill
for the hounds of my eldest son
... This will be a fine subject for
the display of your creative
talents' (*Memoirs*, p. 15). Soane
took this opportunity to create
for such an important potential
client a showcase not only for
his creativity, but also for the
Classical knowledge he had
gained since his arrival in
Rome. The kennel featured the
baseless Greek Doric columns
Soane had seen at Paestum (see
cats 30–34), and the frieze was
borrowed from the Temple of
Vesta at Tivoli (see cat. 19) with
Soane cleverly replacing the
traditional bucrania with dogs'
heads. The form of the
building took as its inspiration
a mausoleum, such as the one
Soane had produced while a
student at the Royal Academy.
Soane further elaborated on
this theme, submitting a
modern version of the kennel
for the annual Royal Academy
exhibition in 1781 (du Prey 1972
[1], p. 161). The 1837 Inventory
of the works of art in the
Museum suggests that this
drawing is a late copy of the
original Soane drawing by
C. J. Richardson, *c.* 1835. HE

27 Designs for a castello
28 d'acqua, in Soane's hand, with
a letter to Thomas Pitt, 1779
Dated on 182r: *Milan Augst. the
1779*
Signed: *J. Soan.*
Pencil, pen and ink:
225 × 373 mm
SM Vol. 42, items 182r, 183r,
mounted together, and 184r

While still in Italy Soane
employed the mausoleum form
seen in his design for a classical
dog kennel in response to a
competition programme for
a castello d'acqua, or
waterworks. These sketches
were contained in one of the
few extant letters Soane sent
from Italy during his
fellowship. The letter was
addressed to Thomas Pitt, the
nephew of the then recently
deceased Earl of Chatham, a
connection that Soane had
made through the Bishop of
Derry. The letter provides a
rare glimpse of Soane's first
efforts to present himself to a
European audience through his
expressed desire to compete
for the Parma gold medal,
which his teacher George
Dance had won a decade and a
half earlier. The subject of the
competition to be held in May
1780 concerned 'Un castello
d'acqua decorato d'una
pubblica fontana'. Although
Soane in the August 1779 letter
to Thomas Pitt professes
himself 'doubtful of the
propriety of [his] ideas
respecting' the subject, it
being, in Soane's words,
'entirely new to me', his two
alternative designs for the
castello reflected to a large
degree his work of a year earlier
considering a mausoleum
design.
Unlike most of Soane's early
student schemes, especially
those for competition,
a reduced version of the
castello d'acqua was ultimately
built at Wimpole (cat. 50). HE

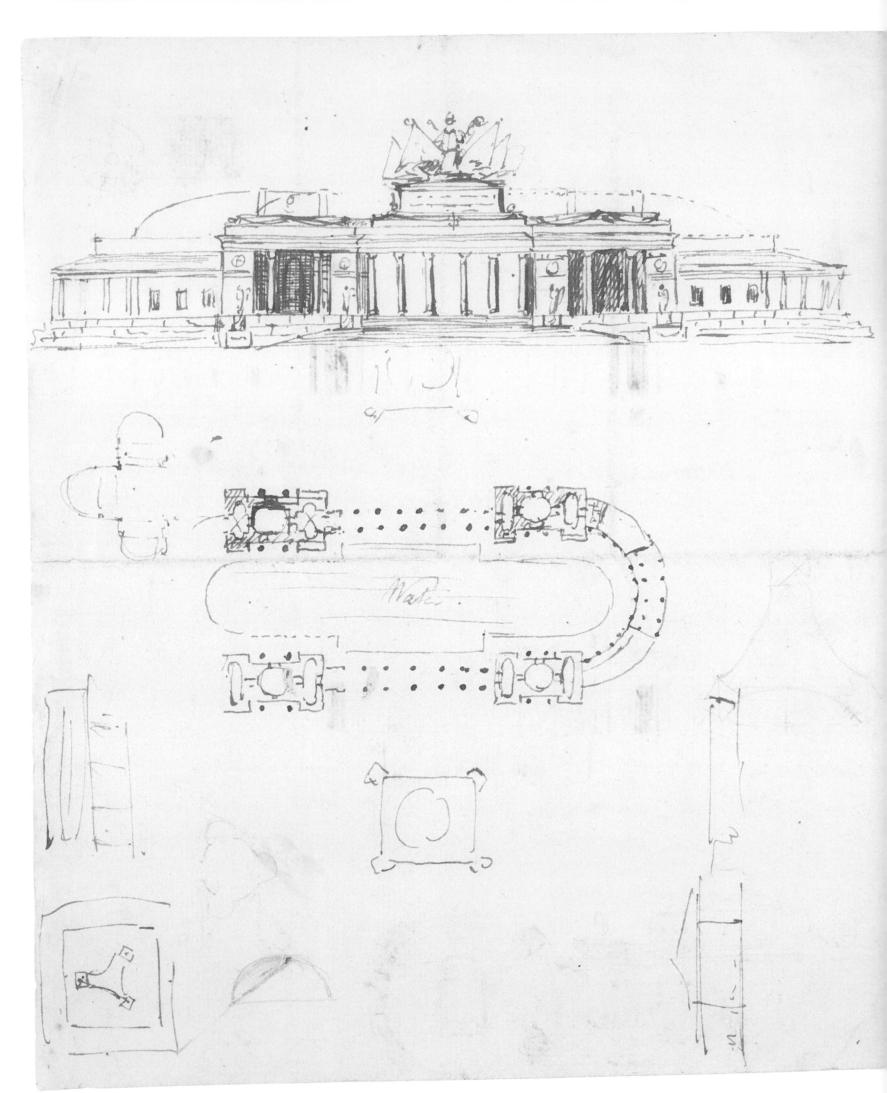

a, Reservoir.

b, Apartment,
for the Keeper.
&c..

c Committee Room

d. Temples to the
4 chief River Gods

e. Fountain

f On each of these
Pedestals a river God

It will be (I believe) necessary to lower the Steps considerably.

The Reservoir will hold ab.t 15,000 Hogsheads of Water. Query
if that is any thing like the Quantity?

I believe the Reservoir must be covered to prevent the water being
heated, in the last page is a design with it open —

The fountains are marked in to shew their situation only, & are supposed
to be much unlike what would be introduced in the fair design.

29 Royal Academy lecture drawing of the Street of the Tombs, Pompeii
Inscr. *STREET OF THE TOMBS POMPEII*
Pencil, pen and watercolour: 705×1257 mm
SM 20/4/7

Excavations of the buried city of Pompeii began in 1749; by the time Soane was visiting a few decades later in 1779, the site was a destination popular with professionals and tourists alike. Soane himself made several study trips to Pompeii during his Grand Tour. Despite the Neapolitan authorities' prohibition of note-taking or drawing, Soane's notebook from the time contains a number of sketches and measured drawings, made, as Soane explained later in his Royal Academy lectures, 'by stealth by moonlight' (Watkin 1996, p. 525). The Temple of Isis, one of the principal sights of Pompeii, and the 'Via delle tombe', the northern approach to the city, were among those aspects of the site Soane studied carefully. HE

The Temples at Paestum
The ruined Doric temples at Paestum, built by Greek colonists in the sixth and fifth centuries BC, are among the best-preserved of all Greek temples. Soane visited Paestum twice in 1779, while spending the winter touring Naples and the south with the Bishop of Derry. He completed a series of measured sketches but found the architecture 'exceedingly rude, the temples at the extremities in particular [having] all the parts of the Grecian doric but not the elegance & taste' (SM 'Italian Sketches, J. Soane, 1779'). Although seemingly unimpressed by the massive, baseless columns of the temples, he greatly appreciated the primitive qualities of the Doric order and the sheer scale

and magnificence of the site. While still in Italy he redrew his Triumphal Bridge using the Greek Doric order as his admission piece for the Parma Academy; nineteen years after his return to England, he designed a Barn à la Paestum (see fig. 111). HD

30 Giovanni Battista Piranesi (1720–1778)
View of the exterior of the Temple of Neptune at Paestum from the north-east, 1778
Pen and wash: 596×774 mm
SM P70

31 Giovanni Battista Piranesi
View of the interior of the Temple of Neptune at Paestum from the north, 1778
Pen and wash: 597×774 mm
SM P74

Piranesi set off for Paestum in 1777–78, the last year of his life, accompanied by his son Francesco (1758–1810) and the architect and cork model-maker Augusto Rosa. Of the series of finished drawings he produced, fifteen are in Soane's collection. The drawings are much more than a detailed archaeological record, conveying beautifully the atmospheric presence and monumentality of the temples as well as the play of light and shade on the crumbling surface of the masonry. They were elaborately executed with a pale wash applied over the initial black chalk outlines after which details were drawn in ink before a darker wash was used for the shadows and the foreground. The figures, some of which may have been drawn by Francesco, were added after the architectural elements were complete. Despite failing health, Piranesi etched all but the title page and two plates of the publication based on the drawings. *Différentes vues de quelques restes de trois grands édifices qui subsistent encore dans le milieu de l'ancienne ville de Pesto*

appeared shortly after his death. Unfortunately, it is not known how or when Soane acquired the drawings. HD

32 Domenico Padiglione, model-maker (*fl.* 1802–1830)
Model of the Temple of Ceres (Athena) at Paestum, after 1802
Cork with terracotta capitals: 320×334×1320 mm
SM MR12

33 Domenico Padiglione
Model of the Temple of Hera (the Basilica) at Paestum, after 1802
Cork with terracotta capitals: 240×617×1335 mm
SM MR22

34 Domenico Padiglione
Model of the Temple of Neptune at Paestum, after 1802
Cork with terracotta capitals: 375×630×1324 mm
SM MR25

Domenico Padiglione made models of all three temples at Paestum for the Naples Museum in *c.* 1805. These post-date the first excavations and restorations of the temples which began in 1802, during which large quantities of accumulated fragments were removed from within the temples. His models remained on view at the Naples Museum until the 1840s and he made numerous copies for private sale despite the fact that his contract with the museum forbade him to do so. The three models in Soane's collection were probably made in the early 1820s; the original inventories of the Soane Museum collection state that they were acquired from his pupil John Sanders in *c.* 1826. HD

35 Model of the Temple of Fortuna Virilis in the Forum Boarium, Rome
Cork: 690×740×1140 mm
SM 1274

This model shows the late second-century BC Temple of Fortuna Virilis standing on a rocky hill, a topographically incorrect setting but one which dramatises and romanticises the subject. Many popular exhibitions in eighteenth- and nineteenth-century London featured such models as part of their displays and this one may have originally come from the model emporium of Richard Dubourg which was first opened in the 1770s and later re-established in Duke Street near Manchester Square by 1798, where its dramatic quality would have been very appropriate. It was probably purchased by Soane from the architect Charles Heathcote Tatham in 1832. HD

36 Model of the Temple of Jupiter Tonans (Vespasian), Rome
Cork: 345×215×200 mm
SM MR 7

The temple of the deified Emperor Vespasian was erected by his son Titus in AD 79–81 on a site at the foot of the Capitoline Hill in the Forum Romanum. Its columns and unusual frieze, carved with instruments of sacrifice and bucrania, have been artificially blackened in this model to convey its ruinous state. HD

37 Joseph Mallord William Turner (1775–1851)
Forum Romanum, for Mr Soane's Museum, 1826
Oil on canvas: 1457×2363 mm
Exh. 1826, Royal Academy, no. 132
The Tate Gallery, London. Bequeathed by the artist, 1856

Soane commissioned this evocative scene overlooking the Forum with the Arch of Titus and the Basilica of Maxentius in the foreground in 1826. He planned to hang it in his Picture Room where the north planes would have opened to reveal this romantic golden view framed within an arch and with Antique fragments scattered in the foreground. When hung at the Royal Academy, however, the work was criticised in the press, along with Turner's other 1826 exhibits: 'In all, we find the same intolerable yellow hue pervading everything ... all is yellow, yellow, nothing but yellow, violently contrasted with blue. With greater invention in his works than any master of the present day – invention which amounts almost to poetry in landscape, Mr Turner has degenerated into such a detestable manner, that we cannot view his works without pain... We ... would wish Mr Turner to turn back to Nature...' (*British Press*, 30 April 1826). In contrast, Sir Augustus Callcott was praised by the *British Press* article for the way he conveyed nature and 'the cool fresh breeze of European scenery'. Perhaps in reaction to this, Soane wrote to Turner in July rejecting the work on the grounds that 'the picture did not suit the place or the place the picture' (SM Archive P.C. II. T.10.4–7). Instead, Callcott was commissioned to paint *A Passage Point*, a nostalgic capriccio with the Temple of Vesta at Tivoli on an Italian lakeside. HD

CATALOGUE 37

CATALOGUE 31
CATALOGUE 34 (PAGES 112–113)

HEXASTYLE·HYPÆTHRAL·TEMPLE. PÆSTUM.

Early Practice:
Country Houses
and the Primitive

FIGURE 108

FIGURE 109

In 1780, Soane prematurely returned from Italy in the mistaken hope that the promises made by his Grand Tour friend the Earl-Bishop of Derry would yield a substantial commission for the reconstruction of Downhill, the Earl-Bishop's house in the north of Ireland. With his aspirations dashed, Soane made his way back to London to start his practice, and had to rely on a network of other friends and acquaintances made in Italy. The building boom of the mid-1770s was over, and Soane's earliest commissions were modest in scale, typified by the pair of estate entrance lodges at Hamels Park, Hertfordshire (cat. 38), his first free-standing structures, constructed in 1781.

Clusters of commissions began to develop, particularly in East Anglia, where Soane's good reputation spread fast. His first country house, Letton Hall, Norfolk, was begun

in 1783, with Saxlingham Rectory (fig. 115, cat. 46) and Tendring Hall following in 1784 (fig. 116, cats 47–48). At the same time, alterations were being made to existing country houses and their estates at a dozen other locations, including two sets of lodges constructed at Langley Park, Norfolk, in 1784 (figs 112, 113). Soane worked unassisted, surveying sites, producing all the design and production-information drawings and the pre-construction estimates as well as monitoring the work on site and checking the tradesmen's bills. Lengthy site visits involved slow and uncomfortable travel by chaise and lasted for weeks at a time, with Soane making more connections and generating more jobs in between. This remarkable effort is recorded in his notebooks, with only a four-day pause during August 1784 when he married Elizabeth Smith in Christ Church,

Figure 111

Barn à la Paestum
(originally the barn on the
Malvern Hall estate,
Warwickshire, now 936
Warwick Road, Solihull):
general view of the
entrance side

FIGURE 111

Figure 112

Langley Park, Norfolk:
the Greyhound Lodges

Figure 113

Langley Park, Norfolk:
the Doric Lodges

FIGURE 112

Lambeth. Soane took on his first pupil in 1784, and
published a volume of his country-house and estate work
in 1788. This was the year that he also secured the
surveyorship of the Bank of England. But it was only in
1790 that his financial position became totally secure,
when his wife's uncle George Wyatt died and left the
couple a considerable amount of property which produced
an income in the form of annual rents.

Throughout Soane's early work a number of themes
emerge: a strong adherence to symmetry; appreciation of
the effects of light and shade; and the potential for
creating 'routes' through buildings. The vista at Tendring
extended from the front door and out into the parkland
beyond, compressed by the flight of steps in the entrance
vestibule, and enlivened by a variety of lighting effects,

FIGURE 113

Figure 114

Pitzhanger Manor, Ealing:
the entrance arch

Figure 115

Saxlingham Rectory,
Norfolk: the entrance
façade

FIGURE 114

FIGURE 115

FIGURE 116

such as the top-lit staircase (see cat. 48). Soane exploited the fine quality of local materials to achieve a crisp articulation of the openings and a sense of 'layering' of his elevations.

These simple effects tied in with Soane's interest in 'primitivism'. This idea had been embodied in the celebrated *Essai sur l'architecture* by the Abbé Marc Antoine Laugier (Paris, 1753, translated into English in 1755), which articulated the suggestion by Vitruvius that the origins of Classical architecture lay in the 'primitive hut' (cats 40–43). It was undoubtedly Soane's clear understanding of the structural logic of classicism that enabled him to strip back details to their essential quality.

Soane's most self-consciously primitive building was the dairy constructed in 1783 at Hamels Park (cat. 39).

It was deliberately 'picturesque', and celebrated the notion of a simple and pure existence, a noble honesty away from the complexities of modern life, akin to the writings of Uvedale Price and Richard Payne Knight. A more literal 'Barn à la Paestum' (fig. 111) was constructed in 1798 for Soane's Grand Tour friend Henry Greswold Lewis as a barn at Malvern Hall, Warwickshire. Instead of logs and roughcast, soft red bricks were used. Soane's 1798 stables at Betchworth Castle, Surrey (cat. 45), combined flint with brick, slate and stone to provide a colourful eyecatcher in the park (fig. 109). So inspired was Soane by this combination of materials that he initially proposed it for his own house at Pitzhanger Manor, before settling for its use on the entrance arch (see cats 60–64).

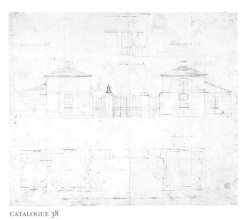

HAMELS LODGES

20 feet
6 metres

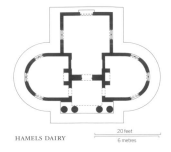

HAMELS DAIRY

20 feet
6 metres

CATALOGUE 38

Hamels Park, Hertfordshire, for the Hon. Philip Yorke, 1781–1783

38 Design, in Soane's hand, for the gateway and lodges, 1781
Inscr. *Elevation next the Road/ Elevation next the Park/Plan of the Bedchamber/Philip Yorke Esq/* and dimensions
Pencil, pen and ink:
486×571 mm
SM 62/8/32

Soane executed several buildings at Hamels for Philip Yorke (later 3rd Earl Hardwicke) for whom he was also to work at Wimpole (see cats 49–50). Some of the Hamels buildings survive, including these lodges, although they have been altered. Soane had met Yorke in Italy where they had visited the ruins of Paestum together.

This is an excellent example of the economy Soane achieved in his working drawings. One lodge is viewed from the road, the other from the park. On the plan below, the ground floor is shown on the left, the first on the right. All the information needed was thus conveyed on one sheet of paper. SA

39 Perspective design for the dairy, as executed, placing it in an imaginary lakeside landscape
Watercolour, the bas-relief of a cow drawn in pencil:
485×700 mm
SM 13/7/10

The dairy was a first wedding anniversary present from the Hon. Philip Yorke to his wife Elizabeth in 1783. 'Fancy dairies' were in fashion for aristocratic ladies interested in the virtues of the 'natural life', encouraged by the philosophy of Jean-Jacques Rousseau.

Soane described this garden structure as 'in the primitive manner of building' (du Prey 1982, p. 248) and its design illustrated the origins of the Doric order, as if he and Yorke were resuming a conversation begun among the ancient colonnades at Paestum. The portico of the dairy illustrated the Abbé Laugier's theories of the origins of architecture in timber construction (fig. 108): the columns are the trunks of trees, retaining their bark, and entwined by woodbines and honeysuckle. Soane's instructions noted that the ends of the rafters should be exposed.

The walls of the dairy were of pebble-dash and the roof of reeds, each a deliberate use of vernacular materials. There were two rooms inside: a dairy, and a parlour for eating strawberries and cream. The building was demolished in the nineteenth century. CW

CATALOGUE 39

CATALOGUE 40

The Primitive Hut

The 'primitive hut' was the central image in Laugier's *Essai sur l'architecture* (Paris, 1753; English ed., 1755), probably the single most influential work of Neoclassical architectural theory, which asserted that Ancient Greek temples derived their form from the wooden huts supposed to be the earliest habitations erected by man. The horizontal beams were supported by tree trunks planted upright in the ground, and the roof was angled to shed rainwater. As civilisation progressed, stone was used, but in a way which symbolised this traditional construction: tree trunks became Doric columns, wooden beams the entablature, and so on.

Although Laugier's story dated back to Vitruvius, the radical application of its lessons was an inspiration for Enlightenment architects in search of first principles of architectural composition. Laugier argued that the hut could be used as a model to separate the structural essentials of architecture from the many features introduced by the changing whims of style. Laugier was the hero of Soane's intellectual theory (Watkin 1996 [1], pp. 115–129). Soane began his Royal Academy lecture series with illustrations of the hut, and when reading the *Essai* (he owned ten copies) jotted: 'Essential – beauty. Necessity – licence. Caprice – defects.' The Barn à la Paestum (fig. 111) and the dairy at Hamels (cat. 39) are didactic illustrations of this theory, designed for Grand Tour clients who could enjoy the intellectual argument. More importantly, perhaps, the theory enabled Soane to reduce the classical style to its essential structural elements in designing utilitarian buildings such as the stables at Betchworth (cat. 45, fig. 109).

40 Royal Academy lecture drawing of the primitive hut, 1807, with figures of primitive tribesmen added by Antonio van Assen
Watercolour: 486×690 mm
SM 23/4/4

Soane's first lecture included a sequence of images showing the evolution of the wooden primitive hut into the stone Grecian Doric temple. Here he noted that the short columns of the upper row, added to support the pitch of the roof, explain the similar upper storey in the early Doric colonnades at Paestum (cat. 31). The topographical artist Antonio van Assen painted the tribespeople in furs, a change from the elegant Regency figures he usually added to Soane's architectural perspectives. CW

41 Royal Academy lecture drawing, showing the origin of the entablature of the Doric order
Pen and watercolour:
610×888 mm
SM 23/4/8

This diagram came later in Soane's first lecture sequence, and showed how the ornamental entablature of the Grecian order is a translation into stone of the wooden roof-beams of the primitive hut. CW

42 Model of a primitive hut
Mahogany: 278×345×531 mm
SM M1298

This was one of the few models used as illustrations in the lectures. Soane's inventory describes it as a 'Small model explanatory of the principle of Construction supposed to have been adopted in the Primitive Huts, and the origin of the several members of the Orders of Architecture'. CW

43 Model of a primitive hut in a more advanced state
Mahogany: 231 × 260 × 430 mm
SM SC1

CATALOGUE 41

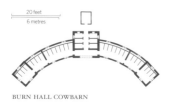

BURN HALL COWBARN

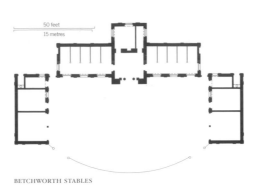

BETCHWORTH STABLES

Cow barn at Burn Hall, Co. Durham, for George Smith, 1783

44 Presentation drawing for a cow barn, in Soane's hand, 1783
Inscr. *Plan of the Hayloft etc/The Elevation of the Principal front next the Road* in Soane's hand
Signed and dated: *June 1783 Soane Archt. Margaret Street Cavendish Square*
Pencil, pen and ink and watercolour: 435×577 mm
Exh: 1784, Royal Academy, no. 489
SM 64/3/100

This drawing was the first design for a farm building to be shown at the Royal Academy.
The cow barn shows Soane miniaturising and simplifying the monumental classical forms of his imagination. The barn's plan is a segment of a curve, echoing the colonnaded crescents in the British Senate House design (cat. 25). Each end pavilion is a perfect cube with a pyramidal roof, and has ventilation openings capped by replicas of Roman altars. The central pavilion has a hayloft behind its pedimented upper storey, and the recess of the Great Arch (inset plan) creates a pool of shadow.

An inexpensive farm building is transformed by the use of classical principles of composition – even the bull pen is placed on the central axis – and elemental geometric forms, enlivened by the changing patterns of light and shade playing across the curving façade. Soane built a second version for Marlesford Hall in Suffolk, another estate in the possession of George Smith. This has burnt down, but the Burn Hall barn has been sensitively converted into housing for a community of monks. CW

Stables at Betchworth Castle, near Dorking, Surrey, for Henry Peters, 1799

45 Presentation design for stables, front elevation and section, 1799
Signed and dated: *June 1799*
Pen and coloured washes: 520×710 mm
SM 64/4/72

This courtyard of stables, since converted into houses, stood in the valley below Betchworth Castle, a hill-top medieval structure which is now a ruin. The challenge was to give a utilitarian, single-storey structure an architectural presence. Soane's design is conventional in plan and outline, but is transformed by the application of a primitivist order of pilasters to add depth to the elevation, and the use of local flint to give invigorating contrasts of colour and texture.

The stables show Soane's primitivism at its subtlest, reinterpreting a vernacular technique to achieve a rigorous, stripped classicism. CW

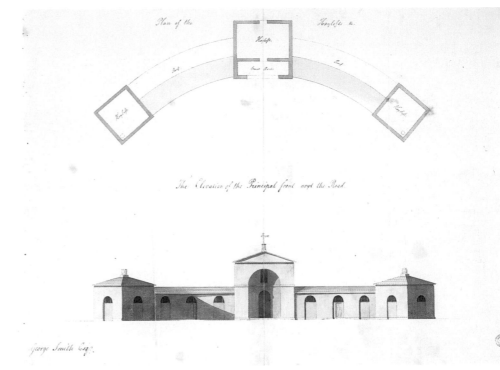

CATALOGUE 44

CATALOGUE 45

SAXLINGHAM

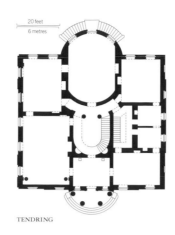

TENDRING

Saxlingham Rectory, Saxlingham Nethergate, Norfolk, for the Reverend John Gooch, 1784–1786

46 Preliminary design sketches, in Soane's hand, June 1784
Inscr. *First floor 4 Bed Rooms & dresg Ro/Attics – 2 Bed Rooms/ 2 Garrets in the Roof*
Sepia pen: 195×380 mm
SM Vol 42, 37

Saxlingham is the most striking of Soane's Norfolk houses for the volumetric purity of its exterior and for the precision of its brickwork. Soane produced four variant designs for his client who had somewhat grander ideas than he could afford: the simplest version was chosen and built of white Norfolk bricks. Elliptical bays in the centre of the north and south fronts rise through both floors to form an attic room above the parapets (see figs 81, 115).

This preliminary sketch, which is close to the final executed design of June 1784, contains the essence of the building and is unusual in showing Soane thinking in plan, elevation *and* perspective at the inception of a design. MR

Tendring Hall, Suffolk, for Admiral Sir Joshua Rowley, Bart., 1784

47 Presentation drawing of the plan and main elevations, in Soane's hand, 1784
Inscr. *The Elevation of the South Front/Plan of the Principal Story of Tendring Hall, Suffolk/The Elevation of the North Front* in Soane's hand
Signed: *J Soane. Arch. Margaret. Street*
Pencil, pen and ink, ink wash and watercolour: 585×471 mm
SM 28/3/1

48 Sectional model of Tendring
Scale 1: 48
Painted wood:
380×600×300 mm
Made in 1999 by Margarida Alexandre, Sandra Videira and Raimundo Moran at Kent Institute of Art and Design (tutor: George Rome Innes)

Tendring Hall was Soane's largest and costliest commission to date. It was also his last as a sole practitioner, responsible for all the drawings; after this he had assistance.

Tendring was built for Admiral (later Sir) Joshua Rowley as a home for his retirement. It was constructed by George Wyatt, the builder whose niece Soane was to marry. How Soane came into contact with the Admiral is not known. The plan is a variant on his earlier Saxlingham (see cat. 46), with a bow on the south front, where Soane uses the East Anglian light to create shadow and modelling on the façade. The plan does not reveal the glory of Soane's design: the stair compartment is lit from a large skylight, the sunshine and shadows opening up the interior. Tendring remained in the Rowley family until World War II when it was requisitioned and ill-treated. In 1955, the house, with the exception of its porch, was demolished. SA

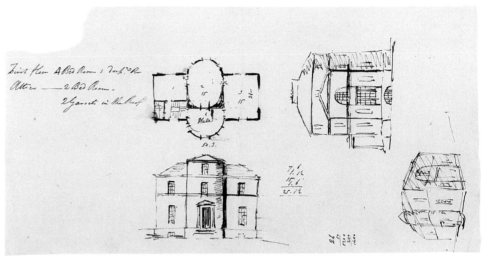

CATALOGUE 46

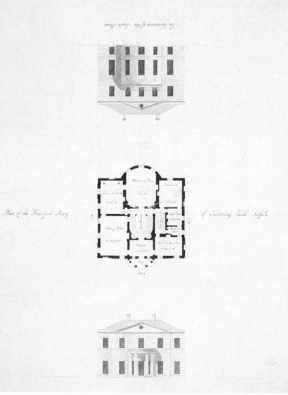

CATALOGUE 47

Wimpole Hall

Figure 117

Wimpole Hall,
Cambridgeshire: the
central block of the south
façade, the seventeenth-
century core of the house,
refaced in the 1740s

Figure 118 (opposite)

Wimpole Hall,
Cambridgeshire:
the Plunge Pool

FIGURE 117

Philip Yorke of Hamels Park (cat. 38) inherited Wimpole in May 1790 and called in Soane less than a month later. The new rooms he created are the most celebrated example of Soane's ability to transform the interior of an existing country house. He inserted several dramatic new rooms without altering Wimpole's doll's-house façades; the six new skylights in the roof are the only external evidence of his remodelling.

Yorke was the first member of his family to go on the Grand Tour and had a perceptive and modern taste in architecture. To him, the principal rooms at Wimpole – rectangular, flat-ceilinged and encrusted with the heavy Palladian ornament in fashion fifty years before – must have seemed as dull as a succession of old shoeboxes.

Wimpole's core was a seventeenth-century house in the form of an 'H', the north and south ranges being the down-strokes of the letter. Earlier in the eighteenth century the house had been extended, with new wings added and the 'H' enclosed. Soane took full advantage of the internal courtyards created as a result.

The Yellow Drawing Room on the ground floor was to be Yorke's principal entertaining space. A barrel-vaulted chamber opens into a soaring circular vault whose dome floats as lightly as a silk parachute; this was Soane's first realisation of his favourite 'canopy' dome (see p. 62). It is slotted between the north and south ranges of the old house, with its glass lantern rising between the rooftops as boldly as a periscope.

On the ground floor, the Yellow Drawing Room displaced a service staircase and some water-closets, and these were shunted into an internal courtyard. But on the first floor the room's double-height space destroyed the circulation route, as well as several bedrooms. While the Yorkes remained in their London house Soane was forced to reshuffle the accommodation of the entire storey, building two new staircases, knocking twelve doors through existing walls, and inserting dozens of new partitions. 'The family will soon be at Wimpole,' Soane wrote to his Clerk of Works (SM 6/1/14, a working drawing dated 5 August 1791), 'do not let a moment be lost in making it complete.' The *coup de théâtre* of the Yellow Drawing Room concealed a measure of backstage panic.

In the second internal courtyard, on the east side, a new Plunge Pool was inserted to make one of Soane's barest and most luminous interiors. It held 2,200 gallons of water, supplied by the castello d'acqua (cat. 50).

Soane also enlarged the 'Book Room', in effect an anteroom to the large library which projects at right angles from the north side of the house. The existing book room was a square space designed by James Gibbs in 1730. Soane preserved Gibbs's coved ceiling but made an opening in its east wall and added two new bays; these were in fact annexed from an orangery which then stood adjacent. The shallow arches of Soane's extension frame the newly created vista.

WIMPOLE HALL (GROUND FLOOR)

Figure 119
Wimpole Hall,
Cambridgeshire: the
'canopy dome' of the
Yellow Drawing Room,
looking south from the
barrel-vaulted chamber
at its entrance

FIGURE 119

Figure 120
Wimpole Hall,
Cambridgeshire: the Book
Room. The ornamental
ceiling in the foreground is
by James Gibbs, 1730.
Soane extended the room
to the west by adding the
two bays with shallow
arches

FIGURE 120

49 Model of Wimpole Hall,
Cambridgeshire
Scale 1: 75
Acrylic and timber:
750 × 1200 mm
Foster Associates, 1999

This model, commissioned
especially for the exhibition,
shows how each of these new
rooms were inserted into the
existing house. Soane's capacity
to resolve the planning and
lighting of each space
individually was typical of his
skill in working with existing
buildings, and would stand him
in good stead for his later work
at the Bank. CW

50 Model of the castello d'acqua,
1793
Painted wood:
H. 150 mm; diam. 260 mm
SM M1148

The castello d'acqua, a
reservoir, supplied water to
the Plunge Pool which Soane
designed for Wimpole Hall (fig.
118). Standing on a wooded hill
in the grounds, the structure is
a folly, designed to resemble a
Roman mausoleum set in an
Arcadian landscape.

Its design synthesised two
ideal projects invented in Italy
in 1779, the classical dog kennel
for the Earl-Bishop of Derry
(cat. 26) and the castello
d'acqua designed for the Parma
Academy competition (cats
27–28), each of which
combined centralised
geometrical planning with
monumental classical forms.

The water is contained in a
circular chamber placed on a
triangular base, and its shallow,
stepped dome is modelled on
that of the Pantheon in Rome
(see cat. 23). The three
pedimented frontispieces
contained cinerary urns,
reinforcing the structure's
sepulchral character. This
souvenir of Soane's Grand Tour
has since been demolished. CW

Tyringham

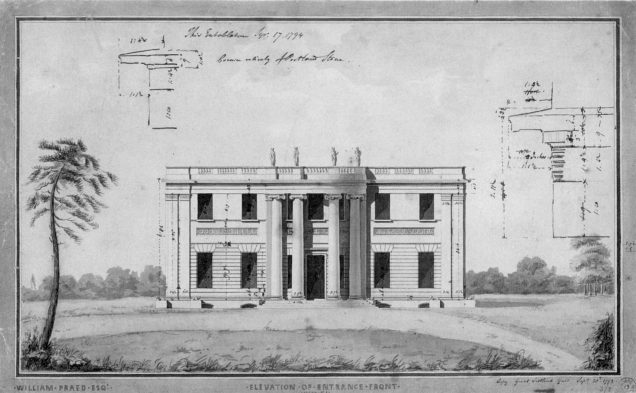

FIGURE 121

Tyringham was designed and built for William Praed, a banker of Fleet Street, and was one of Soane's happier jobs, 'there being no committee of taste with a superintending or controlling power' (Soane, *Designs for Public and Private Buildings*, p. 42).

With its segmental bows on the entrance and garden façades, offices, stables, bridge and gateway, Tyringham still survives, although much altered, and stands as a fine example of a wealthy Soane estate.

The house itself is the largest of the series of eighteen completely new country houses designed by Soane during his career. It was designed and built in 1792–1800 at a period when Soane was engaged in his early work at the Bank of England. Much that is Soane's survives, including the characteristic incised decoration, the giant Ionic columns and the Greek-key frieze, but the house was transformed in 1907–19 by the Austrian architect Ernst Eberhard von Ihne, his French decorator Florian

Kulikowski and the architect Charles Rees, who implemented Von Ihne's ideas. They added the copper-clad dome and made many other alterations as well as completely altering the character of the interior. Soane's vaulted entrance hall, with its Greek Doric columns, and the tribune or inner hall, lit from a dome above, were swept away, although their original dramatic lighting effects are well conveyed in the Gandy perspective (cat. 52).

The stables, bridge and gateway, however, remain unaltered; and the latter in particular is one of Soane's greatest works. Its austere and elemental form was consistently praised in the 1950s and 1960s. Nikolaus Pevsner called it 'a monument of European importance … it is entirely independent of period precedent, a sign of daring only matched at that moment by what Ledoux was designing in France and Gilly in Germany' (Pevsner and Williamson, *Buckinghamshire*, 1994, p. 703).

Tyringham, Buckinghamshire, for William Praed, 1792–1800

51 Joseph Parkins, model-maker
Model of the house,
c. 1793–94
Mahogany: 305×533×482 mm
SM X236

This is a fine example of a 'client' model made before the design for the tribune or inner hall was finalised. It was made from design drawings supplied by Soane and divides horizontally into three layers to show the interiors.

CATALOGUE 51

TYRINGHAM HALL

52 Design perspective of the
interior of the hall, with inset
plans of the hall and chamber
floor, drawn by Joseph Michael
Gandy, February 1798
Inscr. *to shew the manner of
lighting the Tribune and the end of
the Hall*
Pen and watercolour:
845×560 mm
SM 13/5/5

53 Topographical sketch made on
the spot, of the garden side of
the house, showing the offices,
bridge and gateway, drawn by
Joseph Michael Gandy, July
1798
Dated: *ab 2 pm/July 98*
Pencil, pen and watercolour:
246×481 mm
SM Vol. 60, 121

54 Perspective view of the garden
side of the house, drawn by
Joseph Michael Gandy,
August 1798
Dated: *August 24th 1798*
Pen and watercolour:
626×948 mm
SM 13/5/1

55 Perspective view of the
entrance façade, with the
offices on the right, drawn by
Joseph Michael Gandy,
August 1798
Pen and watercolour:
625×949 mm
SM 13/5/3

Gandy worked up this
presentation view from
sketches between 27 July
and 7 August, and entitled
it 'Sunset'.

CATALOGUE 53

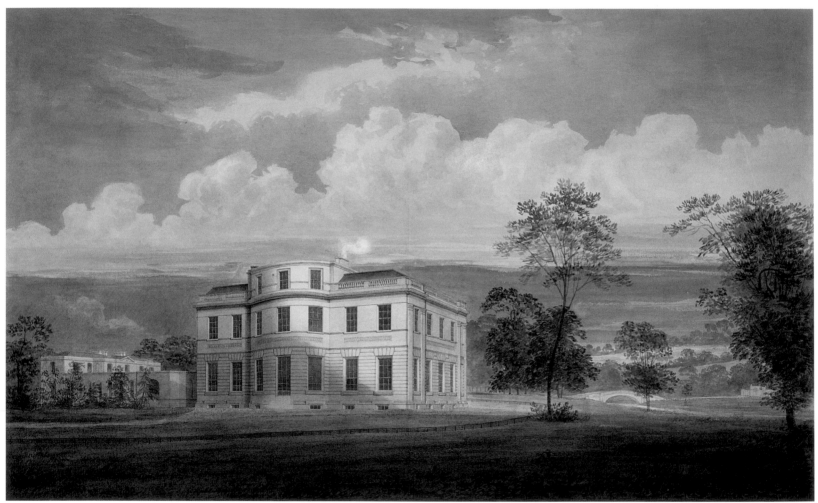

CATALOGUE 54

CATALOGUE 55
CATALOGUE 56 (PAGES 138–139)

Tysingham April 14. 1794

20 feet
6 metres

56 Perspective view of the bridge, with the gateway behind, drawn by Joseph Michael Gandy, September 1798
Pen and watercolour:
580×890 mm
SM 13/5/4

57 Model of the gateway, 1794
Painted pine:
148×470×130 mm
SM DR 4

58 Preliminary sketch of the gateway, in Soane's hand
Dated: *Tyringham April 14 1794*
Sepia pen: 195×368 mm
SM Vol. 42, 164

59 Perspective view of the gateway, drawn by Joseph Michael Gandy, August 1798
Inscr. *Tyringham Park Gates Stormy Effect Joseph Gandy*
Pencil, pen and watercolour:
575×938 mm
Victoria and Albert Museum 2831
Lent by the Trustees of the Victoria and Albert Museum

The view shows the strigilated chimney pots which are no longer in place.

The surviving drawings and documents for Tyringham give a good idea both of the design and construction process in the Soane office and of Soane's relationship with Joseph Gandy.

Soane had first been approached by Praed in 1792 and asked to modernise the Elizabethan manor house at Tyringham which he had inherited through his marriage to Elizabeth Backwell. In December, the office worked on designs for alterations to the old house with Soane also consulting John Haverfield, the Royal Gardener at Kew, about the situation and design of the bridge. Then on 8 June 1793, after a visit to Tyringham with Praed and Haverfield, the decision was taken to build a new house rather than to remodel the existing mansion. The entry in the account Journal of 8 June, 'Settled to have a new house', must have been a welcome one to Soane who now proceeded to work many hours in devising multiple-choice proposals for his client, which was his normal practice. A preliminary design (fig. 121) – close to the final version – shows the kind of drawing Soane would have presented to his client. Soane's drawing technique, and particularly his habit of setting an elevation in a naturalistic landscape, was much influenced by Sir William Chambers; he was also following current picturesque theory in making an architectural drawing into a 'picture' by adding a ruled and washed border. At this early stage Soane would also have dispatched models to the client, being a great believer in the use of models to explain a scheme more clearly and truthfully (cat. 51). During the next four years, work proceeded first on the shell of the house and the gateway, and then on the interiors and offices. Then in July 1798, Joseph Michael Gandy, who had joined the

office as a paid assistant the previous January and who was to become Soane's amanuensis almost immediately, spent nine days at Tyringham making sketch views of the finished house (cat. 53), bridge and gateway at different times of the day to show different lighting effects. On his return from the country on 26 July, Gandy began to work on a series of striking perspectives, all based on his watercolour sketches made on the spot (cats 54–56, 59). MR

CATALOGUE 59

Pitzhanger Manor

Figure 125

Pitzhanger Manor, Ealing:
bird's-eye view, drawn by
C. J. Richardson to
illustrate Soane's *Memoirs*,
1835, showing the retained
Dance wing attached to
Soane's new villa and the
relationship of the house to
Soane's mock Roman ruins
(to the right) and the
entrance arch
(SM Vol. 90, 7)

Figure 126 (opposite)

Pitzhanger Manor: detail of
the façade, showing the
Coade stone caryatids
based on those on the
Erechtheum in Athens

FIGURE 125

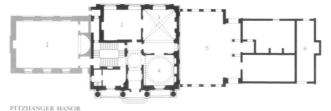

PITZHANGER MANOR

At the age of 15, Soane's first task for his new master
Dance the Younger was to assist in the construction of an
extension to Pitzhanger Manor, Thomas Gurnell's estate
in Ealing. Just over 30 years later, in 1800, Soane purchased
the 28-acre property from Gurnell's heirs for £4,500 (see
fig. 125). For a man so concerned with his place in history,
there was a pleasing symmetry in the establishment of
a dynastic seat for his family in the very place where his
architectural career had begun.

Soane retained the Dance extension, as he admired the
decoration of its interiors and wished to preserve this

memento of his early training. He demolished the
remainder of the house and built a two-storey block and
service wing. Pitzhanger was used as a weekend retreat
from London during hot summers, as a place to entertain
friends, and as a showcase for his growing art collection.

The landscape gardens were redesigned by John
Haverfield, a gardener with whom Soane had collaborated
at Tyringham. The entrance was relocated to the corner of
the site, and the house approached by a curving driveway
edged with trees and flowering shrubs. In the ornamental
gardens to the west of the house Soane and Haverfield
created a lake, an ornamental bridge and a plantation.
A stream well-stocked with fish ran through the property:
Soane was a keen angler.

Pitzhanger can be seen as the genesis of 13 Lincoln's Inn
Fields. In addition to displaying Soane's abilities as an
architect, it was designed to display the finest of his
collection of antiquities and paintings, such as Hogarth's

FIGURE 127

FIGURE 128

A Rake's Progress, and in the basement he created a gallery of Antique fragments and plaster casts intended to educate young architects.

Soane hoped that the house and these collections would inspire his two sons to become architects and that John, the elder, would live there when established in the profession. By the time John junior had graduated from Cambridge, however, it was clear that he did not have a passion for architecture. Soane sold the property in 1810, moving all its contents to Lincoln's Inn Fields. Returning ten years later Soane wrote in his diary: '... walked round poor Ealing. O John, John: what has idleness cost you' (SNB 157, 20 March 1820).

The house has been restored by Ealing Borough Council and was opened to the public in 1987.

CATALOGUE 60

Pitzhanger Manor, Ealing, London, 1800–1802

60 Design perspective for rebuilding Pitzhanger, drawn by Joseph Michael Gandy, 1800
Signed and dated: *Nov 7th 1800*
Watercolour: 660×1065 mm, in a Soane frame
Exh. 1801, Royal Academy, no. 957
SM XP14

This view shows Soane's design for the rebuilding as executed, with minor variations in the decoration applied to the façade. The extension designed by Dance in 1768 is visible on the left.

Some years later, preparing for his Royal Academy lectures, Soane noted that he conceived this entrance façade as a self-portrait: 'a picture, a sort of portrait' of a man who was architect to the Bank of England and a collector of antiquities ('Extracts, Hints Etc. for Lectures', 1813–1818 ff. 134–135). The portico was a deliberate echo of the entrance to the Bullion Court in Lothbury Courtyard at the Bank of England (cat. 138), itself an adaptation of the Triumphal Arch of Constantine in Rome. Three openings are framed by four columns with an entablature projecting from the wall (a feature inspired by the Forum of Nerva, Rome), surmounted by statues of female figures; also identical to those at the Bank are the copies of Thomas Banks's medallions of 'Morning' and 'Evening' embedded in the upper storey (see cats 140–141). The façade was also conceived as an assemblage of Antique motifs, reminiscent of villas in Rome whose walls were encrusted with fragments of antiquity. HE

61 Design perspective for the interior decoration of the breakfast room, drawn by Joseph Michael Gandy, 1802
Watercolour: 970×1295 mm, in a Soane frame
SM P95

This view looks through to the library, where Mrs Soane is reading a letter. For the first time Soane has designed rooms around the objects in his collection, in arrangements prefiguring 13 Lincoln's Inn Fields. On each side of the fireplace, cinerary urns are placed in niches which simulate the shelving of a Roman catacomb.

The sumptuous polychromy of the proposed decoration was inspired by the Roman wall paintings discovered in an ancient villa in the grounds of the Villa Negroni, Rome, in 1778. Soane visited the excavation and later acquired a set of coloured engravings by Campanella. Paint analysis undertaken for the room's restoration in 1989 revealed that, in execution, it was decorated more simply than proposed. Gandy's framing of his painting with a stage curtain, as with the view of the library (cat. 62), reminds us that this is a presentation of a design, not a topographical record. HE

CATALOGUE 61

CATALOGUE 62

62 Design perspective for the decoration of the library, drawn by Joseph Michael Gandy, 1802
Pen and watercolour: 960×1295 mm, in a Soane frame
Exh. 1803, Royal Academy, no. 562
SM P94

This view looks east into the breakfast room, where Mrs Soane stands in front of the window on the entrance façade. The groin-vaulted ceiling of the library is painted in *trompe-l'oeil* with a trellis and flowers, repeating the design of the ceiling of the breakfast room at 12 Lincoln's Inn Fields (cat. 65).

Gandy has presented the room as a showcase for Soane's work as an architect, intending to impress visitors to the annual Royal Academy exhibition. Perspective views of designs for public projects and the Bank of England are hung framed on the walls and more drawings are spread on the table, including Gandy's own view of Lothbury Court (cat. 138) and a plan of the Tivoli Corner at the Bank of England. HE

63 View of an unexecuted design for alterations to the conservatory on the garden front, *c.* 1806–10
Pencil, pen and watercolour: 258×338 mm
SM Vol. 60, 69

Pitzhanger had a single-storey conservatory at the rear of the house, entered from the library. Filled with Antique statues and cinerary urns as well as vines and other plants, the conservatory was integral to Pitzhanger's role as a place of entertainment, display and repose. Hughson's *Circuit of London* (1808) described the conservatory as a place where the 'antiquary and the artist may be usefully gratified, in ascertaining the inscriptions on the several Roman altars, and curious urns, which Mr Soane has collected into this place; in contemplating the fine statue of the Dea Naturae; or, in looking over the fine landscape at the back of the house...' The conservatory was demolished *c.* 1901, when the house was refitted to serve as a public library.

This undated drawing represents unexecuted designs to add a second storey to the conservatory. HE

CATALOGUE 63

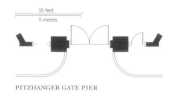

PITZHANGER GATE PIER

64 Sketch designs, in Soane's
hand, for ornamental detailing
of the entrance gateway as
executed, 1801
Inscr. *Take this*, to marginal
sketch showing finial of gate
pier (see opposite)
Signed and dated: *Novr. 17th.
1801.*
Pencil, pen and ink with
coloured washes: 470×588 mm
SM 32/1/14

The gateway is placed to frame
the view of the façade of the
house, surmounted by the neo-
Antique motif of an eagle
framed by a laurel wreath.

This sheet of paper records
Soane's restless search for
perfect detailing, and the final
design shows the refinement of
what might be called his
'primitivist' order of
architecture (see cats 38–45,
pp. 114–117). Pilasters of
knobbly flint stand proud of
the red-brick arch, and courses
of white Portland stone are
inserted to delineate the
pedestal and entablature.

Soane's marginal sketch
shows light playing on a surface
varied in texture and profile,
and in particular the line of
shadow created by the
retracted necking. This
gateway also introduces his use
of a shallow, domed lid as an
ornamental finial, a miniature
version of the canopy to his
tomb (cat. III). CW

CATALOGUE 64 (DETAIL OPPOSITE)

12–14 Lincoln's Inn Fields

Figure 130

The façades of 12–14 Lincoln's Inn Fields, London

Figure 131 (opposite)

13 Lincoln's Inn Fields: detail of the Breakfast Room, showing the imaginative use of convex mirrors in the corners and on the edges of the dome

In 1792, Soane bought 12 Lincoln's Inn Fields, perhaps influenced by its proximity to the Royal Academy which was then at New Somerset House on the Strand. Between 1792 and 1794 he demolished the existing house, in the centre of a terrace, and rebuilt it as his own residence. Although his new house conformed to the building line of the north side of the square his façade was distinctive, having a rustic brick cornice at the top and being built of white Norfolk bricks which would have stood out like stone among the surrounding London stock-brick houses. The plan of the new house retained the idea of a residence at the front of the site with a small central courtyard, but, at the back, the stable block was replaced with a purpose-designed two-storey architectural office.

In 1807, Soane purchased No. 13, the house next door to the east, explaining to the owner that he wished to acquire the stable block at the rear and was prepared to buy the whole house to do so. The sitting tenant remained in the existing house and Soane demolished the stables across the rear of the site and constructed a double-height 'museum' area for the display of plaster casts and marbles

FIGURE 130

(figs 132–136) and a new architectural office. These new buildings at the rear of No. 13 were entered via No. 12 and Soane provided the tenant of the front part of No. 13 with a passageway at the east end of the new rear buildings to give him access to Whetstone Park, the mews behind.

Soane made it clear in his sixth Royal Academy lecture that it had been following his appointment as Professor of Architecture in 1806 that he 'began to arrange the Books, casts and models in order that the students might have the benefit of easy access to them' (Watkin 1996 [1], p. 579). It seems to have been that appointment that led to his desire to acquire the No. 13 site to expand his Museum.

By 1812 the Museum at the back of No. 13 was full up: Soane was constantly acquiring more objects and had also incorporated into the display his collections from Pitzhanger Manor (sold in 1810). He therefore negotiated with the tenant of No. 13 to take over the whole house: the tenant was offered No. 12 on a long lease in return for vacating No. 13. In July 1812, Soane began work on his plans for the rebuilding of the front part of No. 13 and the demolition of the existing house on the site started on the 17th of the same month. The rebuilding of No. 13 was largely complete by the end of the year. The new No. 13 was a three-storey brick house with a distinctive projecting Portland stone open loggia, or verandah, on the front. Behind the house Soane reduced the width of the central courtyard, constructing rooms on either side (the Breakfast Room to the west and the Study and Dressing Room to the east) which he linked through to his Museum and Office at the back of the site, making adjustments to the floor levels in these existing areas to make this possible.

At his Royal Academy lecture on 6 January 1812, Soane announced to the students that they could visit his house the day before and the day after each of his lectures to inspect the drawings and other collections. Such visits would not have taken place during 1812 as Soane did not deliver another lecture until January 1813, as a consequence of his dispute with the Royal Academy. His house was referred to for the first time in the *European Magazine* of November 1812 as an 'Academy' of architecture.

After the completion of the front part of No. 13, Soane continued to live in the house until his death, making constant alterations to enhance the poetic and picturesque qualities of his interiors and to incorporate new acquisitions. In 1821 he altered his Office, reducing it in

Figure 132

13 Lincoln's Inn Fields: design sketches in Soane's hand for his 'plaister room' or Museum at the back of the house, June 1808. The two sketch sections show the earliest form he envisaged for the main dome (SM 32/2A/1A)

Figure 133

13 Lincoln's Inn Fields: design section of the Upper Drawing Office, a recently identified drawing which is unique in showing in Soane's own hand the concept of his Office as a floating box, free of the main walls, c. 1821 (SM 32/3/52 verso)

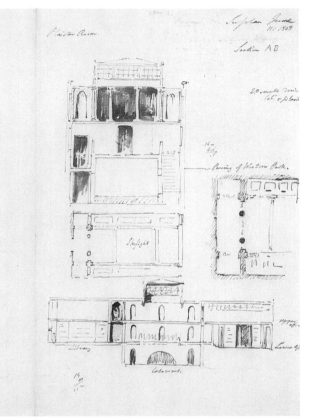

FIGURE 132

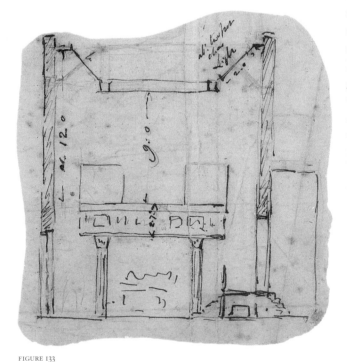

FIGURE 133

size to just the 'upper' office and thereby expanding the space available for his collection.

On 14 October 1823, at the age of 70, Soane expanded his premises again by buying 14 Lincoln's Inn Fields for £1,480. This purchase was probably prompted by the urgent need for space to house his growing collection of paintings and in particular to accommodate the four large paintings of William Hogarth's *An Election*, purchased in June 1823. For a brief period from 1819 until the acquisition of No. 14, Soane had taken back for his own use the ground-floor room at the rear of the No. 12 site which he had turned into his first Picture Room. This had enabled him to hang his large Canaletto, *Riva degli Schiavoni*, and Hogarth's *A Rake's Progress*, but the room could not accommodate the *Election* pictures.

As soon as he had acquired No. 14, and despite the death of his elder son a few weeks later, Soane set to work on plans for the rebuilding of the stable block at the back of the house to create a Picture Room on the ground floor with a mock-Gothic 'Monk's Parlour' (also known as the 'Parloir of Padre Giovanni', a play on Soane's name) below. The courtyard of No. 14 became the romantic 'Monk's Yard' (fig. 139), paved with pebbles into which patterns of glass bottle-tops and bottle-bottoms were laid. Medieval fragments were brought from the Palace of Westminster and re-erected in a picturesque manner to create the so-called ruins of the fictitious monk's monastery. Space was also made in the yard for a column, on axis with the Pasticcio in the Monument Court (cat. 77), containing the grave of the monk's 'faithful companion', the dog Fanny (see fig. 140), in fact Mrs Soane's dog, who died in 1820. Soane's careful plans for the rear buildings of No. 14 also enabled him to rationalise the existing staircases leading from his rear Museum area to the basement and to the Upper Drawing Office (figs 133, 135) by moving them to a narrow space on the west side of the Picture Room.

Soane was intensely proud of his Picture Room, being able to boast that through the use of the 'moveable planes', resembling giant cupboard doors, with 'sufficient space between for pictures ... the small space of thirteen feet eight inches in length, twelve feet four inches in breadth and nineteen feet six inches in height, which are the actual dimensions of this room, is rendered capable of containing as many pictures as a gallery of the same height, twenty feet broad and forty-five feet long' (*Description*, 1835). The design of the Picture Room, as a square suspended within

Figure 134

**13 Lincoln's Inn Fields:
detail of the Dining Room**

FIGURE 134

Lincoln's Inn Fields 1796
1 Office
2 Courtyard
3 Breakfast Room
4 Dining Room

Lincoln's Inn Fields 1810
1 Former Office, now a study
2 Passageway across Courtyard
3 Breakfast Room
4 Dining Room
5 Museum or 'Dome'
6 The Lower Office
7 Stairs to basement
8 Stairs to Upper Office

Lincoln's Inn Fields 1822
1 The First Picture Room
2 Courtyard
3 Breakfast Room
4 Dining Room
5 Museum or 'Dome'
6 Display area beneath the
  Upper Office (formerly a lower office)
7 Stairs to basement
8 Stairs to Upper Office
9 Dressing Room
10 Study
11 Library–Dining Room
12 Breakfast Room
13 Monument Court

Lincoln's Inn Fields 1837
1 The First Picture Room (No. 12)
2 Courtyard (No. 12)
3 Breakfast Room (No. 12)
4 Dining Room (No. 12)
5 Museum or 'Dome'
6 Colonnade
7 Stairs to basement
8 Stairs to Upper Drawing Office
9 Dressing Room
10 Study
11 Library–Dining Room
12 Breakfast Room
13 Monument Court
14 Corridor
15 Picture Room
16 Monk's Yard

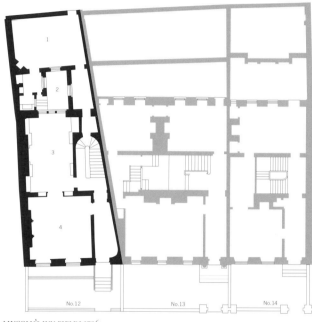

LINCOLN'S INN FIELDS 1796

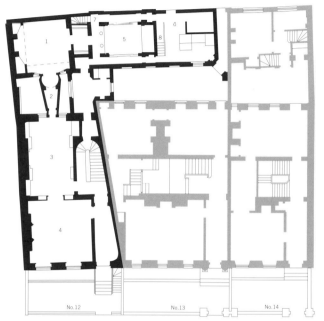

LINCOLN'S INN FIELDS 1810

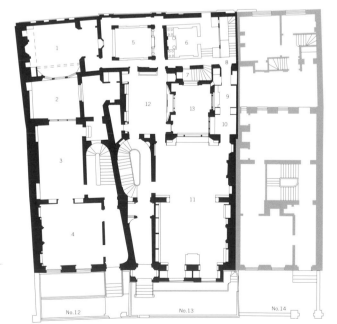

LINCOLN'S INN FIELDS 1822

LINCOLN'S INN FIELDS 1837

50 feet
15 metres

Figure 135

13 Lincoln's Inn Fields:
the Upper Drawing Office

FIGURE 135

Figure 136

13 Lincoln's Inn Fields:
sectional perspective
design for the Museum at
the rear of the house,
drawn by James Adams on
25 June 1808, and showing
the atmospheric contrast
Soane envisaged between
his ground floor Museum
and basement Crypt or
Catacombs
(SM Vol. 83, 37)

Figure 137

13 Lincoln's Inn Fields:
sectional perspective of
the dome area looking
east, drawn by John Soane
junior, c. 1809–10. This is
the earliest surviving view
of Soane's new Museum
as executed and was the
first image of it to be shown
in public when it was used
to illustrate his sixth
Royal Academy lecture,
read for the first time on
12 February 1810
(SM 14/6/6)

Figure 138 (opposite)

13 Lincoln's Inn Fields:
the Dome area

FIGURE 136

FIGURE 137

the larger square of the Monk's Parlour, with its south wall unsupported from below and the space of the Parlour wrapping round it and interconnecting with it, expanding and contracting via the opening and closing of the planes, is the most spatially imaginative and exciting part of Soane's Museum (see figs 141–142).

Once the rear buildings had been constructed, Soane rebuilt No. 14 and immediately let it. He never occupied it and on his death it was bequeathed to his family. For the rest of his life he continued to focus on improvements to Lincoln's Inn Fields, and to expand his collection. In 1824–25 he created a small, narrow Anteroom on the ground floor interconnecting via an aperture in the floor with Catacombs below designed like Roman *columbaria* (square or rectangular niches designed to hold urns containing the ashes of the dead) and in 1834–35 he converted his large wine cellar beneath the office into a funereal Crypt. The first published guidebook to the

Museum, by Soane's friend the antiquarian John Britton, appeared in 1827 under the title *The Union of Sculpture, Architecture and Painting* – describing exactly what Soane aimed for in the imaginative synthesis of objects in his interiors and what he believed was essential for the proper education of architects.

In 1833, Soane negotiated an Act of Parliament to settle and preserve the house and collection for the benefit of 'amateurs and students' in architecture, painting and sculpture. On his death in 1837 the Act came into force, vesting the Museum in a board of trustees. A crucial element in the act was the stipulation that the Museum be maintained 'as nearly as circumstances will admit in the state' in which it was left at the time of Soane's death in 1837, with free access to allow visitors to 'consult, inspect and benefit' from the collections.

Since Soane's death in 1837, successive curators have sought to preserve and maintain Soane's arrangements as

Figures 139, 140

13 Lincoln's Inn Fields:
the Monk's Yard looking
east, 22 August 1825,
showing the picturesque
monastic ruins Soane
created using fragments
from the medieval Palace
of Westminster and the
column incorporating the
tomb of 'Fanny', Mrs
Soane's lap dog, against
the east wall
(SM Vol. 82, 71)

FIGURE 139

FIGURE 140

Figure 141

The Picture Room, looking
east, with the moveable
planes on the north and
south sides partly open to
show how the design of the
room enabled Soane to
hang three times as many
paintings as a space of this
size would normally hold

Figure 142

The Monk's Parlour, drawn
by Joseph Michael Gandy,
12 August 1825, showing
its complex spatial
relationship with the
Picture Room (top right)
(SM Vol. 82, 67)

FIGURE 141

FIGURE 142

Figure 143 (opposite)

13 Lincoln's Inn Fields: the
Breakfast Room looking
north, showing the dome
with its incised decoration
and the convex mirrors
added in the 1830s

and the coloured glass in the Museum skylights, has been restored, and his colour schemes – amongst them Turner's patent yellow in the drawing rooms and olive green in the Picture Room – have been reinstated.

Soane's Museum is one of the most celebrated buildings in the history of architecture. It encapsulates in miniature his mastery of small spaces and his love of the picturesque vista (upwards to the elaborate roofscape, from one room to another and via a series of windows from the west side of the Monument Court to the east wall of the Monk's Yard). More particularly it displays his genius for theatrical and spatial effects: space expanding and contracting as the planes open in the Picture Room; rooms able to alter in appearance as mirrored doors are opened and closed; the ground floor of the Museum area removed beneath the Dome to create the double-height tribune. The subtle blending of reflection and reality in his use of mirrors, particularly in the No. 13 Breakfast Room where they also enhance the feeling that its dome is floating above the space, is magical.

Numerous influences were at work in the creation of Sir John Soane's Museum over more than half a century but each idea was used imaginatively to create just the 'effect' that was required. For example, in the Dining Room Soane transformed reflections of the interior into works of art through the use of framed convex mirrors in almost the same way as the adherents of the picturesque movement used hand-held convex 'Claude' glasses to transform landscapes into framed views reminiscent of the tranquil paintings of Claude and Poussin. The mirrors are placed next to niches displaying casts of Antique busts. The niches are lined with flat mirror, an idea inspired by the Villa Albani in Rome where Soane sketched just such an arrangement in 1778, but the effect is imaginatively amplified by the sequence of reflections created by the adjacent convex mirrors (see fig. 134).

In 1836, Soane's friend Isaac D'Israeli wrote to him to thank him for the gift of a copy of the 1835 *Description*. His letter concluded: 'Your Museum is permanently magical, for the enchantments of Art are eternal. Some in Poems have raised fine architectural Edifices, but most rare have been those who have discovered when they had finished their House, if such a House can ever be said to be finished, that they had built a Poem. All this you have accomplished ... What the nation wanted your hand has bestowed. Euge! Euge!'

he wished. Major changes were made to the building in the 1880s and 1890s during the curatorship of James William Wild, who removed Soane's stained glass windows, extensively remodelled the basement Crypt and was only prevented by his death from applying to the trustees for permission to demolish the Upper Drawing Office along with the main Dome and other skylights to create a single gallery across the back of No. 13. Other curators altered Soane's finely balanced colour schemes, for example painting the staircase and the Museum green at the end of the nineteenth century. A recent five-year restoration programme (1990–95) has sought to restore Soane's arrangements and effects where they have been lost. As a result, much of Soane's stained glass, including the original arrangements in the Dining Room and the Monk's Parlour

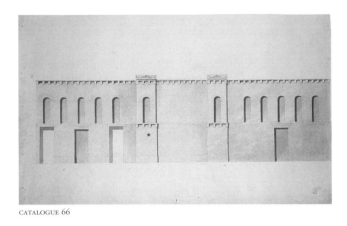

CATALOGUE 66

---

12 Lincoln's Inn Fields, London

65 View of the breakfast
room, drawn by Joseph
Michael Gandy, November
1798
Watercolour: 645×650 mm
SM 14/6/1

The distinctive trellis ceiling,
painted by John Crace, is the
earliest of Soane's shallow,
starfish, cross-vault ceilings,
perhaps inspired by similar
ceilings (such as those at
Cranbury Park, Hampshire,
c. 1780) by George Dance (who
probably based his on a plate in
Pietro Santi Bartoli's *Gli
Antichi Sepolchri*, Rome, 1768).
The insertion of the
asymmetrical band at the left-
hand edge of the ceiling,
decorated with bronzed
medallions, enabled Soane to
place the cross-vault on axis
with the adjacent front room,
the dining room, which was
painted Pompeiian red and in
which the oak floorboards
were shaped to create a
perspective effect along the
main axis and through into the
breakfast room. This sequence
of rooms, when combined with
the very dark black stippled
effect in the windowless
staircase void, must have been
startling in the 1790s. Soane
designed variations on such
ceilings for many of his
interiors, including the library
at Pitzhanger Manor (see cat.
62) and the dining room at 10
Downing Street. The breakfast
room also served as Soane's
library and contained the large
desk made for him by John
Robins (see cat. 80). HD

13 Lincoln's Inn Fields, London

66 Design for the rear elevation
of 12–13 Lincoln's Inn Fields
onto Whetstone Park, late
July–August 1808
Pen and pencil with grey and
cream washes: 451×726 mm
SM 32/3/43

When No. 12 was rebuilt in the
1790s, Soane seems to have
retained the existing wall onto
the mews, Whetstone Park,
inserting an office door. In
rebuilding the rear premises of
No. 13 in 1808, Soane designed
this elegant rear façade for
both No. 12 and No. 13, built
of yellow stock bricks and
articulated with a series of
shallow niches and a restrained
slight projection indicating the
position of the Museum
tribune or 'Dome'. The rustic
qualities of the façade made
reference to the site of former
stables and the use of carved
blocks based on the lids of
Antique cinerary urns
expressed the character of the
catacomb-like Museum within.
Soane used such segmental
pediments adorned with
beribboned wreaths on a
number of tomb designs (see
fig. 155). The brick cornice is
a feature which Soane used
frequently elsewhere (for
example in the stables at
Chelsea Hospital, see cat. 104).
The evolution of the design
of Soane's rear buildings for
No. 13 during the construction
process is reflected in the fact
that Office doors indicated on
early design plans are shown on
this elevation but shaded dark
to indicate that they have
already been blocked up,
within a month or two of
construction, as Soane was
experimenting with the
interior layout of his Office.
HD

CATALOGUE 65

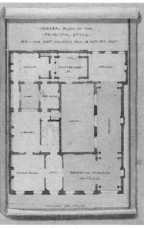

CATALOGUE 67 (DETAIL)

67 Sectional perspective of the Dome area looking east with inset small section looking east, basement and ground floor plans (lower left-hand corner) and 'General plan of the principal story' (lower right-hand corner), drawn by George Bailey (1792–1860)
Inscr. *View of various architectural subjects belonging to John Soane Esqre as arranged in May MDCCCX*
Signed: *George Bailey Fect*
Watercolour: 960 × 625 mm
SM 14/6/3

Although the inscription on this drawing records it as showing the Museum as it appeared in May 1810, entries in the Office daybooks show that Bailey worked on it for 25 days between January and March 1811, in time for the Royal Academy summer exhibition.

The double-height central tribune of the Museum, windowless, with its many surfaces covered with architectural fragments and top-lit through a single skylight fitted with coloured glass, is seen as an interior ruinscape evoking Antique ruins, open to the sky and lit by a golden Mediterranean light. The area is dominated by a large cast of the entablature of the Temple of Castor and Pollux (see cat. 22) on the east wall and high shelves to north and south (shown in section) display tiered arrangements of cinerary urns and vases, accessible through doors leading into Soane's Upper Drawing Office to the east. In the basement Crypt, funereal objects flank the door to Soane's wine cellar.

The small subsidiary drawings on the sheet are shown as if unfurled for presentation. The plan (lower right) illustrates Soane's scheme of *c*. 1809–11 for the future use of his two houses. He envisaged the idea of taking over the whole of No. 13 and combining it with No. 12 so that he could continue to live at No. 12 and No. 13 could become a museum space with collections displayed in an academic and rational manner in galleries each devoted to particular kinds of works: architectural models, casts or drawings. The idea was put forward in an early draft of Soane's sixth Royal Academy lecture (Watkin 1996 [1]) and is also shown in one perspective (see fig. 137) but was essentially impractical because it would have involved demolishing much of No. 12 to straighten the party wall with No. 13. Had it been carried out, the character of Soane's Museum would have been utterly different to that preserved today. Instead Soane continued to acquire casts, marbles, natural curiosities, books, models and drawings, displaying them in an inspirational rather than a rational manner. HD

CATALOGUE 67

68 View of the Dome area by lamplight looking south-east, drawn by Joseph Michael Gandy, 1811
Pen and watercolour:
1190 × 880 mm
SM 14/6/5

This atmospheric watercolour was drawn early in 1811 and shows the Dome by night, dramatically lit by a hidden light source in the Crypt, illustrating exactly the kind of *lumière mystérieuse* that appealed to Soane. The striking light, exaggerated perspective and low viewpoint, which increase the apparent scale of the interior, are again reminiscent of Piranesi's views of the ruins of Rome. Both the piling up of fragments and the juxtaposition of diverse elements seem to owe something to Piranesi's fantasies. Not only does the pile of fragments jut forward over the central space of the Dome area to the left, but another pile projects forward to the right topped by a model of one of the temples at Paestum. On the far north side of the Dome is the figure of Soane himself, dwarfed by his creation and gesturing to invite the spectator to view his collection.

Cats 68 and 69 are views made before the opening up of doors through to No. 13 in 1812 and illustrate clearly Soane's original intention to mimic a windowless catacomb or crypt, top-lit and piled high with fragments. They also show the dark-brown colour of the Dome area as originally conceived – this survives *in situ* behind some fragments although the area seems to have been repainted in a lighter colour by the 1820s. HD

CATALOGUE 68 (DETAIL OPPOSITE)

CATALOGUE 69

69 View of the Dome area looking east, drawn by Joseph Michael Gandy, 1811
Watercolour: 1370×800 mm, in a Soane frame
SM P384

This dramatic view looks up into Soane's Dome from the Crypt below; the arches are shown springing straight from the ground, almost as if in a partly excavated catacomb filled with Antique fragments. The exaggerated perspective heightens the Piranesian quality of the arrangements which now incorporate a pile of fragments topped by the cork model of the Temple of Vesta at Tivoli (cat. 19) placed on the east side of the Dome and projecting forward over the central void. The high shelves are now supported by elaborate metal columns, perhaps for strengthening purposes. HD

70 Design perspective for the front elevation of 13 Lincoln's Inn Fields, drawn by Joseph Michael Gandy, late August 1812
Watercolour: 780×445 mm
SM 14/6/2

In July and early August 1812 Soane was experimenting with ideas for the treatment of the upper parts of the projecting loggia he proposed to build on the new façade of No. 13. There are eight other drawings in the Soane Museum showing the variety of his ideas, including one with a large domed finial over the central feature and another with four caryatid figures.

This drawing shows the Portland stone 'virandah' or 'loggia' almost as executed, with open arches on three floors and the upper section flanked by balconies, on the parapets of which are two female caryatids based on those of the Erechtheum in Athens. The design is the epitome of Soane detailing with its clear incised lines, controlled elegance and smooth, finely cut finish in white Portland stone. Recent research has shown that when built in 1812 there was a third storey to No. 13 in the form of a half-garret, behind the top parapet. In 1825, four fourteenth-century corbels from the front of Westminster Hall were set into the façade and the front brick wall of the house was built up to create a complete third storey. This in fact rather unbalanced the astonishing design of the projecting front which some contemporaries found 'a palpable eyesore' but which Soane justified in terms of the picturesque, envisaging it as an eye-catcher in the centre of the uniform building line of the north side of Lincoln's Inn Fields. HD

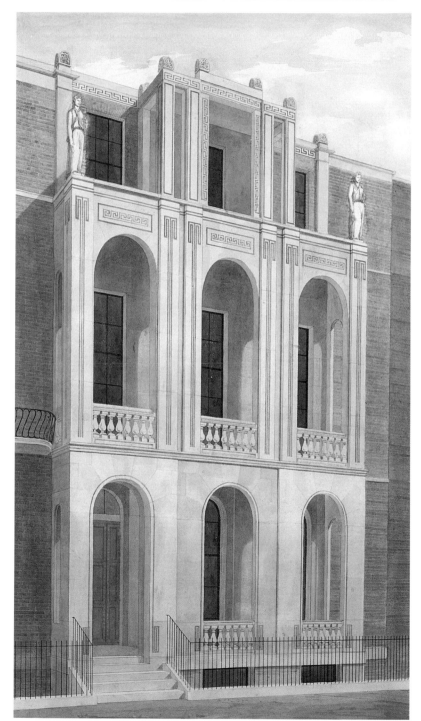

CATALOGUE 70

71 Model of the façade of
13 Lincoln's Inn Fields, 1812
Painted pine:
245×185×45 mm
SM M1242

Before beginning the
construction of the projecting
façade of No. 13, Soane had to
notify the District Surveyor,
William Kinnard, of his
intentions, so that he could
confirm that the setting out of
the foundations conformed
with the Building Act of 1774
which prohibited all
projections apart from
porticoes, steps and fences.
Soane's notebook records on
12 August 1812: 'Kinnard called
and behaved impudently'
(Soane Archive 7/A/8). No
doubt Soane responded
forthrightly and the surveyor
then retaliated by bringing a
court action on the grounds
that Soane had contravened
the Building Act. A summons
arrived on 26 September and
after postponements on 28
September and 7 October the
case was eventually heard on
12 October. *The Sun* of 15
October reported that during
the case Soane's lawyer had
'stated that so far from Mr
Soane's building (of which he
exhibited a model) being an
injury, it was an ornament to
the Square, and he produced
models of two other buildings,
namely Mr Pearce's and
Surgeon's Hall, of far greater
projection, the one which had
received the sanction of the
Magistrates upon a similar
information having been laid
and the other had never been
complained of at all.'
Judgement was given against
Kinnard and Soane was able to
complete his façade to his
intended design. This small,
schematic model of the façade
is the one displayed at the
court hearing; a view of Soane's
Drawing Office made in 1812
shows it on display along with
two other models used in the
case, which have since

disappeared. Despite the fact
that the Building Act
prohibiting projections was
still in force, Soane did
eventually progressively
enclose the loggia in the 1820s
and 1830s, incorporating it into
the rooms behind on each
level. HD

72 Design for an extended
elevation for 13–15 Lincoln's
Inn Fields, drawn by Joseph
Michael Gandy, 1813
Watercolour: 765×1112 mm
Exh. 1813, Royal Academy,
no. 812: 'Design for three
houses, intended to form a
centre, on the north side of
Lincoln's Inn Fields, in part
erected'
SM 74/4/1

This drawing shows an
imaginary scheme for a
grandiose central projecting
façade in the centre of the
north side of Lincoln's Inn
Fields. It incorporates a version
of Soane's own No. 13 façade
but is extended to include Nos
14 and 15 with a grand Ionic
colonnade at first-floor level.
The figures on the balcony of
No. 13 are presumably Soane
and his wife, whilst the small
figure in the street below,
accompanied by a dog, is
probably the Lincoln's Inn
Fields scavenger or rubbish
collector. Joseph Gandy was
paid £50 for this drawing on
30 January 1813; it was drawn
with the assistance of another
drawing of the same scheme by
George Bailey dated *January
19th 1813*. HD

73 Two honeysuckle acroteria
74 from the façade of 13 Lincoln's
Inn Fields, 1812, removed
during restoration in 1992
Portland stone:
450 × 450 × 450 mm
SM X1233, X1234

CATALOGUE 71

CATALOGUE 72

75 View of part of the north wall of the Dome area, drawn by Henry Parke
Signed and dated: *H. P./May 12 1818*
Watercolour: 703×506 mm
SM Vol. 83, 9

This view was drawn over six days in April–May 1818, looking from Soane's Upper Office through an opening in the east wall of the Dome area and along a high shelf running east–west along the north wall of the Dome. The volute brackets which appear to support the shelf are in fact largely decorative: the shelf is built rather like a simple wooden bench, with its ends supported on the structural walls at either end behind the main piers of the Dome. Strong yellow light is shown coming from the main Dome skylight and illuminating the objects on the pier. This is a marvellous illustration of Soane's stated belief that the uniformity of sculpture could be enlivened by the effects of light. The verticality of the view has been emphasised by using the full height but only part of the width of the sheet. HD

76 Sectional perspective of the Dome area and Breakfast Room looking east, drawn by Frank Copland (*fl.* 1817–1820), 1818
Signed and dated: *Drawn by F. Copland, June 1817* (in George Bailey's hand)
Pen and watercolour: 545×640 mm
SM Vol. 83, 1

This section was, according to the Office daybooks, drawn by Frank Copland in 1818 rather than 1817 as the later inscription states. It conveys well the dual nature of Soane's house as residence and museum. On the left is the double-height and top-lit Museum, piled high with Antique fragments, sculpture and vases, whilst the Breakfast Room, on the right, with its pendentive dome, belongs more to the domestic front part of the house and is hung with capriccios of Roman ruins by Clérisseau and four engravings of Roman frescoes by Campanella. To the right of the main window, in front of a large mirror, is the model of the Temple of Vesta at Tivoli (cat. 19), previously in the Dome area (see cats 68–69).

The Breakfast Room is lit by an octagonal lantern incorporating stained glass and two flat-topped skylights, presenting what Soane called 'a succession of fanciful effects which constitute the poetry of architecture' (*Description*, 1835). The concept of the Breakfast Room is a miniature version of one of Soane's great banking halls at the Bank of England. The variety of changing effects is extraordinary in such a tiny space. These were partly created by the device of a square dome within a rectangular plan, which enabled the creation of skylights at either end, with their coloured glass, and partly by the use of double doors in each of the entrances to the room from the Dome area, one containing clear glass, the other mirror glass. By the simple means of opening or closing these mirrored doors, or setting them at different angles, a variety of combinations of reflections and vistas was possible; the second door in each case, containing clear glass, prevented draughts of cold air from entering the room.

Soane altered the Breakfast Room many times over a quarter of a century to enhance his picturesque effects. In this view the corners of the Dome are decorated with plaster angels in relief: these were removed by 1825 and large circular holes punched through each corner to admit four shafts of yellow light. By the time of Soane's death these had been filled in with large convex mirrors (fig. 131); many tiny convex mirrors had been added to the edges of the Dome, and six even inserted into the marble fireplace. Soane had also added strips of mirror to bookcases and filled in the pilasters beneath the four corners of the Dome with mirror glass to make it appear to float, unsupported, above the room. The window recess was also altered in the 1820s to incorporate shallow recesses on either side, fronted by shutters or planes, which could be opened to reveal works of art hung within, set into mirror. HD

CATALOGUE 76 (DETAIL ON PAGES 168–169)

Drawn by F. Copland, June 1817.

CATALOGUE 77

77 Composite view of Lincoln's Inn Fields: plan of the ground floor and views of the Monument Court looking north, the façade, the Library and Dining Room looking north and south, the Study looking north and the Breakfast Room looking south, drawn by Joseph Michael Gandy, 1822
Inscr. *THE PLAN AND INTERIOR/OF THE/ GROUND FLOOR/OF A/ TOWN HOUSE* and in pencil on the *trompe-l'oeil* corner of the view of the Breakfast Room: *IOHN SOANE [...?] ARCHITECT/ R.A. F.S.A. SURVEYOR/ TO HIS MAJESTY/ BOARD OF WORKS/ &C. &C.*
Signed and dated: *MARCH MDCCCXXII* (on plan) and *IOSEPH GANDY A.R.A. FECIT* (in lower right hand corner)
Watercolour: 930×1500 mm, in a Soane frame
Exh. 1822, Royal Academy, no. 875
SM P86

This series of views, although described as a design when exhibited at the Royal Academy, records the Museum as it actually looked in 1822 and demonstrates especially clearly Soane's sense of vista in the planning of the very small spaces at 13 Lincoln's Inn Fields.

The two central views show the combined Library and Dining Room, decorated in Pompeiian red, which served as the main reception room on the ground floor. A series of arches runs around the Library end of the room to differentiate it subtly from the Dining Room. High up are busts placed in niches backed with mirror glass, an idea sketched by Soane at the Villa Albani during his Grand Tour but here extended by the addition of adjacent convex mirrors (see fig. 134). Many

features introduced later by Soane are missing, including the ceiling paintings by Henry Howard (added in the 1830s) and the large areas of mirror glass installed in 1828 surrounding both Lawrence's portrait of Soane above the fireplace and a painting by Reynolds above the sideboard. The desk (see cat. 80) is shown at the far end of the Library.

The view of the Monument Court looking north (on the left) shows how Soane used this small yard as an external room, setting sculpture into the walls and combining statues, full-scale models of elements designed for the Bank of England, a Coade stone vase salvaged during the demolition of Carlton House and ammonite fossils on the parapets and skyline to create a picturesque roofscape visible from the north window of the Library. In the centre of the yard is the architectural Pasticcio, a column of fragments including a full-scale copy of one of the capitals from the Temple of Vesta at Tivoli, intended to act as a symbolic pivot for the Museum, representing the history of architecture. The Pasticcio was removed in 1896 after it became dangerously unstable. HD

78 Benjamin Louis Vulliamy (1780–1854)
Eight-day chiming quarter clock
Walnut with enamel face, ormolu columns and decorative panels: 480×300×300 mm
SM XF146

The Swiss firm of Vulliamy was known for high-quality case design rather than for mechanical innovation. However, for this clock, commissioned in 1835, Soane must have provided the design for the case, which is unlike any other produced by Vulliamy. Its shape reflects the Soanean dome of the Breakfast Room in which it stands, and it incorporates lunettes of yellow stained glass, matching that of the skylights above. HD

79 Door to the large front room on the second floor of No. 13, originally Mrs Soane's bedroom and Soane's Model Room at the time of his death
Mahogany, incorporating a convex mirror set within panels of flat mirror:
2130×930×45 mm
SM

CATALOGUE 78

The Office

When Soane rebuilt
12 Lincoln's Inn Fields in
1792–94 he constructed
a carefully planned Drawing
Office on two floors at the rear
of the site with its own
entrance on Whetstone Park.
Here, Soane's pupils occupied
themselves with all the work of
a busy architectural practice
while Soane himself probably
worked at his desk in the
Breakfast Room (see cat. 65).
When Soane bought No. 13 in
1808 he constructed a new
Office on two floors at the
back of that house to the east
of the Dome area. Once Soane
had moved entirely into No. 13
in 1813 he was able to work in
his little Study (see cat. 77) with
its adjacent Dressing Room,
leaving the pupils in the Office
under the supervision of his
chief clerk.

In 1818, 1821 and 1823–24
Soane modified his
arrangements, sacrificing the
Lower Office to the needs of
his ever-expanding collection
of works of art and
constructing the Upper
Drawing Office in the form in
which it survives today – an
astonishingly innovative
floating space, unattached to
the main walls of the Museum
(see figs 133, 135). HD

80 Pedestal desk, copy made by
Hatfields, 1993–94
Mahogany:
770×1190×825 mm
SM XF307

This is a copy of the desk made
by John Robins for Soane in
the 1790s; it is shown in the
Breakfast Room at 12 Lincoln's
Inn Fields in Gandy's view of
1798 (see cat. 65). The original
desk was moved to Chelsea
some time after Soane was
appointed Surveyor to the
Royal Hospital in 1807,
returning to 13 Lincoln's Inn
Fields in 1812–13, where it was
placed at the south end of the
Library–Dining Room to serve
as a pier table and modified to
include three panes of mirror
glass set into the front (see cat.
77). *In situ*, these are
ingeniously arranged so that
two reflect the carpet while the
central piece, which is set at an
angle, reflects the stained glass
in the window at the other end
of the room. HD

81 Book-carrier in three
compartments with a tray top
with fixed brass handles on
either side, slots on the back for
optional hanging on a wall, and
bun feet, early nineteenth
century
Mahogany: 255×150×205 mm
SM XF2

Soane owned three such book-
carriers. They enabled him to
transport small books and
writing or drawing equipment
around the house to various
desks, for example that in the
Breakfast Room or the small
circular table tucked into the
base of his plaster cast of the
Apollo Belvedere. At the time of
his death all three were listed
among the contents of his
Study. HD

82 Antiquarian tee-square with
tapered blade, c. 1820
Mahogany: 1450 mm long
SM X1198

This tee-square would have
been used in conjuction with a
drawing board and large
antiquarian-sized sheets of
paper to draw straight lines.
Carefully seasoned mahogany
was used to ensure that the
accurate alignment of the blade
to the vertical 'stock' was
maintained. HD

83 A parallel ruler
Mahogany with brass:
47×380 mm (closed)
SM X283

Parallel rules were introduced
in about 1700 to assist with
drawing parallel lines. They
could be used without a tee-
square and were moved up the
drawing by hand. HD

84 A pair of proportional dividers,
probably made by Jeremiah
Sisson, c. 1780
Inscr. *J. Sisson, London*
and marked up for *circles,
plans & solids*
Brass with metal tips:
165 mm long
SM X1207

Soane can be seen holding a
similar pair of dividers in cat. 1.
HD

85 Circular seal, engraved with the
initials *J S*
Brass with a wooden handle:
H. 93 mm; seal diam. 22 mm
SM X280

This was used for stamping
drawings with Soane's initials
prior to their leaving the
Office. HD

86 Small tapered pocket
instrument case with a flip-top
and spaces for a scale, pen and
two other instruments (all
missing), c. 1800
Inscr. *J S* (on the top)
Wood covered with green
shagreen (shark skin) with
brass and silver mounts:
210×40×20 mm
SM X296

87 Six-inch drawing scale, with
divisions for fractions of an
inch to one side and decimals of
an inch to the reverse side
together with a diagonal scale
of 1/100th part of an inch (used
for land measures), c. 1800
Inscr. *Elliott Bros of the Strand,
London*
Ivory: 42×152 mm
SM X1205

88 Ink-pot with attached ink-well
Ceramic and brass:
55×110×85 mm
SM X287

89 Quill cutter
Mahogany with brass fittings:
9×104×18 mm
SM X286

90 Circular stepped paperweight
with decorative lion's head top
to knob
Metal with brass knob:
H. 44 mm; diam. 80 mm
SM X297

91 Two mahogany pyramids
92 165×165×178 mm in plan,
89 mm high
SM X1209, SM X1210

These were probably used by
Soane to demonstrate
geometrical solids or, if used in
conjunction with adjacent
lamps, the effects created by
shadows. HD

93 Travelling case for documents
or small drawings
Inscr. *I S*
Tin: 275×118×88 mm
SM X1213

94 Cylindrical roll case for
drawings
Tin: H. 760 mm; diam. 106 mm
SM X1216

These cases were used by Soane
to transport documents and
drawings around the country to
his various clients. HD

95 Model of 12–14 Lincoln's Inn
Fields
Unpainted wood:
46×61×107 cm
Made by Peter Mullan and
Thomas Gluck, 1996–97
SM

CATALOGUE NUMBERS 86, 88, 89 AND 93

Dulwich Picture Gallery

Figure 144
Dulwich Picture Gallery:
Soane's original west
façade, showing the
Mausoleum in the centre

Figure 145 (opposite)
Dulwich Picture Gallery:
the south wall, showing
the simple layering of
brickwork

FIGURE 144

Although considered today to be one of Soane's most influential buildings, Dulwich Picture Gallery (formerly Dulwich College Picture Gallery) as built represented a disappointment to its architect. Celebrated as an important project in Soane's composite drawings and books, the building was a much-reduced version of what Soane had originally envisaged. In spite of recent re-evaluations which suggest that Soane never intended such a minimally decorated building, both the exterior and interior of the astylar structure which emerged from the Gallery's complicated building history have made a major impact on postwar architects on account of the very constraints that were imposed on Soane. Dulwich is now one of the most potent prototypes for the art gallery in the Anglo-Saxon world.

The Gallery resulted from an unusual commission. In 1811, Sir Francis Bourgeois RA (1756–1811), a painter of modest abilities, bequeathed to Dulwich College, then a small charitable foundation south of London, a collection of Old Master paintings. Many of the pictures had originally been bought for Stanislaus Augustus, the last King of Poland, who was deposed in 1795 before the works of art reached him. Bourgeois and his friend and collaborator Noel Desenfans (1745–1807) had previously kept the paintings in their house in Charlotte (now Hallam) Street, close to Portland Place. There in 1807 Soane, a close friend of Bourgeois, had designed a mausoleum for Desenfans.

Bourgeois intended to create a national gallery at a time when no such institution existed in Britain, although his choice of Dulwich as beneficiary was to prove not altogether wise. The bequest brought various conditions, including the appointment of Soane as architect. Soane was particularly attached to this commission, partly from friendship and partly because it required him to design not only a gallery but also a mausoleum for the founders. He was fascinated by both building types, which he explored on a number of occasions elsewhere (see cat. 96).

Figure 146
Dulwich Picture Gallery:
preliminary design, 1811
(SM 65/4/36)

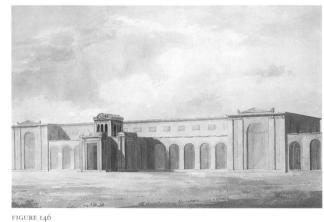

FIGURE 146

Figure 147
Dulwich Picture Gallery:
interior of the gallery,
showing the enfilade of
arches

FIGURE 147

Soane's work began in January 1811 with the production for Dulwich College of plans and elevations (fig. 146). It was his hope that the new gallery would form the principal side of a quadrangle, flanked by the college buildings. Numerous drawings in Sir John Soane's Museum and elsewhere illustrate the architect's attempt to find a satisfactory plan: the version approved showed a building at ninety degrees to the college's central block. The relationship between the two buildings was of central importance to Soane, who hoped that the gallery would be linked to its neighbours by arcades. He tried to create a modern version of the college's Jacobean architecture (traditionally attributed to Inigo Jones), combining this attempt with essays in advanced, not to say eccentric, Greek Revival architecture. The foundations were laid in

October 1811, but Soane continued to alter the scheme while work advanced. The exterior was completed in September 1812. Soane's part largely ended in 1813, and completion was entrusted to George Tappen. Dulwich Picture Gallery opened to visitors in 1817, seven years before the National Gallery.

The ambition of Soane's earliest schemes was thwarted by a shortage of funds. The original quadrangle became a single block, and the rich decoration of the earlier versions was reduced to a severe astylar functionalism. The building was remarkable in being almost a container for works of art. In accordance with prevailing thought in Britain and with Soane's own ideas, it was top-lit. The Gallery was constructed of London stock brick, which plays an important role in elevations only minimally adorned with Portland stone. Its final form resembles contemporary constructions such as Soane's stables and Infirmary for the Chelsea Hospital, and dock buildings in London and Liverpool, rather than structures associated with the arts or government, law or finance. Internally the building is extremely simple, minimally decorated and spatially articulated by alternating cubes and double cubes which form a single enfilade. At the centre of the building, to the west, stands the Mausoleum of the founders, originally flanked on either side by almshouses for the elderly cared for by Dulwich College.

Since its completion the Gallery has been considerably altered. In the late nineteenth century the almshouses were converted for gallery use. A new suite of rooms was added on the east front around 1910 by E. S. Hall, who altered the lantern lights. After bomb damage in 1944 the entrance was moved from the south end, where, contrary to Soane's intention, it had been sited since the Gallery's opening, to the centre of the east front. The most recent stage in the Gallery's history is the creation of a conjectural version of the original east façade, and the addition in the garden of a new 'cloister' to accommodate modern gallery facilities such as a lecture room, a classroom and a café, to the designs of Rick Mather.

Figure 148
Dulwich Picture Gallery:
one of the roof lights

FIGURE 148

FIGURE 149

Figure 149
Dulwich Picture Gallery:
a door on the exterior of the
Mausoleum, a fine example
of Soane's abstraction in
detailing

96 Design perspective of the mausoleum at 38 Charlotte Street (now Hallam Street), London, for Sir Francis Bourgeois, 1807
Inscr. *To. THE. MEMORY. OF NOEL. DESENFANS. ESQR/ "HIS. SALTEM. ACCVMVLEM. DONIS. ET. FVNGAR. INANI. MVNERE."*
Signed and dated: *John Soane Archt/1807*
Pen and coloured washes: 646×650 mm
SM 15/2/1

This mausoleum was built by Sir Francis Bourgeois at the back of his house to receive the coffin of his benefactor, Noel Desenfans, as well as that of Mrs Desenfans and his own. Replicated later at Dulwich, it was therefore the prototype for the Dulwich Mausoleum. It had no external elevations. The mausoleum was planned as a private chapel leading to the burial chamber, where Desenfans was initially interred.

This drawing shows a richer scheme of decoration than the one executed, but the essential character of the chamber did not change. Both mausolea are remarkable in creating the illusion of a large space within a small area, and for their effect of *lumière mystérieuse*. GW

CATALOGUE 96

1 Mausoleum
2 Galleries
3 Almshouses

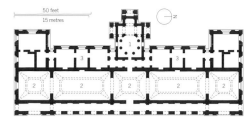

DULWICH PICTURE GALLERY

Dulwich Picture Gallery, College Road, Dulwich Village, London, for the Master, Warden and Fellows of Dulwich College, 1811–1812

97 Preliminary design in perspective, drawn by Joseph Michael Gandy, *c.* 1812
Pen and watercolour:
740×1280 mm
SM 15/2/3

This drawing shows the essential character of the executed building but is considerably embellished, reinforcing Soane's hope that the structure would be more elaborately decorated. The facing of the Mausoleum in Portland stone, the carved panels, the arcade on the roofline and the neo-Jacobean windows all reflect his original aspirations. Notable is the strong lighting applied to the Mausoleum, emphasising its crucial role, and intensifying the drama with which this monument to art and death was imbued. The drawing shows a design which differs in detail from the final version which was probably made for exhibition at the Royal Academy in 1812. GW

CATALOGUE 97 (DETAIL ON PAGES 180–181)

SIR FRANCIS BOURGEOIS
M DCCCXII

98 A pupil at work on a progress view inside the domed entrance to the Mausoleum, drawn by a fellow Soane pupil, July 1812
Pen and watercolour:
238×168 mm
SM Vol. 81, 23

A series of construction views was made in the summer of 1812 by Soane's pupils, including George Basevi, Charles Tyrell and R. D. Chantrell. This drawing, taken from the burial chamber of the Mausoleum, shows the view through the 'chapel' and the small lobby to the main gallery, with the college garden seen beyond. It illustrates the intended contrast between the gloom of the Mausoleum and the Gallery's clear light. This contrast was precious to Soane, who intended that entry into the Mausoleum should be a fundamental element of the experience of visiting the Gallery and was furious that the space was barred off by the college authorities. GW

99 Royal Academy lecture drawing showing a progress view of the west front of the Gallery, *c*. 1815
Pen and watercolour:
525×891 mm
SM 15/2/10

This drawing, which is based on a progress view dated 6 July 1812, records the exterior just before it was completed. It shows the west front, with the rustic college buildings beyond. The Mausoleum is flanked by the wings for the almshouses, with two-storey blocks at each end. Soane's original idea of an arcade linking the Gallery to the college is reflected in the large arched openings, which are more pronounced than in the completed building. GW

CATALOGUE 99

100 Composite views of Dulwich Picture Gallery and Mausoleum, drawn by Joseph Michael Gandy, 1823
Top left: *Angular view from the Entrance Court agreeably to the original design*; centre left: *The Picture Gallery*; bottom left: *The plan of the building in its present unfinished and altered state*; top centre: *View of the Entrance Front in its present unfinished state*; centre: *Central view from the Entrance Court agreeably to the original design*; bottom centre: *View of the Lawn front of the building with the omission of the temporary entrance at the South-East corner*; top right (title): *Dulwich College. The Picture/Gallery and the Mausoleum erected pursuant to the Will and at the expense of the late Sir Francis Bourgeois/This assemblage has been made to illustrate the doctrine of the Rev. T. F. Dibdin lately/promulgated respecting the advantages to the Public of liberal criticism and the unshackled freedom/of the Press*; centre right: *The Mausoleum*; bottom right: *The plan of the/building agreeably to the/original design*
Pen and watercolour:
900×1460 mm
Exh. 1823, Royal Academy, no. 1056
SM P265

This large drawing by Gandy, exhibited at the Royal Academy in 1823 and since 1835 in the North Drawing Room of Soane's house, was partially intended as a justification of his Dulwich commission. The building was not admired by contemporaries, and partly to draw attention to the Reverend T. F. Dibdin's outrageous criticism ('say what you please, and you cannot say anything so delightfully monstrous as is the exterior in question' [quoted in *Designs for Public and Private Buildings*, 1828, p. 47]), Soane published in various forms the building he had wanted, in comparison to that executed.

This drawing is conceived in the same spirit. It shows, top left and centre, the planned building, with the Mausoleum balanced by another tower which would have served as the entrance hall, and an arcade. By contrast the top central drawing illustrates the executed building, with a much-reduced version of the arcade and no central feature. Bottom right is the proposed plan of the building, with the Gallery as a central feature of the college quadrangle. The central bottom drawing illustrates the executed building, with the fenestration required for the almshouses. The rare interior view illustrates important elements: the monitor lights with their solid sloping roofs (subsequently altered), the minimal architectural articulation, the red walls and the floor covered in green oilcloth. The large objects in the centre of the room are part of the heating system. GW

CATALOGUE 100 (DETAIL)

The Royal Hospital, Chelsea

Figure 150
The Royal Hospital, Chelsea: the Clerk of Works's house before Soane's alterations showing it abutting Wren's old stables (SM Vol. 76, 58)

Figure 151 (opposite)
Construction work in progress in the long ward of the Infirmary, c. 1814 (detail of cat. 103)

FIGURE 150

Soane became Clerk of Works to the Royal Hospital at Chelsea in 1807, after a successful petition in the weeks following the death of the incumbent, Samuel Wyatt. He held the post for thirty years, until his own death in 1837. The position at the hospital (an institution for the care of retired soldiers) entailed the upkeep and maintenance of the existing complex (predominantly designed by Sir Christopher Wren), and other building work as needed; the perquisites included an annual salary of £220 and a house on the property. Soane was required to report once a month to the Chelsea Board of Commissioners, and to keep careful records of all expenses.

Within two years the first major building project of Soane's Chelsea career materialised, though its beginnings were marred by bureaucratic manoeuvrings. The Chelsea Board proposed to replace the inadequate accommodation for the Infirmary then located over the Great Hall by adapting the newly acquired, early eighteenth-century Walpole House for this purpose. Soane found the residence unsuitable and instead introduced an entirely new design for a monumental arcaded building facing the

river. His selected site for this new building, however, had been clandestinely leased by the Governor, and another architect had been hired to build a villa for a high-ranking official. Deliberations over the project continued for a year. Ultimately, Soane was forced to modify his design to create a smaller building incorporating Walpole House. The new Infirmary (cat. 102) as built established the vocabulary of Soane's work at Chelsea: a 'primitive' handling of form, yellow stock brick, an abstraction of architectural ornament, round-headed arched openings and a distinctive chimney-stack design (see cat. 106).

These architectural qualities were even more pronounced in the building that followed, the stable block of 1814–17 (figs 82, 88 and 154), widely acknowledged as 'the most quintessentially Soanic of all his exteriors', in the words of Henry-Russell Hitchcock (Stroud 1961, p. 16). The front elevation of the stable block in particular exemplified this minimalist or primitive aesthetic, with its concentric brick-arched openings and an elemental cornice of brick triglyphs (cat. 104, detail).

Figure 152

Photograph taken by John
Summerson of the
Infirmary after the bombing
of 16 April 1941, looking
north-east, with sand-bags
piled among the ruins and a
barrage balloon overhead.
The Infirmary was
subsequently demolished

FIGURE 152

At about the same time, Soane undertook alterations to the old Clerk of Works's house, converting that building into a symmetrical composition. Its radically simple form was punctuated (cats 105–106) by a series of prominent and unusual chimney-pots, ridiculed as 'raisin jars' in a scathing article which appeared in September 1815 in the newspaper *The Champion*, whose anonymous author was Soane's second son, George. Entitled 'The Present Low State of the Arts in England and more particularly of Architecture', the article singled out Soane, and specifically his architecture at Chelsea, for criticism. It condemned the lack of distinction between building types, explaining that, 'buildings so different in their nature [as an infirmary, stable block, and a house] must require a difference of construction'. Soane, from the start at Chelsea, had introduced his own architectural language, without any compromises towards Wren. While appealing to the modern eye, Soane's abstracted forms and reduction of detailing baffled and disturbed many of his contemporaries.

Perhaps as a result of this critical censure, the Soane buildings erected after 1815 were cloaked in the stylistic vocabulary established by Wren, relegating the distinctive Soanean design to the interior spaces. The Chelsea Board specifically requested that the secretary's office of 1818 be in keeping with the old construction, the two Wren pavilions (the old guardhouse and gardener's house) flanking it. Likewise, the surgeon's house of 1821 was a large-scale design undertaken in a Wren style, in red brick with stone quoins. The last building at Chelsea, erected in 1834, was the only departure from this restricted avenue of design. A simple garden shelter (fig. 153) of proto-Doric construction originally with a thatched roof, it was very similar to one of Soane's earliest buildings, the dairy at Hamels Park of 1783 (see cat. 39). A tribute to the origins of architecture, which had fascinated Soane all his life, the garden shelter was a fitting conclusion at Chelsea to a collection of buildings expressive of his explorations of primitive form.

Figure 153

The Royal Hospital,
Chelsea: the Doric garden
shelter

FIGURE 153

Figure 154

The Royal Hospital,
Chelsea: one of the layered
brick arches in the stables

FIGURE 154

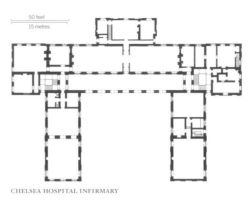

The Royal Hospital, Chelsea, 1807–1837, for the Commissioners of the Royal Hospital

101 Royal Academy lecture drawing showing a progress view of the Infirmary with Walpole House on the right, *c.* 1814
Pencil, pen and watercolour:
606×1203 mm
SM 14/7/1

This drawing is based on a progress view by George Underwood dated *28 Sept 1810.*

102 Royal Academy lecture drawing of the completed Infirmary, made by Henry Parke, 1816
Dated: (on verso) *6th Febr. 1816*
Pencil, pen and watercolour:
700×1285 mm
SM 14/7/2

103 Royal Academy lecture drawing showing a progress view of construction work in the long ward of the Infirmary, *c.* 1814
Pen and watercolour:
628×877 mm
SM 14/7/5

This drawing is based on a progress view by Robert Chantrell (1793–1872), dated *16–24 Oct 1810.*

The Infirmary was Soane's first major building project at the Royal Hospital. The Chelsea Board requested in 1809 that Soane adapt the early eighteenth-century Walpole House in the hospital grounds for use as an infirmary.

The two in-progress drawings (cats 101, 103) reveal the incorporation of the eighteenth-century Walpole House into the new building. Eventually, the only significant part of the house retained was the ground-floor drawing room with its coffered ceiling and marble chimney surround. In cat. 103, which shows the construction of the long gallery inside the Infirmary, the trussed beams of the original roof structure of Walpole House are visible embedded in the brick wall on the left.

These two drawings were prepared after the building was completed, from sketches made on site during construction, to illustrate Soane's Royal Academy lectures. Soane often sent his students out to sketch buildings as they were being constructed (see cats 98–99, 144, 166), explaining that by, 'attending the progress of buildings and by making drawings of them in their different stages of progress, the student will not only attain great skill in the mechanism of buildings, but at the same time discover many effects of light and shade which a close observation of nature alone can give' (Watkin 1996 [1], p. 657).

The Infirmary displays the architectural qualities that came to characterise much of Soane's work at Chelsea: yellow stock brick, bold simplified forms, a minimalist approach to detail and striking chimney-stack designs. HE

CATALOGUE 101

CATALOGUE 102

CATALOGUE 103

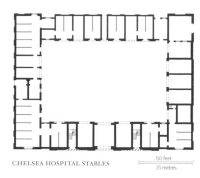

CHELSEA HOSPITAL STABLES

50 feet
15 metres

104 Composite perspective of the
Royal Hospital, Chelsea, drawn
by Joseph Michael Gandy, 1818
Inscr. *A. VIEW. OF. THE.*
NEW. BUILDINGS.
FORMING. THE.
PRINCIPAL.
ALTERATIONS. AND.
ADDITIONS. IN. THE.
ESTABLISHMENT. OF. THE.
ROYAL. HOSPITAL. AT.
CHELSEA. PARTICULARLY.
THOSE. NOTICED. IN. THE.
CHAMPION. OF. THE.
TENTH. AND.
TWENTYFOURTH. OF.
SEPTEMBER. MDCCCXV.
Pencil, pen and watercolour,
framed: 745×1070 mm, in a
Soane frame
Exh: 1818, Royal Academy,
no. 908
SM P387

Soane commissioned this
drawing from Gandy for
exhibition at the Royal
Academy's annual exhibition in
1818 in part – as evinced by the
title – as a response to the
vitriolic criticism of Soane's
architecture published
anonymously in *The Champion*
of 1815. Although it seems
curious that Soane wished to
draw people's attention three
years later to the withering
attack, which had in fact been
written by his son George, the
picture is evidence that Soane
had been deeply wounded by
the article. Gandy's composite
perspective was designed to
impress the viewer with all of
Soane's work at Chelsea (up
until 1818): in the foreground
on the left are the stables, and
on the right the Clerk of
Works's house. In the middle
ground is the Infirmary.
Floating beyond the trees,
placed in view but not
reflecting their actual
locations, are the secretary's
offices to the left and the
riverfront elevation of the
Infirmary to the right. HE

CATALOGUE 104 (DETAIL OPPOSITE)

The Clerk of Works's house at Chelsea

105 View of the house from Royal Hospital Road showing the addition of a new bay on the left, the stables on the far left and the Infirmary in the background
Signed and dated: *Sept. 1833/ C. J. Richardson*
Pencil, pen and watercolour: 255×420 mm
SM Vol. 79, 1

106 View of the back of the house, showing the chimneys, with the rear of the stables on the right
Signed: *C. J. Richardson*
Pencil, pen and watercolour: 256×422 mm
SM Vol. 79, 3

When Soane acquired this house in 1807 as one of the perquisites of the position of Clerk of Works for the Royal Hospital, it was a small, irregularly shaped building adjoining the west end of Wren's stable block (fig. 150). The demolition of Wren's old stables enabled Soane to carry out substantial alterations to the house, transforming it into an elegant, symmetrically arranged two-storey villa. Soane added a two-storey bay to the east (where he placed his office), and a large addition at the rear facing the garden (for a study, central stair and a chamber). The house was especially notable for its prominent chimney-pots at the rear.

The Clerk of Works's house, derided in that article as a 'monster in the art of building', in fact became a refuge for Soane; after the death of his wife in November 1815, he spent increasing amounts of time there, escaping the melancholy of Lincoln's Inn Fields. These views are part of a series painted at Chelsea in 1833 by C. J. Richardson, a former pupil who remained in the office until Soane's death

in 1837. The house, which stood on the site of the present National Army Museum, was demolished in 1853. HE

107 Chimney-pots from the Clerk
108 of Works's house, 1815
Terracotta: 750×500×500 mm
The Commissioners of the Royal Hospital, Chelsea

These chimney-pots were singled out for ridicule by Soane's son, George, in his anonymous article: 'On the top [of the Clerk of Works's house] at the back are two large raisin jars; let us not be understood to speak jestingly; we say in all the gravity of truth, that there are two large raisin jars, fresh to all appearance, from the grocer's shop. Fronting them, ranged in military array, appears a little regiment of chimney-pots with white heads, like so many well grown cauliflowers' (*The Champion*, 10 September 1815). HE

CATALOGUE 105

CATALOGUE 106

The Soane Family Tomb

Figure 155

The Soane family tomb: preliminary sketch for the *ouroboros* coiled round the drum below the finial (detail of cat. 110b) (SM 63/7/3)

Figure 156 (opposite)

The dome of the tomb may have inspired the K2 telephone kiosk by Sir Giles Gilbert Scott (detail of cat. 110a)

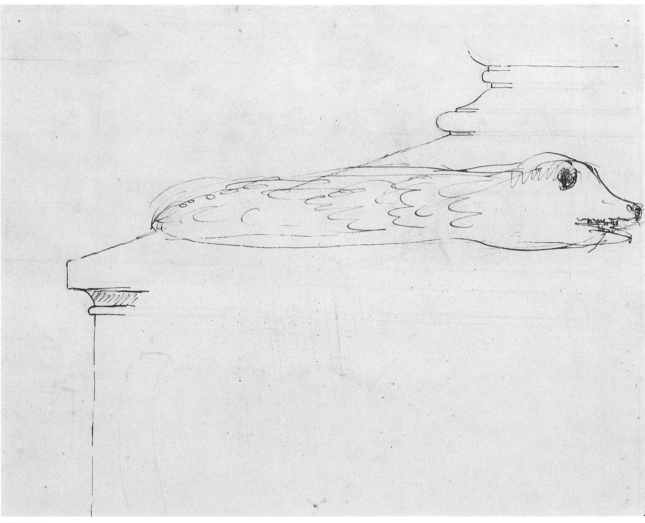

FIGURE 155

Soane was buried in this tomb in 1837 but it had originally been designed for his wife, Eliza, who died in November 1815. She was buried in a plot purchased by Soane in the cemetery at St Pancras, an overspill burial ground for their parish of St Giles-in-the-Fields. The domed monument has no practical purpose, being a symbolic superstructure placed above the subterranean brick vault. Its design was the boldest of any churchyard monument then in London.

The core of the design is an upright double cube of Carrara marble, with Eliza's epitaph inscribed on its north face. This is enclosed by a quadruple aedicule, formed of four Ionic columns supporting pediments, also of marble, which in turn is sheltered by a dome of Portland stone supported on four piers of the Doric order. The structure is nine feet high.

Soane's design contrasts the heavy, protective weight of the dome with the delicacy and transparency of the inner aedicule; the visitor's gaze is drawn to the inner sanctum but physical access is denied. The tension between enticement and resistance, openness and enclosure, gives this diminutive structure a mesmerising presence.

The monument was erected in April 1816 at a cost of £425. It was restored by the Soane Monuments Trust in 1991 but, sadly, has recently been vandalised. Sir John Soane's tomb has a claim to popular fame as it may have inspired Sir Giles Gilbert Scott's design for the K2 telephone kiosk in 1923. It is also one of two tombs in London to be listed Grade I; the other is Karl Marx's in Highgate Cemetery.

3

2:3

6

CATALOGUE 110A

The Soane Family Tomb, St Pancras Gardens, London, 1816

109 Preliminary design, 1816
Pencil and coloured washes:
435×370 mm
SM 63/7/26

Soane began to design the monument in the afternoon of Sunday 11 February. This is his first design and shows the essence of his conception. Its core is the marble memorial bearing the inscription to Eliza, the delicacy of which is in deliberate contrast to the ruggedness of the protective canopy. Its dome is a monolith of almost oppressive weight and at this stage its surface is bare of ornamentation. To Summerson it seemed 'brutally crude and primitive – almost dolmen-like' (Summerson 1990, p. 136). CW

110a Preliminary design showing the elevation, with sketches in margin
Signed and dated: *14 Feby 1816*
Pen, pencil and coloured wash:
535×370 mm
SM 63/7/3

110b (verso) Preliminary sketch for the *ouroboros*, 1816
Pen and ink

The basic form conceived in cat. 109 was overlaid with symbolism in a drawing made three days later. No traditional Christian symbol of death is in evidence. The iconography chosen by Soane is the direct result of the study of Enlightenment theory that he had made in preparation for the Royal Academy lectures.
    The finial of the monument is in the form of a pineapple, commonly used in Roman tombs as a symbol of regeneration. Coiled around the drum below the pineapple is a serpent swallowing its tail, an ancient emblem of eternity known as an *ouroboros* and sketched by Soane on the

reverse of this drawing. Its use was extremely rare in Neoclassical Britain, and Soane was the first architect to use the device so boldly – to encircle an entire structure. The wavy line incised into the outer face of the dome is probably a Freemasonic symbol; Soane had been appointed Grand Superintendent of Works to the United Grand Lodge in 1813. CW

CATALOGUE 109

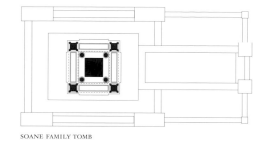

SOANE FAMILY TOMB

111 Perspective design showing the monument in an imaginary landscape, drawn by Joseph Michael Gandy
Watercolour: 665×970 mm
Exh. 1816, Royal Academy, no. 709 or 810
SM 14/4/8

Gandy emphasises the contrast between the duller texture of the stone canopy and the shimmering surface of the block of precious Carrara marble, which glows like a translucent block of ice.

As this view shows, Soane considered adding a gateway over the steps descending to the vault but abandoned the idea. Perhaps he remembered how small the structure really was: the mourning figures painted by Gandy would be 18 inches in reality. Soane did decide to surround the structure with a stone balustrade and, in execution, its parapet was monumentalised by the addition of acroteria and ornamental ridging. The balusters themselves are from a Coade stone catalogue, the only off-the-peg element in the design.

Visible on the north face of the monument is a skeleton hurling a spear. This Christian symbol was becoming extinct in funereal iconography and Soane did not propose its inclusion in the executed design. Rather, Gandy adds this melodramatic anachronism to dramatise the melancholy atmosphere of his painting. CW

112 Model of Soane's tomb
Scale 1: 2
Plaster: 760 mm square, over 1750 mm high
Nicholas West, 1999

CATALOGUE 111

John Wibberley,
Barry Clayton

Pell Wall

Figure 157
Pell Wall, Staffordshire: this
photograph of the garden
façade, taken before 1875,
shows the offices with their
high picturesque tower on
the right (Anthony Griffin)

Figure 158 (opposite)
The domed ceiling in the
ladies' dressing room
(detail of cat. 116)

The three sentences which John Soane penned to accompany the publication of engravings illustrating 'The Seat Of Purney Sillitoe Esq. Near Market Drayton, Salop' (Soane, *Designs for Public and Private Buildings*, p. 43) encapsulate not only the importance which Soane himself attached to this building, but also his approach to design, construction and the profession of architecture.

'In composing the Plans of this Villa, my best energies have been exerted, intending that, when it was completed, my private professional labours should cease. The materials used in this Work are of the best and most durable kind, – the construction as substantial as possible, – and the interior finishings and fittings keep pace with the exterior. If the situation of the Mansion, with its attached and detached Offices, together with the principal approaches thereto, are not properly connected, it is the fault of the Architect; if the several Buildings, considered together, do not form a suitable and convenient Residence for its liberal-minded, wealthy owner and his family, the faults are not to be charged on Mr and Mrs Sillitoe, further than in their having placed the most unbounded confidence in the professional character of their Architect.'

Soane saw Pell Wall as his country-house swansong. It was designed in 1822 at a time when he was much occupied with larger public buildings. Due to a close relationship with his client, a wealthy iron merchant, he was able to realise a final reworking of his earlier country-house designs.

The plans and elevations show both the development and the variation of earlier themes in Soane's work. The north-west façade continues his interest in the curved

FIGURE 157

bombé front but takes advantage of a 'panorama over unspoiled parkland', which 'must rank as one of the grandest "picturesque" settings in nineteenth-century western European civilisation' (du Prey in Save 1987). The tripartite entrance elevation had also been used previously, but at Pell Wall the pilaster strips and incised details have been pared down to a token order. Internally, a strongly axial plan links a series of interior spaces unmatched in Soane's other country houses. They could well have been designed to illustrate the full range of his decorative techniques, but show a new, picturesque and even Gothic quality.

As with other aspects of his practice as an architect, Soane's approach to construction was heavily dependent upon precedent. A clear understanding of a relatively limited palette of tried and tested materials and techniques enabled the architect to concentrate on the specific needs of each client on each site.

Pell Wall was typical of Soane's earlier country houses in many respects. A semi-basement built directly off the bearing strata obviated the need for deep foundations and elevated the principal floor. Load-bearing masonry walls were used, diminishing in thickness from basement to chamber floor with local sandstone (from Grinshill) bonded to the internal brickwork at the pilasters and on alternate ashlar courses. A central chimney core and a stairwell deep within the building shell provided bearings for optimum joist spans with a cantilevered stone main stair linking the principal and chamber floors, with a decorated iron balustrade and lantern light over. A back stair linked all storeys, again in stone but devoid of architectural detail and to a steeper pitch, with a basic square-section balustrade and simple skylight. Fanlights, internal windows and mirrors took natural light into the heart of the building, and heating was provided by fireplaces in every room (and a stove in the stairwell); several walls were warmed by the tortuous flue routes to the central chimney. There was also an attic floor in a mansard roof (in Westmoreland slate) with lead-lined dormer windows.

Soane achieved quality control on a site 154 miles and 2 days' travel away from Lincoln's Inn Fields by making occasional site visits at critical stages of the programme. He employed trusted clerks of the works who were expected to provide weekly progress reports and issue working drawings, and used the services of London

FIGURE 159

tradesmen and suppliers for specialist work, with materials brought to Staffordshire on the new canal system. Another feature of Pell Wall's design and construction was the active involvement on the site by the client who described the bricks Mr Wade had delivered as 'so infamously bad that they are not fit to be used for any building' (letter from Sillitoe to Wade, SM Priv.Corr. VII.B.1.7.2).

The estate at Pell Wall provided Soane with further opportunities to demonstrate and develop his style. Linked to the house on the secondary axis are three brick pavilions, comprising the service wing or 'offices'. These are surmounted by a 'monumental chimney-stack' which John Summerson described as 'a specific reminiscence of Vanbrugh, whom Soane held to be the "Shakespeare of Architects"' (Summerson in Save 1987). On the same axis but up the hill to the south is the brick stable building with a clock tower and weather-vane, contemporary with similar features on Soane's London churches. To the west, beyond the lake which gave the house its name, is a simple gardener's house and a walled garden with glasshouses.

There were two lodges on the estate. One was constructed in red brick with a shallow, slated roof. The stone lodge, Soane's final work at Pell Wall, illustrates how the Soane order could be adapted to accommodate the Gothic style. Proper connection between this unique collection of buildings is assisted by a series of gateposts around the grounds, the caps of which are carved with pendentive domes, echoing those on the parapet of the main house.

On 25 August 1828, Purney Sillitoe wrote to Soane, announcing that he had moved into his new home, made it 'tolerably comfortable' and that it was ready for 'the pen of the artist' (letter from Sillitoe to Soane, SM Priv.Corr. VII.B.1.31). These drawings, together with archaeological evidence on site, documentary records at the Museum and, critically, precedent studies, have recently allowed the shell of the house to be restored by the Pell Wall Preservation Trust, following a disastrous fire in 1986. It would be a fitting epitaph to both Purney Sillitoe and John Soane if Pell Wall's interiors could now be returned to their former glory.

Figure 160
Pell Wall: the entrance front
in 1998, showing the roof
restored and the Victorian
additions demolished in
work undertaken by the
Pell Wall Preservation Trust

FIGURE 160

1 Breakfast Room
2 Drawing Room
3 Eating Room

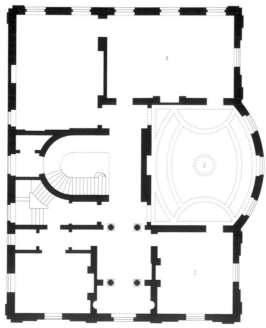

PELL WALL HOUSE

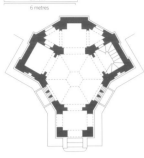

PELL WALL LODGE

CATALOGUE 113

Pell Wall, Staffordshire, for Purney Sillitoe, 1822–1828

113 View of the lodge at Pell Wall, with the house in the background, drawn by Joseph Michael Gandy
Dated: *Tuesday Sepr 9 1828*
Pencil and watercolour: 290×435 mm
SM Vol. 61, 17

The north lodge at the bottom of the drive leading up to the house from Market Drayton can be seen as a further, final experiment by Soane to unite the classical and the Gothic. In plan, the building is an equilateral triangle with square projections. The triangular theme is carried through to the pointed arches to the porch and window surrounds, the stone balustrades and even to reeded timber mouldings. The central hexagonal room has stone-mullioned windows with leaded sash windows. The hexagonal lantern light over contains yellow glass and is surmounted by a weather-vane. JW, BC

114 View of the entrance front, drawn by Joseph Michael Gandy
Dated: *Sat Sept 13 1828*
Watercolour: 295×470 mm
SM Vol. 61, 8

The imposing north-east front is divided into three equal bays by giant flat pilasters with incised grooves and token capitals. The ashlar walls are of Grinshill sandstone with a rusticated basement storey. Incised semicircular and Greek-key decoration surrounds the recessed windows at the principal floor level. The projecting cornice is also decorated with a Greek key and supports a parapet with incised pedestals and domed caps surmounting the pilasters. The entablature of the central Ionic portico carries a double console with rosettes and shell and serpent ornament as used at the Bank of England. Market Drayton parish church dominates the skyline to the north. JW, BC

CATALOGUE 114

115 View of the eating room, drawn
by Joseph Michael Gandy
Dated: *20 Sept 1828*
Watercolour: 290×460 mm
SM Vol. 61, 9

In terms of decoration, this is
the most elaborate room in the
house. Three windows are
balanced by two mahogany
doors flanking a 'black and gold
marble' chimneypiece. Walls
are painted vermilion and a
pendentive arcaded frieze with
inverted pineapple drops runs
round the cornice, a motif used
by Soane in his own Dining
Room at 13 Lincoln's Inn
Fields. The flat-panelled ceiling
design incorporates a central
circular device with smaller
circles, each with central
plaster rosettes and ball
beading. The mahogany
sideboard was adapted from
one acquired by Soane. JW, BC

116 View of the ladies' dressing
room, drawn by Joseph Michael
Gandy, September 1828
Pencil and watercolour:
290×465 mm
SM Vol. 61, 13

This room, placed in the
centre of the south-west front,
is spatially the most complex
room in the house. The
shallow domed ceiling features
mouldings in concentric circles
with a central rosette and
winged figures (as at 13
Lincoln's Inn Fields [see cat.
69], Pitzhanger Manor and
Wotton) in the spandrels.
The walls are painted in a grey-
green colour. The simple
chimneypiece is grey-veined
marble with triangular shafts.
The long wardrobe on the
right is finished in grained
satinwood. Doors to either
side of the window lead to the
adjacent bed chambers. The
curtains appear to be made of
crimson- and white-patterned
silk with crimson fringes.
JW, BC

CATALOGUE 115

The Bank of England

Daniel Abramson

Figure 161

A 1739 engraving, by W. H. Toms, of the Bank built by George Sampson between 1731 and 1734 (Bank of England Museum)

Figure 162 (opposite)

The Bank of England: photograph by Frank Yerbury of the Colonial (formerly the New Four Per Cent) Office in the 1920s, as built by Soane in 1818–23

In 1694, a group of entrepreneurial City of London merchants lent William III £1.3 million for his war against France. In exchange, Parliament sanctioned the establishment of a commercial, joint-stock bank. For the next forty years, the Bank of England occupied a rented medieval livery hall. In 1734, near the Royal Exchange, the surveyor George Sampson completed the Bank's own first building: a traditional City of London courtyard complex corseted in classical garb (fig. 161).

The Bank of England's efficiency soon earned it the trust of London's mercantile community as well as management of Britain's national debt. Continued war with France increased the size of both the national debt and the Bank's building, which, from 1765, was enlarged by the Continental-minded, sculptor-turned-architect Robert Taylor (figs 163–164). By 1788, the year John Soane become the Bank's architect, its amalgamation of halls, offices, courtyards, and vaults already embodied Britain's fiscal might and London's commercial prowess.

Soane's labours at the Bank of England are here introduced thematically, since chronology illuminates little about five decades' worth of overlapping building campaigns. We begin with the Bank's centrality within Soane's career, the architect's relation to the client, and other circumstances effecting the building's production. The architecture itself is studied from the outside in: we look first at Soane's screen walls, then at the compound's planning, and conclude with the interiors' ornamentation. Soane poured a lifetime of passion for decorative experimentation, structural daring, technological innovation and spatial complexity into the Bank. Ultimately, his work there illustrates the difficulty of Soane's appropriation and the possibilities for a twenty-first-century legacy.

For forty-five years, from 1788 to 1833, Soane renovated and expanded this largest, most renowned and most public of all his buildings. The Bank of England in Soane's self-representation always occupied pride of place: in dozens of Royal Academy exhibition and lecture drawings; in the architect's monograph and *Memoirs*; and in the models, mementoes, and hundreds of drawings filling his Lincoln's Inn Fields home. In the 1820s, several writers close to Soane planned monographs on his most exemplary work.[1] No other project intertwined with quite the same richness the architect's aesthetic and professional ambitions. Personally, too, the Bank made the man, providing Soane

with a substantial annual income and introducing the Reading bricklayer's son into the society of London's mercantile élite.

At the beginning, however, Soane was not altogether pleased at having won the Bank post. Instead he dreamed traditionally of prestigious state patronage. 'I am sorry you lost Greenwich', consoled Soane's patron Thomas Pitt referring to the Greenwich Hospital surveyorship, 'but at your time of life the Bank is such a step gained that it ought to reconcile you to your disappointment.'[2] Pitt's cousin, William Pitt, the Prime Minister and Chancellor of the Exchequer, probably supported Soane's application. Like several Bank directors, Pitt had employed Soane in the 1780s for country-house work.

Soane's architectural credentials were impeccable, his élite training was of the highest calibre, and his recent country houses were of the most sophisticated elegance. While Soane initially believed employment by a commercial corporation lowered his professional status, the directors' selection of Soane enhanced their social rise from entrepreneurial City outsiders into an established oligarchy residing in the suburbs and the country.

Over time, Soane worked for and befriended several Bank of England directors, particularly the overseas merchant Samuel Thornton of Clapham and Albury Park. The modern social convergence of commercial client and professional architect polished the directors culturally and educated Soane professionally. The Bank's mien of efficient probity probably influenced Soane's ethical stance in the face of Britain's increasingly competitive architectural marketplace.

In more immediate ways, too, the Bank of England directors steered their architect's efforts, determining programmes and layouts, and encouraging economy and consultation. As long as Soane met the directors' practical requirements, the City businessmen supported his aesthetic experimentation, proving impervious, for example, to public criticism of Soane's 1790s renovations.

Extenuating circumstances organised Soane's five-phased career at the Bank of England. From 1791 to 1797, Soane rebuilt three of Taylor's rotting, wooden, east-wing halls in fireproof brick and stone, including the famous Bank Stock Office. Simultaneously, from 1793 to 1802, he extended the Bank's walled premises to the north-east around the Lothbury Court, in order to accommodate the wartime national debt business and to insulate the Bank

FIGURE 161

Figure 163

The Bank of England: a plan of the complex in 1788, the year in which Soane took over from Sir Robert Taylor as architect to the Bank (Bank of England Museum)

FIGURE 163

Figure 164

The Bank of England: engraving of the Threadneedle Street Façade, 1797, showing George Sampson's building in the centre and the flanking wings built by Sir Robert Taylor, architect to the Bank from 1765–88 (Bank of England Museum)

Figure 165 (opposite)

View of the Tivoli Corner, 1807 (detail of cat. 162)

FIGURE 164

against its combustible wooden neighbours. Soon after, Soane began laying out a new north-western addition (1800–08), including the Tivoli Corner, in order to accommodate wartime production of low denomination banknotes, which swelled the Bank's workforce to nearly one thousand and for the first time put paper money into the pockets of common Britons.

Exhausted by its war efforts and physical expansion over a three-and-a-quarter-acre island site, the Bank put off until 1818–23 the replacement of Taylor's remaining east wing stock transfer halls, including the New Four Per Cent (later Colonial) Office. Finally, between 1823–27, when the postwar Bank emerged as the bulwark of Britain's banking system, the septuagenarian Soane finished wrapping the whole of the Bank's exterior in his own design, including the original Threadneedle Street frontage, capping a career of truly monumental proportions.

In October 1833, forty-five years to the day after his first appointment, the nearly blind architect submitted his resignation to the Bank's Court of Directors. Some months earlier Soane had written to the Bank's Governor: 'The moment I cease to be the architect to the Bank, that moment will be one of the most trying and painful of my life.'[3] Over the course of half a century, the private Bank of England had risen nearly to the level of a public institution, and Soane had learnt that in the modern world supportive corporate clients often offered the best opportunity for ambitious architecture.

To look at the Bank's architecture, we start from the outside in, with the high stone walls, windowless against fire and attack, and in Soane's hands expressive of their structural separation from the interior warren of spaces. Beginning with the mid-1790s north-east extension, Soane

rendered the Portland stone walls as thin, independent screens, elegantly rounded and grooved in a French manner, and also as fortified bulwarks, raised upon a high socle and surmounted by an abstractly castellated skyline of syncretic Greco-Roman acroteria and attics (fig. 168). Contrasts and mixtures of form, style and character increased visual pleasure, Soane believed, and made the Bank's architecture decidedly 'picturesque', critics noted.[4]

Curiously, the grandest portion of the Bank of England's quarter-mile circuit occurred at the rear, north-west Tivoli Corner (named after the Corinthian order from the round Roman temple at Tivoli) (fig. 165). Wrapping the Bank's industrial printing works and overlooking a cramped back-street intersection, the ebullient Tivoli Corner (1803–05) had less to do with existing reality than with a great urban scheme to staunch the commercial élite's suburban exodus, authored in 1800–02 by George Dance the Younger, architect to the City of London and Soane's early mentor (fig. 166). Into his printed copy of Dance's plan – with its residential circus and broad new avenues – Soane sketched the Bank's projected north-west angle. The non-functional Tivoli Corner thus appears as a landmark terminus symbolising the Bank of England's primacy within the City of London and remedying London's urban mediocrity. 'It is humiliating indeed', Soane lamented, 'to see how much more numerous, more extensive, and more magnificent the public buildings are in all the great cities on the continent than in London.'[5] Eventual construction of Finsbury Circus (1815) and Moorgate Street (1830s) partially realised Dance and Soane's collaborative dreams.

Soane's screen walls also expressed the institution's general character of 'opulence, strength and security', as the critic John Britton put it in 1827. The thick and forceful Corinthian order from Tivoli connoted 'masculine energy and luxuriant richness'.[6] By the mid-nineteenth century, however, observers saw other less appropriate meanings. John Ruskin slyly chided as overly commercial the exteriors' pencilled rustication: 'typical of accounts'. Soane's successor, C. R. Cockerell, criticised the Threadneedle Street elevation's plethora of doors and windows as 'common domestic arrangements'.[7]

Soane's failure by Victorian standards to classify properly the Bank of England's institutional character threatened the visual legibility of the modern city and implicitly then its social order. Soane's crowded amalgamation of Grecian, Roman, French and abstractly medieval forms aimed

Figure 166

The Bank of England:
engraving of a plan drawn by
George Dance the Younger
in 1802 showing
'Improvements Proposed by
the Honourable Corporation
of London Between the
Royal Exchange and
Finsbury Square', annotated
by Soane with a sketch of
the Bank's projected north-
west angle (SM 9/1/15)

Figure 167

The Bank of England: a plan
dated 1833, the year Soane
retired as architect
(SM P350)

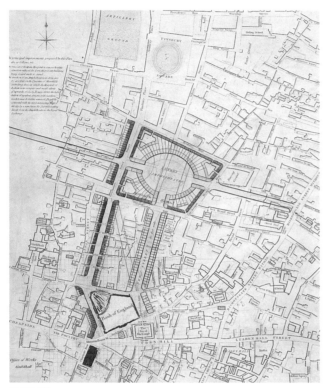

FIGURE 166

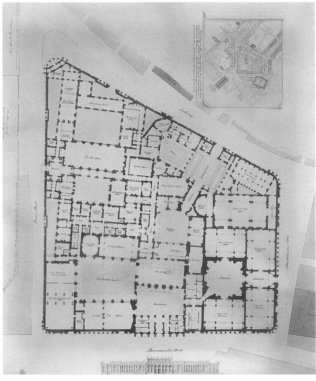

FIGURE 167

primarily at visual pleasure, poetic affect and general
character. It did not lend itself to easy typological legibility
or conventional reproduction. For these reasons, the
Bank's idiosyncratic exteriors produced few successors
either in the history of bank architecture or in modern
classicism generally.

Soane's aesthetic of amalgamation worked better as
an internal planning strategy, in which a loose-jointed
assemblage of spaces and buildings were compounded
together with uncanny equilibrium (fig. 167). Beginning
with the north-east extension around the triumphalist
Lothbury Court (1796–1802), and continuing with the
northwesterly renovations and expansions (1801–08),
Soane aggregated within the expanding site's awkward
angles a diversity of halls, offices, courtyards, residences,
vaults, printing works, storehouses, barracks, stairwells and
corridors. Axiality, symmetry and concatenation, derived
from classical anthropomorphism and Roman-bath
planning in particular, joined their opposites: diagonality,
irregularity and figural fragmentation, derived from
Hadrian's Villa at Tivoli, the more recent examples of
Piranesi, and the domestic planning of the Adam brothers
and French designers like Ledoux.

As more areas of the Bank of England were given over
to specialised circulation and reception spaces, Soane
concentrated on the network of interlinking corridors.
From the new, western Princes Street entrance, for
example, a 350-foot sequence of vestibules, loggias,
corridors and lobbies spiralled deep into the Bank's
executive nerve centre, discretely conveying awed private
visitors and spatially compartmentalising the directorate
from the rest of the staff. Unexpectedly, the Bank of
England's bureaucratic corridors of power also possessed
equal measures of affective pleasure. The variety and
diversity of successive architectural experiences embodied
what contemporaries called the picturesque, which Soane
simply denoted the 'poetry of architecture', a 'succession
of fanciful effects', the architect explained, characterised
by 'pictorial breaks of light and shade'.[8]

At the Bank of England, Soane's 'poetry of architecture'
attained its apotheosis in the remodelled passage (1814–15)
(fig. 170) from the Threadneedle Street courtyard to the
east-wing Rotunda. Miraculously vaulted layers of
stretched shells and impossibly thin domes float within
a mysterious light of infinite transcendence. Soane's
architectural poetics sublimated the Bank of England's

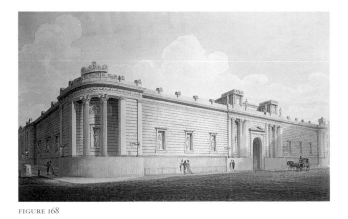

FIGURE 168

1 Front Court
2 Pay Hall
3 Rotunda
4 Old Four Per Cent Office
   (later Old Dividend Office)
5 New Four Per Cent Office
   (later Colonial Office)
6 Bartholomew Lane Vestibule
7 Bank Stock Office
8 Four Per Cent and Five Per Cent Office
9 Consols Transfer Office
10 Consols Library
11 Lothbury Court
12 Printing House Court
13 Accountants' Office (later £5 Note
   Office; later Public Drawing Hall)
14 Governor's Court
15 Governor's Room
16 Committee Room
17 Court Room
18 Bill Office
19 Reduced Annuity Office
20 Cheque Office
21 Dividend Warrant Office
22 Garden Court
23 Bullion Court
24 Chief Cashier
25 Bullion Office
26 Bullion Gateway, Lothbury Façade
27 Residence Court
28 Princes Street Vestibule
29 Tivoli Corner

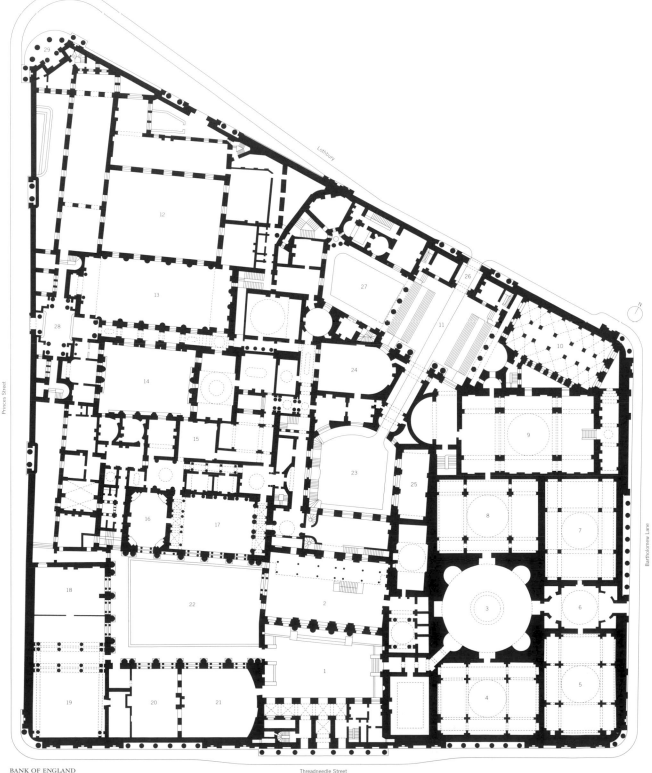

BANK OF ENGLAND

Threadneedle Street

Figure 170 (opposite)
The Bank of England:
photograph by Frank
Yerbury of a detail of the
ceiling of the passage
leading from the front
courtyard to the Rotunda in
the 1920s, as built by Soane
in 1814–15

FIGURE 171

Figure 171
The Bank of England:
photograph by Frank
Yerbury of the corridor from
which the Court Room Suite
was entered, looking south,
in the 1920s, as built by
Soane in 1805–06

Figure 172
The Bank of England:
photograph by Frank
Yerbury of the Old Dividend
(previously Old Four Per
Cent) Office in the 1920s, as
built by Soane in 1818–23

FIGURE 172

Figure 173
The Bank of England: the
Rotunda during demolition,
The Times, 1 May 1925

FIGURE 173

Figure 174
The Bank of England in
c. 1980, as built by Herbert
Baker between 1921 and
1945 (Bank of England
Museum)

FIGURE 174

real work in the production of capitalist economic and social power. The conjunctive spaces, even when they operated as picturesque corridors of pleasure, thus remained corridors of power.

Soane's planning strategies at the Bank of England naturalised architecture through the simulation of landscape scenery's irregularity and mutability, its chiaroscuro of light and shadow, and its successive surprises and contingent effects. The picturesque's naturalism thus substituted for the Enlightenment's loss of faith in classicism's orthodox anthropomorphic proportions. At the level of planning, the picturesque transgression of bodily order and classical wholeness vitally enlivened the Bank of England's architecture. Transposed to the level of interior decoration, Soane's innovations disturbed critics deeply.

Soane began the Bank of England's east-wing remodellings in 1791–93, with the Bank Stock Office just north of the Bartholomew Lane vestibule, where brokers and investors registered trades in Bank of England stock and several government funds (fig. 169). Retaining the pre-existing dimensions and foundations of Taylor's *cortile* hall, Soane erected a monumental Roman-bath-like space composed of four cut-stone piers defining a pendentive-domed crossing flanked by lower aisles roofed with incombustible hollow clay pots. Ideas for the Bank Stock Office's vaulting and lighting schemes, pyramidal composition and reductive ornament were all contributed by Soane's mentor Dance, helping to create collaboratively what John Summerson once called 'the key building of [Soane's] entire career', in 'the most original architectural language in Europe at that moment'.[9]

Subsequently, Soane elaborated the Bank Stock Office's decorative innovations in the structurally identical Four Per Cent Office (1793–97), New Four Per Cent (later Colonial) Office (1818–23) and Old Four Per Cent (later Old Dividend) Office (1818–23), as well as in the new-built Consols Transfer Office (1798–99), the renovated Brokers' Exchange Rotunda (1794–95) and Bullion Office (1806–08). Over time, Soane progressively reduced or eliminated ornamental mouldings in search of an appropriately sober commercial character imbued with the Neoclassical virtues of simplicity (fig. 162). At the stylistic level, Soane's increasingly taut, plastic interiors syncretised the grandeur of monumental Roman massing, the elegance of Grecian ornament, and, in the later halls, the attenuated dematerialisation of the Gothic. The result was a sophisticated 'Soanean' style, contrived to distinguish Soane's work in a design marketplace increasingly filled with derivative amateurs and pattern-book builders.[10]

Unfortunately for Soane, his first decorative assays aroused his professional colleagues' ire. In Soane's absence, at a small dinner in May 1796, a pair of satirical poems were read aloud excoriating Soane's 'pilasters scor'd like loins of pork' and the 'barbarous stile' of incised decoration '[n]o longer able to give the form and grace of Nature/To the objects of her imitation'.[11] Fundamentally, the poems charged Soane with having unnaturally abstracted the ideal classical body, robbing the orders of both their figural coherence and tectonic logic: 'To see the Order in confusion move/Scroles fixed below and Pedestals above.' In effect, Soane's crime was to have transgressed classical architecture's categorical distinctions between the figural, the tectonic and the decorative.

A few months later Soane caught wind of this mirth at his expense. He was livid, even more so when he learned that the offending verses had been published. In 1799, the legendarily sensitive Soane initiated a libel suit against the verses' publisher, the builder Philip Norris. He lost. This unprecedented legal action hints at just how influential commercialised print media was becoming to architects' reputations in modern marketplace discourse.

Published criticism of the Bank of England renovations must have been particularly galling to Soane since it was precisely there that he most fully put into practice his highest professional ideals. In his Royal Academy lectures, Soane preached that ethical responsibility and technical proficiency would distinguish the modern architect from

1 Letter from Joseph Gandy to John Soane, 17 July 1821, quoted in Bolton 1927, p. 347. The monographs included: Britton 1827, p. 60, and W. H. Leeds in Britton and Pugin 1828, p. 251.

2 Letter from Thomas Pitt to John Soane, 6 February 1789, Soane Museum Archive, Personal Correspondence, 4/2/31 (reprinted in Bolton 1927, p. 25). Contemporary accounts report eleven contenders for the Bank of England job: Soane, Holland, Samuel or James Wyatt, Thomas Leverton, James Peacock, Nathaniel Wright, Willey Reveley, James Lewis, Samuel Pepys Cockerell, Charles Beazley, and Richard Jupp. Horace Walpole, *Anecdotes of Painting in England*, vol. 5, Frederick W. Hilles and Philip B. Daghlian, eds, New Haven, 1937, pp. 199–200; and Samuel Bosanquet's memorandum book, quoted in Darley 1999.

3 Letter from John Soane to John Horsley Palmer, 8 April 1833, Soane Museum Archive, Personal Correspondence, XIV/J/1.2.

4 See especially Britton 1827 and Leeds 1828.

5 Soane, Royal Academy lecture eleven, in Watkin 1996 (1), p. 637.

6 John Britton, *The Original Picture of London*, London, 1826, p. 124, and Leeds in Britton and Pugin 1828, p. 246.

7 John Ruskin, *The Stones of Venice*, vol. 1, New York, 1860, p. 321; and Cockerell quoted in Abramson 1994, p. 126.

8 *A New Description of Sir John Soane's Museum*, London, 1991, pp. 44 and 52; Soane, Royal Academy lecture eight, in Watkin 1996 (1), p. 598; Donaldson 1837, p. 14; and Britton 1827, esp. pp. 13–14 and 20.

9 John Summerson in Soane 1983, p. 14; and Summerson 1983, p. 472. See also Summerson 1984 and Daniel Abramson, unpublished catalogue of the Bank of England Bank Stock Office drawings (1997), Sir John Soane's Museum Library.

10 George Wightwick, *The Palace of Architecture*, London, 1840, pp. 191–194.

11 'The Modern Goth' and 'Inscription for a Monument To The Memory of Sir William Chambers', reprinted in Bolton 1927, pp. 62–65.

12 Joseph A. Schumpeter, *Capitalism, Socialism, and Democracy*, 2nd edition, Harper & Brothers, New York and London, 1947, p. 83.

Figure 175

The Bank of England: the Bank Stock Office as re-created by Higgins Gardner, 1986–88, to house the Bank of England Museum (Bank of England Museum)

FIGURE 175

his commercial competitors. At the Bank, Soane served the directors disinterestedly, evolved his plans after close consultations, and incorporated into the building a broad range of technological solutions and innovations including iron skylights and tie-rods, gas lighting and hypocaust heating systems, economical artificial Coade stone ornament and incombustible hollow-clay pot vaulting used previously in Britain only at industrial mills.

The representation which comes closest to encapsulating Soane's achievement at the Bank of England is Joseph Michael Gandy's 1830 Royal Academy exhibition watercolour (cat. 119). As an allegory of the architect's ambitions, the aerial view depicts the Bank of England's building both poetically in ruins, like a Piranesi print, and professionally under construction, its walls, vaults and arches all freshly laid. The view illustrates the complex totality of Soane's greatest accomplishment and invests it with naturalistic authenticity. Gandy's view equates the Bank with the venerated ruins of antiquity, gifts London with urban grandeur and seizes representational control of Soane's architecture back from the commercial media. In effect, Gandy's view narrates Soane's lifelong struggle to construct for himself a modern professional identity, as both a poetic genius and a consummate professional.

The other fable told by Gandy's image is that of the Bank of England itself, which is here misleadingly represented as a transparently public national institution.

In the nineteenth century, the private Bank of England did in fact emerge as the financial pivot of imperial Britain's gold-backed currency. Yet only after nationalisation in 1946 did the Court of Directors formally cede control to the British government and begin making the Bank's operations fully transparent. Ultimately, Gandy's view renders the Bank as the embodiment of modern capitalism itself, in Joseph Schumpeter's classic formulation as the 'process of Creative Destruction', always and forevermore simultaneously in ruins and under construction.[12]

In less than a hundred years – a capitalist eternity – Soane's Bank of England really would be in ruins (fig. 173). After a century of architectural somnolence, World War I quadrupled the Bank's workforce and compelled the directors and their architect Herbert Baker to reconstruct the building nearly entirely, save for Soane's screen wall and some re-created interior motifs, now dwarfed within a seven-storey, steel-framed, stone-clad superstructure (fig. 174). The destruction of Soane's Bank of England earned Baker the enmity of posterity and further fuelled Britain's architectural preservation movement. Ironically, Baker's Bank (1921–42) is now a Grade-I listed building. In 1986–88, English Heritage supervised Higgins Gardner's painstaking re-creation of the Bank Stock Office as a public museum, symbolising the Bank's hope for popular sympathy in the age of European monetary union, as well as the ongoing valorisation of Soane's reputation (fig. 175).

Heroising Soane compresses the real complexity of the Bank of England's architectural history and perhaps deadens the richness of the architect's legacy. Likewise, the portrayal of Soane through the Bank of England's lens gives a distorted view of his overall career. Still, the Soane revealed at the Bank of England offers some basic lessons about his aims, principles and struggles.

Up until 1930, the Tivoli Corner embodied Soane's reputation as a great classical architect. After 1950, the Bank Stock Office represented his apparent proto-modernism. Now, looking at the totality of Soane's Bank, we glimpse a Postmodernist, even Deconstructivist, sensibility, concerned with renovation and contingency, collaboration and consultation, fragmentation and synthesis, blurred boundaries and ambiguous expression, and, perhaps above all else, the professional architect's intractable struggles within capitalist society. On the verge of the twenty-first century, the Bank of England continues to reinvigorate Soane's legacy.

The Bank of England, Threadneedle Street, City of London, for the Governor and Company of the Bank of England, 1788–1833

117 William Hamilton and
P. W. Tomkins
Engraving to show the illumination of the Threadneedle Street Façade, 24 April 1789
Engraving with added coloured washes: 230×673 mm
SM 10/1/2

In April 1789, George III's recovery from madness was celebrated with a festoon of yellow lamps, garlands, medallions and stars. In the centre, William Hamilton's allegorical painting depicted the City of London guiding Britannia's triumphal chariot. The scheme was designed and executed with lamps and transparent paintings under Soane's direction. This must have been one of Soane's earliest tasks at the Bank after his appointment in 1788 and shows the existing architecture: George Sampson's neo-Palladian centre-piece with Sir Robert Taylor's lateral wings. MR

118 Thomas Malton junior
View of the South (Threadneedle Street) front of the Bank of England, 1798
Watercolour: 370×480 mm
The Governor and Company of the Bank of England

This is the preparatory watercolour for plate 63 of volume 2 of Malton's *Picturesque Tour*. The view looks towards the main façade of the Bank of England with George Sampson's central building flanked by Robert Taylor's single-storey Italianate wings. Soane commented on the striking difference in style between the work of these two architects. HD

119 Aerial cutaway view of the Bank of England from the south-east, drawn by Joseph Michael Gandy, 1830
Pen and watercolour: 845×1400 mm, in a Soane frame
Exh. 1830, Royal Academy, no. 1052
SM P267

Soane exhibited Gandy's watercolour in 1830 to illustrate the results of nearly forty-five years' labour. The view inventively conflates conventions of the Renaissance aerial cutaway perspective with the eighteenth-century Piranesian ruinscape to create an image of the Bank of England ambiguously both in ruins and under construction. Gandy's view aggrandised the institution and its building as imperial monuments, and celebrated Soane's poetic genius as well as the professionalism of the Bank's fireproof structural systems. DA

120 Bird's-eye perspective of the Bank of England from the north, 1810
Watercolour: 469×703 mm
SM 1/8/12

This eccentric, rearward perspective obscures the Bank of England's older southern portions by George Sampson and Robert Taylor. Instead, represented in the foreground from left to right are Soane's domed Rotunda and top-lit Transfer Halls (1792–99) (see cats 128–134, 144–151); the triumphal Lothbury Court (1796–1801) (see cats 137–142); and the final 1802–08 extension around the Printing House Court and high-arch-windowed Accountants' (later £5 Note) Office. At the bottom, Soane's screen wall wraps the three-acre complex's Lothbury front, fenced at the west against loiterers and wheeled traffic. DA

CATALOGUE 120

121 George Elgar Hicks (1824–1914)
Dividend Day at the Bank of England, 1851
Oil on canvas: 130×170 cm
Exh. 1859, Royal Academy,
no. 519
The Governor and Company
of the Bank of England

George Elgar Hicks set his
painting, showing payment of
dividends in 1850, in the Old
Four Per Cent (later Old
Dividend) Office, remodelled
by Soane in 1793–97 (see cat
128), just north of the Rotunda.
Quarterly dividend days
became renowned as
picturesque assemblages of
modern metropolitan life,
helping to engender, like
Soane's grandiose public
architecture, the Bank of
England's populist Victorian
mythology. After 1869,
dividends could be mailed to
stockholders and Soane's halls
eventually became more
private clerical work spaces. DA

122 Model of the Bank of England
Scale 1: 72
Cast acrylic:
1076×1587×1857×1768 mm
Andrew Ingham & Associates,
1999

This model has been
generously funded by Morgan
Stanley Dean Witter and
donated to the Governor and
Company of the Bank of
England.

CATALOGUE 121
CATALOGUE 122 (PAGES 224–225)

The Bank Stock Office, 1791–1792

123 George Dance the Younger
Early studies for the Bank
Stock Office, November 1791
Pencil and sepia pen with
monochrome washes:
335×513 mm
SM 10/4/19

George Dance the Younger,
Soane's teacher and friend,
vitally contributed to the Bank
Stock Office's renovation.
In this sheet Dance explores
various single- and triple-dome
alternatives and decorative
possibilities. For the moment
Dance ignores the hall's pre-
existing dimensions and
foundations, while
adumbrating the eventual
ornamental plasticity. Soane
had already proposed to the
Bank of England directors his
own scheme with three domes,
each with its own lantern, like
that at the sheet's base. DA

124 George Dance the Younger
Preliminary studies for the
Bank Stock Office, December
1791
Dated: *Recd at Barnet/decr 11
1791* in Soane's hand
Pencil and sepia wash:
207×320 mm
SM Archive 14/80/1

Soane received several sheets
by Dance at Barnet, north of
London, on 11 December 1791
for the Bank Stock Office's
renovation. Dance's basilica
plan here significantly proposes
the use of clerestory lunettes,
which would be incorporated
into the built hall as flanking
elements for the climactic
pendentive dome. To the
collaboration with Soane,
Dance brought a receptivity
both to Roman vaulting
schemes and to the drama of
variegated light sources. DA

125 Longitudinal section of the
Bank Stock Office with cellar
and foundation, as executed,
c. 1792
Pencil, pen and coloured
washes: 526 × 650 mm
SM Vol. 74, 12

This sheet, which can be
attributed to either William
Lodder or Christopher Ebdon,
meticulously depicts Soane's
technical solutions for the
remodelled Bank Stock Office,
including its brick and stone
vaulting and the underlying
cellar foundations. Within the
centre bay's timber flooring are
ducts for the hypocaust
heating system. Above are the
iron-framed lantern and some
unrealised transverse piping,
possibly connected to roof
drains. DA

126 Joseph Parkins, model-maker
Design model of the Bank
Stock Office, as built, 1793
Painted wood, copper and
yellow glass: 325×375×275 mm
SM MR 20

In order to lighten the
innovative Bank Stock Office's
incombustible superstructure
and to maximise illumination,
Soane, with his mentor George
Dance the Younger, designed
a pyramidal composition of
attenuated arches, vaults,
clerestories, a pendentive dome
and a circular iron lantern.
This model assessed the hall's
proportions, stability and
lighting effects. The interior
depicts the annular clerical
counters and abstracted plaster
ornament. DA

127 View of the Bank Stock Office
looking north, as built, drawn
by Joseph Michael Gandy, 1798
Dated: *June 7th 1798*
Pen and watercolour:
568×941 mm
SM 11/4/1

Gandy accurately depicted the
Bank Stock Office's signage,
counters and central stove,
while exaggerating the hall's
monumentality and play of
light and shade. The view
embodies Soane's fusion of
traditional Roman grandeur
with an affective picturesque
naturalism independent of
the canonical classical orders,
here simplified beyond
almost all recognition. Soane's
experimentation aroused
contemporary controversy;
in the twentieth-century his
abstraction has been
misunderstood as proto-
functionalism. DA

CATALOGUE 123

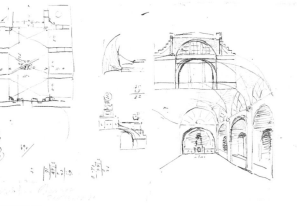

CATALOGUE 124

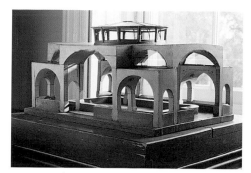

CATALOGUE 126

CATALOGUE 127

227

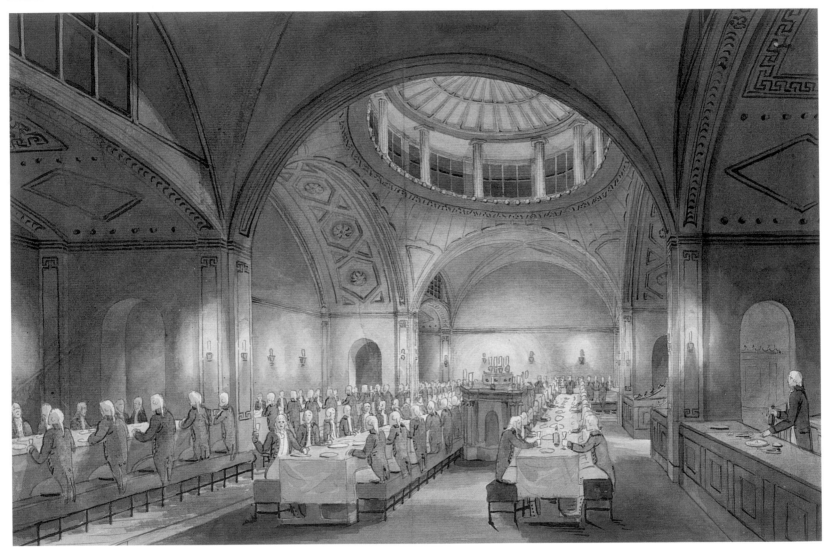

The Four and Five Per Cent (later Consols Dividend) Office, 1793–1797

128 View of the Bank Volunteer Association dinner in the Four Per Cent Office, 2 September 1799, drawn by Joseph Michael Gandy
Pen and watercolour:
492×647 mm
SM 1/8/7

The Four Per Cent Office (1793–97), north of the Rotunda, hosts a dinner of the Bank Volunteer Association during the Napoleonic Wars. Soane duplicated the Bank Stock Office's structure, applying a more intimate décor of scalloped pendentives and astylar pilasters. Between 1798 and 1814, anxious patriotism motivated the Bank's 500-strong ceremonial self-defence corps, manned by clerks, officered by directors and department heads, with Soane as quartermaster. DA

129 Scroll ornament for cupboards in the Four and Five Per Cent Office
Painted plaster:
265×915×55 mm
SM H10

This ornament was designed as the scroll cresting for the tops of cupboards in the interiors of the Four and Five Per Cent Office. The scrolls were cast in plaster and painted to simulate wood. HD

The Rotunda, 1794–1795

130 Elevation of part of the Rotunda, with sketches of ornament, 1795
Dated: *July 7 1795*
Pencil, pen and blue washes:
318×524 mm
SM Vol. 74, 102

Soane, with Dance's minor collaboration, outlined the renovated stock-exchange Rotunda with sinuous runs of incised Grecian wave and key patterns. The décor's disembodied attenuation scandalised Soane's professional colleagues as being 'scor'd like loins of pork' (Bolton 1927, pp. 62–65). They feared the seemingly unnatural freedom from canonical classicism's anthropomorphic proportions and full-bodied substantiality. DA

131 Henry Provis, model-maker
Constructional model of a niche in the Rotunda, 1794
Painted wood:
39.5×60×32.5 cm
SM M606

Soane highly recommended the use of models to assess complicated three-dimensional structural systems, for example where the renovated Rotunda's niche arches transferred the heavy incombustible dome's weight to the thickened walls below. This fourteen-piece model was probably fabricated by Henry Provis in 1794–95 and later used by Soane as an instructional tool in his Royal Academy lectures. DA

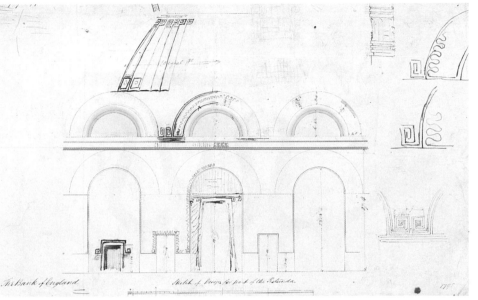

CATALOGUE 130

132 View of the Rotunda as built, drawn by Joseph Michael Gandy, 1798
Pen and watercolour:
630 × 690 mm
SM 9/2/1C

Gandy monumentalised Soane's renovated Rotunda (1794–95) in sombre tones focusing on the picturesque play of light and shade across scooped niches, thick lunettes and the caryatid-ringed lantern. In reality, the Pantheon-inspired hall was thronged daily by brokers, jobbers and investors in government and Bank securities, who then registered trades in the surrounding stock transfer offices. Here only the clock and lantern wind-dial index the commercial purpose. DA

133 An imaginary view of the Rotunda in ruins, drawn by Joseph Michael Gandy, 1798
Pen and watercolour:
660 × 1020 mm, in a Soane frame
SM P127

The Bank of England's renovated Rotunda and Four and Five Per Cent Office (see cats 128–129) appear as ruins in this 1798 view, exhibited at the Royal Academy thirty-four years later under the title 'Architectural ruins: a vision'. The idea of the future ruin blended picturesque visual pleasure with the sublime frisson of temporal doom consoled by architectural immortality. Soane's Rotunda joins the revered remains of Roman antiquity. DA

CATALOGUE 133

134 Section through the Rotunda flanked by identical Four Per Cent Offices, 1805
Inscr. *Consols Dividend Office/The Rotunda/The 4£ per Cent Office (as designed)*
Dated: *August 14 1805*
Pen and watercolour:
651×1229 mm
SM 11/6/1

The sheet's centre and right-hand side accurately depict Soane's renovated Rotunda (1794–95) and northern Four and Five Per Cent Office (1793–97); the left-hand side duplicates the latter hall prior to the southern hall's real 1818–23 renovation. The section vividly illustrates the thickened Rotunda dome and Soane's overall composition, which builds up pyramidally within each hall and between the three as a concatenation of arches, vaults, domes and lanterns. DA

CATALOGUE 134 (DETAIL OPPOSITE)

"the Rotunda".

CATALOGUE 135 (FACING INTO LOTHBURY COURT)

The Bullion Gateway, Lothbury Façade, leading into Lothbury Court, c. 1796

135 Double-sided model of a preliminary design for the Bullion Gateway, *c.* 1796
Painted wood:
405×567×200 mm
SM M1375

Soane's design for the gateway from Lothbury into the Lothbury Court and Bullion Court presented an appropriate image of stout fortification with its eight-foot-high socle and parapeted attic. At the same time, the recessed Corinthian orders, pencilled rustication, and taut archway embodied institutional refinement. Soane relished the picturesque contrast and critics applauded the polysemous expression. The entrance lodge behind held Soane's office at the Bank. DA

Lothbury Court, with Residence Court adjoining on west, 1797–1800

136 Design model for the Residence Court's window frames, 1797
Painted wood:
513×349×82 mm
SM M1287

The unusual window frame studied in this model, with its tabernacle pediment elegantly recessed within a blank segmental arch, illustrates Soane's penchant for structural attenuation and spatial nestling. It also marked the Residence Court's distinctive character as home to several of the Bank's staff and their families. In 1804, upwards of forty people lived on the premises, for reasons of safety, convenience and local tradition. DA

137 Preliminary design perspective of Lothbury Court looking east from the Residence Court, drawn by Joseph Michael Gandy, *c.* 1798–99
Inscr. *View of a Design for the Lothbury Court etc looking towards the South-East*
Pen and watercolour:
849×652 mm
SM 12/3/14

The north-east expansion of the Bank of England between 1797 and 1801 afforded Soane the opportunity to design a picturesque pair of grandiose colonnaded courtyards, one for the shipment of treasure into the Bank's vaults and the other for lighting a series of residences and offices. The impression of an ideal Roman urbanism underscored the Bank's insularity and aggrandised what functionally were only rear service yards. DA

138 Preliminary design perspective of Lothbury Arch, looking south from the Lothbury Court into the Bullion Court, drawn by Joseph Michael Gandy with figures added by Antonio van Assen, 1798–99
Pen and watercolour:
646×952 mm
SM 12/3/13

The Lothbury Arch celebrated the Bank of England's emerging national identity during the Napoleonic Wars. Soane's design simplified the fourth-century Arch of Constantine and added allegorical statues of the four continents, caducei symbolising commerce and a resplendent seated Britannia (unrealised in the built version). DA

139 Model of the Arch of Constantine, Rome, late eighteenth century
Cork with terracotta or plaster roundels: 295×310×170 mm
SM MR29

The Arch of Constantine, the largest of the three surviving triumphal arches in Rome, was erected to commemorate Constantine's victory over Maxentius on 28 October 312. Much of its sculpture was assembled from other locations, with the exception of the circular roundels showing the Emperor himself. The form and decoration of the Arch of Constantine, together with that of the Forum of Nerva, provided the inspiration for the entrance to the Bullion Court from Lothbury Court (see cat. 138) and for the façade at Pitzhanger Manor (see cat. 60), the latter intended to echo Lothbury and thus to remind visitors that the house was the residence of the architect to the Bank. HD

CATALOGUE 135 (ON LOTHBURY)

140 Thomas Banks RA (1735–1805)
Model of a bas-relief of 'Morning' or the 'East', after the Antique in the Arch of Constantine, Rome
Plaster in a wooden painted frame: 755 × 755 mm (roundel 610 mm diam.)
SM M16

141 Thomas Banks
Model of a bas-relief of 'Evening' or the 'West', after the Antique in the Arch of Constantine, Rome
Plaster in a wooden painted frame: 755 × 755 mm (roundel 610 mm diam.)
SM M32

Soane commissioned a pair of roundels from Banks after those of Sol and Luna (sun and moon), on the short west and east sides of the Arch of Constantine (AD 312–315), for the Lothbury Court in 1801 where they occupied important positions between the columns flanking the great archway. The original Roman roundels are about eight feet in diameter and the full-size Banks versions were just over four feet across (full-scale casts survive in Sir John Soane's Museum). These smaller versions, modelled later by Banks, are half the scale of those used at the Bank. After Banks's death in 1805 Soane continued to use these sculptures in his work: casts were fixed to the pendentives of the domed ceiling of the Old Four Per Cent (later Old Dividend) Office (1818–23) and were used again in the Royal Gallery at the Palace of Westminster in the 1820s. HD

142 Preliminary design model of Lothbury Court, east, south and west sides, 1799
Painted wood:
320 × 575 × 475 mm
SM M1384

At the Lothbury Court, colonnades defining an open square created an ideal image of monumental order and unity in front of otherwise irregularly shaped, utilitarian buildings and courts. An unrealised public processional way through the passage on the left into the Consols Transfer Office would have rivalled the Bank's main Threadneedle Street entrance. The model helped Soane to align the Court's elevations and imagine the views through its columnar screens. This model shows Lothbury Court without the Bullion Gateway that occupied its north side, and without the Court's extension – beyond the columnar screen to the west – later known as the Residence Court (see plan on p. 213). DA

143 Thomas Malton junior (1748–1804)
View of the North (Lothbury) elevation of the Bank of England, 1797
Aquatint: 560 × 435 mm, framed
The Governor and Company of the Bank of England

This view of Soane's Lothbury Façade was published in Malton's *A Picturesque Tour through the Cities of London & Westminster*, plate 65, volume 2.
HD

CATALOGUE 138

CATALOGUE 144

The Consols Transfer Office, 1798–1799

144 View of the Consols Transfer Office showing the walls unplastered and the dome constructed up to the base of the lantern, drawn by Joseph Michael Gandy, 1799
Inscr. *3% Office*
Dated: *April 28th 1799*
Pen and watercolour:
720 × 1018 mm
SM 11/6/6

Incombustibility was the Bank of England's primary architectural imperative, since the institution's true treasure lay in its paper records. As shown in Soane's unplastered Consols Transfer Office (1798–99), sturdy stone piers and arches carried an innovative fireproof superstructure of brick and lightweight, hollow clay pots, distinguished by their circular sections and previously used in France and England mainly for domestic and industrial architecture. DA

145 Eight hollow cones used in the construction of vaults at the Bank of England
Terracotta: H. 190 mm;
diam. 107 mm
SM M609, X260, X261, X262, X263, X264, X265, X266

146 Hollow half-cone used in the construction of vaults at the Bank of England
Terracotta: H. 190 mm;
diam. 105 mm
SM M610

These are examples of the terracotta hollow cones or 'pots' used by Soane to lighten his fireproof vaulting at the Bank of England. Soane drew particular attention in his Royal Academy lectures to the fact that the vaults at the Bank were constructed of a variety of fireproof materials: stone, brick and terracotta; above all, no timber was permitted. The cones were made at a kiln on the construction site at the Bank. Two full-scale examples were kept by Soane for his Museum. The others were salvaged by a Bank employee in the 1920s and donated to the Museum in 1989. HD

147 View of the Consols Transfer Office as built, drawn by Joseph Michael Gandy with figures added by Antonio van Assen, 1799
Pen and watercolour:
719 × 1018 mm
SM 11/4/3

The Bank of England's most common type of public hall is represented here by the Consols Transfer Office. The term 'consols' refers to a number of separate government funds grouped together at a three per cent rate of interest and collectively known as the three per cent consolidated annuities, or consols for short. The clerks behind the counters transacted business with the public and kept the books for these annuities, carefully registering the frequent transfers of ownership and arranging the semi-annual dividends. Numerous departments in the Bank were involved in managing the extensive number of government funds, of which the consols represented just a fraction; the largest departments gave their names to the half-dozen halls of the transfer type. DA

CATALOGUE 147 (DETAIL ON PAGES 238–239)

148 Unrealised design for the Consols Transfer Office pilaster cap ornament, *c.* 1798
Pen and monochrome washes: 527×660 mm
SM Vol. 74, 88

Large-scale drawings of ornamental details transmitted Soane's ideas to plasterers executing the design. Here, Soane schematised an Ionic capital, which can be seen in cat. 147, into an anthemion device flanked by a pair of Greek key-frets and sinuous scrolls. Soane believed in grafting the virtuous simplicity of Grecian décor onto monumental, Roman-inspired structures, though the results sometimes unsettled critics. DA

149 Design for Consols Transfer Office soffit ornament, as built, *c.* 1799
Pen and monochrome washes: 668×522 mm
SM Vol. 74, 89

Soane plastered the undersides of the Consols Transfer Office's side-arm arches with this assemblage of conventional and full-bodied bead and Greek-fret mouldings and Roman rosette and oak-leaf motifs. Soane here stepped back momentarily from his abstract mid-1790s innovations – stung perhaps by colleagues' and critics' attacks – before resuming experimentation in the final, late-1810s transfer hall renovations. DA

150 Design for the Consols Transfer Office cornice, *c.* 1799
Pen and monochrome washes: 656×521 mm
SM Vol. 74, 90

For the Consols Transfer Office's entablature, Soane employed an Ionic tri-fascia architrave and dentilled cornice, omitting the intervening frieze as unnecessary to a utilitarian interior space. The cornice's deep projection underlined the hall's overall horizontality and solidity. The lion's-head and acorn motifs conventionally connoted strength and stability; they do not make reference to the Bank of England's particular commercial character. DA

151 Lion's mask cornice decoration, probably from the Consols Transfer Office, *c.* 1799
Coade stone on an oval wooden backboard: 350×300×200 mm
The Governor and Company of the Bank of England

The Accountants' (later £5 Note) Office, 1802–1806

152 Design model for the Accountant's (later £5 Note) Office, 1803
Painted wood: 460×332×865 mm
SM M1481

The 96-by-40-foot Accountants' Office represented by far the largest space in the Bank of England's 1802–06 north-west expansion. Sandwiched between the Governor's Court and Printing House Court, its five, high-arched, northern windows illuminated the hunched labours of scores of clerks, out of nearly a thousand employed by the Bank (see plan on p. 213). This back office's surprisingly magnificent interior ornament, featuring elegant Ionic half-columns, compensated for the work's quotidian drudgery. It was later to be known as the Public Drawing Office. DA

CATALOGUE 148

The Bank of England.   Ornaments in the Soffites of Side Arches in the Consols Transfer Office. 1799.

CATALOGUE 149

The Governor's Court, 1803–1805

153 Preliminary design perspective of the Governor's Court, looking into the north-west corner, with figures added by Antonio van Assen, 1803
Inscr. *View of a Design for the Waiting Room Court*
Dated: *Augt 13 1803*
Pen and watercolour:
630×882 mm
SM 11/5/1

The Bank of England's extension northward from the executive Parlours included the ample Governor's Court (1803–05), circumscribed by various offices, including the Governor's, and initially articulated with Grecian Ionic colonnades. In the built design, Soane placed more inventive, high, plank-like antae along the northern loggia, which functionally linked the Princes Street Vestibule to the Bank's interior. Strolling tourists were barred from this private precinct. DA

154 Design model for the Governor's Court, as built, 1803
Painted wood:
398×490×510 mm
SM M1366

This model helped Soane to align the multi-storeyed elevations of the Governor's Court, belying the single-storey expression of the Bank's exterior screen walls. Basement vaults supported three older ranges of private offices, while the new fourth side formed an open loggia linking the Princes Street Vestibule and the interior of the Bank. The austere, plank-like antae expressed the precinct's utilitarian function and shielded the new Accountants' Office's southern windows (see cat. 152). DA

CATALOGUE 153 (DETAIL OPPOSITE)

The Princes Street Vestibule, 1803–1808

155 Preliminary design perspective for the Princes Street Vestibule, with figures added by Antonio van Assen, 1803
Dated: *July 29 1803*
Pencil, pen and watercolour:
742×639 mm
SM 11/4/4

In 1802, the Bank of England's Governor Job Mathew suggested that a private entrance from Princes Street be opened into the Bank's new north-west extension. The result was the imposing Doric Vestibule (1803–08), Soane's most conventionally Grecian set-piece for the Bank. Later, in his Royal Academy lectures, Soane apologised for the interior placement of an exterior Grecian Doric entablature mixed, worse still, with a Roman dome. DA

156 Preliminary model of the Princes Street Vestibule, north section, 1803
Painted wood:
465×700×282 mm
SM MP224

Soane's two-part model of the Princes Street (Doric) Vestibule assessed this large volume's structural relation to its adjacent subdivided spaces. This half of the model represents the Vestibule's northern wall. One side shows the bi-level, columnar Vestibule itself, plus the eastern bays of the Governor's Court loggia. On the obverse, the wall frames the high-vaulted Accountants' (later £5 Note) Office, plus lower offices and corridors. DA

CATALOGUE 155

CATALOGUE 160

157 Preliminary model of the
Princes Street Vestibule,
south section, 1803
Painted wood:
465×700×270 mm
SM MP226

The southern section of the
two-part Princes Street (Doric)
Vestibule model shows the
bi-level Vestibule's stepped
approach into the high, antae-
framed Governor's Court
loggia (cat. 154). The obverse
depicts the Court's north-west
corner, its columnar east
elevation, two storeys of offices
behind, a lower office and a
narrow corridor abutting onto
an open yard. Together with its
other half, the model assessed
the area's lighting, spatial
organisation and structural
stability. DA

158 Model of fret ornament for the
Princes Street Entrance
Plaster: 455×670×55 mm
SM X126

The Tivoli Corner and the
Lothbury Façade, 1803–1805

159 Model of the centre bay of
the north (Lothbury) façade,
as built, c. 1803
Painted wood:
550×575×115 mm
SM MP215

Soane extended the screen wall
along Lothbury to twice its
original length in 1802–03 and
during the process gave
considerable thought to the
central bay. A proposal for a
Corinthian hexastyle portico
was rejected and he eventually
settled for the more modest
projection shown in this
model, although he did
produce another model
showing an alternative design
for the attic (SM M264). HD

160 Preliminary 'square' design
model for the Tivoli Corner,
October 1804
Painted wood:
615×550×325 mm
SM M1482

Soane carefully studied the
problem of wrapping the Bank
of England's new, acute north-
west angle. In the penultimate
design, Soane envisioned a full-
blown architectural confection
of splayed wings flanking a
layered colonnade surmounted
by a high, three-stage attic,
with only a vestigial sub-grade
doorway. The corner's
nickname derived from the use
of the full-bodied Corinthian
order modelled on the Roman
Temple of Vesta at Tivoli
which Soane had recorded
in 1778–79 on his Grand Tour
(see cat. 19). DA

161 The 'circular' design model for
the Tivoli Corner, as built, 1805
Painted wood:
615×500×250 mm
SM MP225

Soane's final design
acknowledged the north-west
corner's non-functionality by
omitting the earlier doorway,
and heightened its picturesque
movement by projecting a
concave colonnade framed by
angular columnar wings and a
pedimented attic. Before mid-
twentieth-century Modernism
the Tivoli Corner's classical
confection was considered
Soane's greatest masterpiece:
an inspired classical
amalgamation of undulating
Baroque massing, Roman
columnar monumentality,
Grecian simplicity in the attic
and an exuberant Vanbrughian
skyline. DA

CATALOGUE 161

John Soane Arch. 1807   ·THE·BAN

CATALOGUE 163

---

162 View of the Lothbury Wall and
Tivoli Corner, 1807
Signed and dated: *John Soane
Archt. 1807*
Pen and watercolour:
319×917 mm
SM 12/1/7

The Tivoli Corner represented
the Bank of England's most
spectacular exterior element,
yet it marked no entrance at
the building's rear and
overlooked a cramped back-
street intersection. In fact,
Soane coordinated the design
with an 1802 urban planning
scheme by George Dance the
Younger (Soane's collaborator
again), which, with Moorgate's
completion in the 1830s, made
the Tivoli Corner the pivot of a
monumental new avenue into
the centre of the City of
London. DA

The Bullion Office, 1806–1808

163 Design model for the
Bullion Office, *c.* 1807
Painted wood:
219×361×195 mm
SM M281

This model of the renovated
Bullion Office, located deep
in the Bank complex for
transhipping treasure, allowed
Soane to test the proportions
and structure of the transverse
barrel vaults and broad
supporting arches. In the
finished hall, the arches were
articulated as semicircles
without impost mouldings,
adumbrating the revolutionary
plasticity of the later 1810s
Bank Transfer Halls, as well as
Soane's arch treatments at
Chelsea and Dulwich. DA

The New Four Per Cent (later Colonial) Office, 1818–1823

164 Design model of the New Four
Per Cent (later Colonial)
Office, as built, *c.* 1818–23
Painted wood and metal on a
fixed stand: 725×473×340 mm
SM MR16

The model illustrates Soane's
intentions both for rebuilding
Taylor's 1760s south-east
corner screen wall, in a simpler
monumental style, and for
remodelling the interior New
Four Per Cent Office. The
interior hall's triple-aisle plan
replicates the Bank Stock
Office renovation twenty-five
years earlier. But now the
arches are more regularly
hemispherical and the
octagonal lantern and flanking
clerestories raised for better
illumination, distorting the
antetype's pyramidal harmony.
DA

165 Perspective design of the New
Four Per Cent (later Colonial)
Office, drawn by Joseph
Michael Gandy
Pen and watercolour:
717×971 mm
SM 11/4/2

This watercolour depicts
significant changes in the
evolution of Soane's
architecture. Here the thirty-
year-old domed office
prototype received its final
refinements. Soane leavened
the heavy Roman nature of the
Consols Transfer Office with a
new effect of Gothic lightness
and with a conspicuous
adoption of Greek
ornamentation as seen in the
ring of Greek Ionic columns
around the lantern and the
prominent Greek-fret pattern
incised over the front and back
arches. DA

CATALOGUE 165 (DETAIL OPPOSITE)

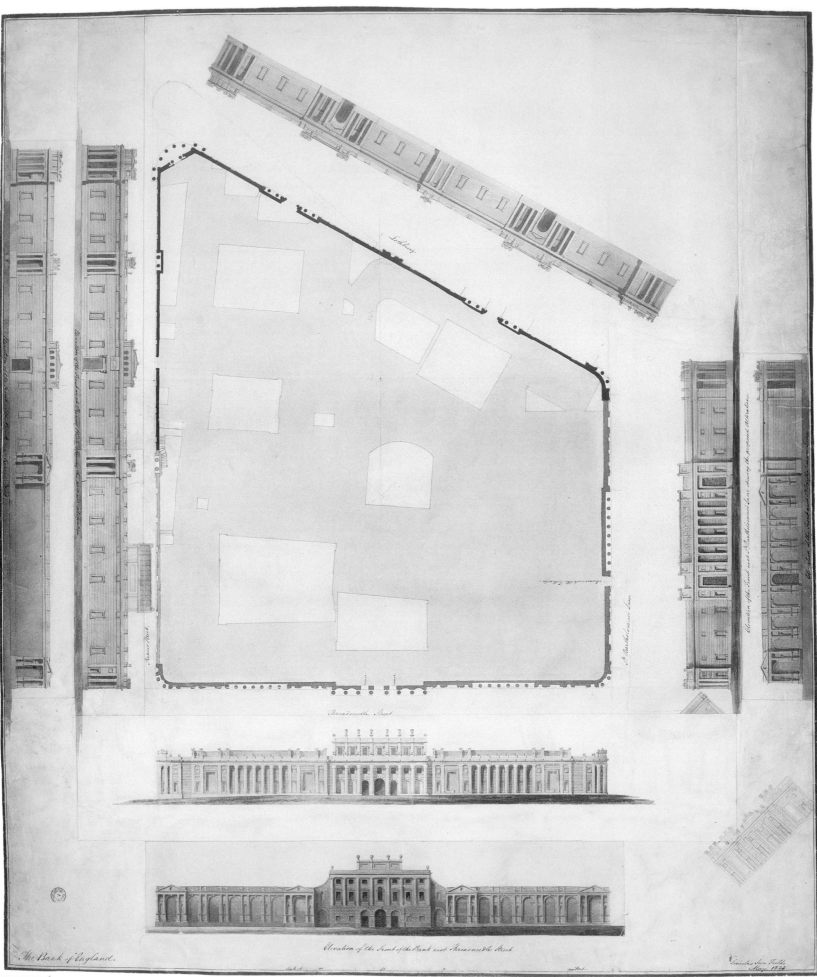

The Bank of England.

Elevation of the Front of the Bank next Threadneedle Street

Lincoln's Inn Fields
May 1824

Old Four Per Cent
(later Old Dividend)
Office, 1818

166 Progress view of the old
Four Per Cent Office during
demolition, looking east at
basement level, drawn by
Arthur Mee, 1821
Inscr. *View of the Old
4% Office/taken down 1821*
Dated: August 1821
Pencil and watercolour:
304×398 mm
SM Vol. 60, 31

Soane dispatched pupils to
draw and learn from the Bank
of England's reconstruction.
In August 1821, nineteen-year-
old Arthur Mee clambered into
the excavated basement of the
Old Four Per Cent Office.
Taylor's 1760s hall was stripped
of its decayed wooden flooring
and domed superstructure, in
this, the final phase after thirty
years, of the east wing's
rebuilding. The elevated
platform led north to the
Rotunda. DA

167 Block plan and comparative
elevations of the Bank, nearly
as built, 1823
Dated: *Lincolns Inn Fields/
May 1823*
Pen and monochrome washes:
867×734 mm
SM 9/2/1

In one image, Soane
summarised his achievement
at the Bank of England,
expanding and renovating the
three-and-a-quarter-acre
complex within a quarter-mile
circuit of walls. The block plan
delineates seven major courts
and thirteen minor yards. The
collage of double elevations
illustrates the existing
elevations by Sampson and
Taylor below, with Soane's
renovation of the Bank's
unified exterior above, as well
as the articulation of the main
Threadneedle Street front
versus the plainer side and rear
façades. DA

Threadneedle Street
Façade, 1816–1826

168 View of the Threadneedle
Street Façade, drawn by Joseph
Michael Gandy, *c.* 1825–27
Pen and monochrome washes
within a washed border:
748×1322 mm
SM 12/1/8

Soane's last major project at
the Bank of England involved
recasing George Sampson's
crumbling 1734 Threadneedle
Street entrance block (see fig.
161). Frameless arches, a spiky
skyline, and eight ground-level
Corinthian columns integrated
the three-storey building into
the Bank's quarter-mile
exterior circuit, now
completely authored by Soane.
According to critics, however,
who thought the Bank's
character demanded a grander,
more public expression, the
horizontal emphasis decreased
the front's monumentality. DA

169 Study model for the spacing of
the columns of the
Threadneedle Street Façade,
c. 1824–27
Wood: 380×810×44 mm
SM M1364

170 Design model of the East Wing
of the Threadneedle Street
Façade as built, *c.* 1823–1825
Wood: 502×1865×180 mm
SM SC4

Between 1824 and 1827, Soane
refaced the Bank of England's
crumbling Threadneedle Street
elevation. While Soane
despised Taylor's original 1760s
wing arcades as fussily
inappropriate, he recognised
the value of colonnades in
breaking up the monotony of
the 370-foot fronts (see fig.
164). In each of Taylor's rebuilt
wing façades, Soane recessed
six Corinthian orders flanked
by a pair of flat, triumphal-arch
type pavilions. Soane's more
rectilinear, stylistically eclectic
and monumental design
rounded off the corner towards

Bartholomew Lane (cat. 173).
The study model (cat. 169) was
almost certainly used to study
the spacing of the recessed
Corinthian orders. DA

171 Design model of the central
elevation of the Threadneedle
Street Façade, 1825
Wood: 650×1160×130 mm
SM SC3

Soane lauded Sampson's 'grand
style of Palladian simplicity'
(see fig. 161) when he recased
his predecessor's 1732–34
Threadneedle Street main
entrance block. Each bay and
storey is clearly articulated and
proportioned, and the skyline
is relatively subdued. Soane
retained Sampson's upper-
storey windows, the only
openings on the whole exterior,
which subtly recalled the
original architectural
conception of the Bank of
England as a traditional City of
London business house. DA

172 Design model of the whole
Threadneedle Street Façade
as built, 1825
Painted plaster:
415×2773×175 mm
SM MR4

This model records the Bank's
completely rebuilt
Threadneedle Street Façade
(1823–27) in which Soane
unified Sampson's centre and
Taylor's wings beneath a strong,
continuous entablature.
Besides amalgamating Roman
orders with simplified Grecian
attic forms, Soane lavishly
employed for visual effect
numerous blank doors and
windows. Soane's successor,
C. R. Cockerell, thought the
screen walls inappropriately
domestic in expression. This
highly detailed model was
produced by the plasterers
Thomas Palmer and John
Bayley in 1825 to permit the
consideration of ornaments
on the south front. DA

Bartholomew Lane Façade,
1825

173 Design model for the
Bank's Bartholomew Lane
Façade, 1825
Wood: 510×2900×105 mm
SM MP216

In 1796, Soane first extended
the Bank of England's
Bartholomew Lane wall
northwards (to the right), and
then thirty years later rebuilt
Taylor's southern two-thirds in
front of the Stock Transfer
Offices and Exchange
Rotunda. On the narrow side
street, Soane decreased the
scale of his Threadneedle
Street scheme (see cat. 167),
here with a single columnar
screen, narrower framing units
and plainer wall surface. DA

Ornament and Furniture

174 Lattice-back chair with arms,
designed by Soane and made
by David Bruce, 1809
Wood: 875×575×575 mm
The Governor and Company
of the Bank of England

175 Ballot box designed by Soane
in the form of a Roman
cinerary urn, *c.* 1800
Wood: 325×300×350 mm
The Governor and Company
of the Bank of England

176 Square anthemion or
honeysuckle ornament
Portland stone: 370×445 mm
SM MY5

177 Half anthemion or
honeysuckle ornament
Portland stone:
370×460×215 mm
SM MY9

These are full-scale examples of
the anthemion blocks which
appear in a variety of modes on
the skyline of the Bank (see figs
168, cats 162, 172). HD

178 Model of the anta capital used
at the Bank of England
Painted plaster:
410×865×180 mm
SM M1420

A full-scale model of the capital
used throughout the Bank
Façade and in the Lothbury
and Governor's Courts. HD

179 Model of an Ionic capital for
the Discount Office Lobby
Plaster: 230×450×280 mm
SM M1443

This full-scale model is a study
for the Ionic capitals of this
lobby, which was completed by
June 1806. HD

The Processional Route

Figure 176
Design perspective for the
exterior of the new Royal
Entrance to the House of
Lords, *c.* 1823. This shows
how Soane used the style
and form of James Wyatt's
castellated office range
(seen in the background),
in extending the existing
arcade to form a curved
'cloister' leading to the
Scala Regia (on the right)
with a central entrance
portal carefully positioned
to align with the approach
of the King's carriage
(SM Vol. 61, 26)

Figure 177 (opposite)
Design perspective of the
Scala Regia, drawn by
Joseph Michael Gandy,
1800 (detail of cat. 181)

In the aftermath of the Napoleonic Wars, John Soane became an architect of national stature. The Bank of England was recognised as a 'great national structure', as he termed it, and his on-going work there brought him a measure of fame, particularly in June 1814 when he met Tsar Alexander I at the Bank during the celebrations marking the Allies' initial victory. That same month Lord Liverpool's government restructured the Office of King's Works and named Soane as an Attached Architect, along with John Nash, the Prince Regent's favourite architect, and Robert Smirke, the darling of the Royal Academy and the Tory landed élite. This public appointment provided Soane – then in his sixties – with the opportunity to realise his youthful ambitions to construct monumental civic structures. Or so he thought.

Soane's appointment, with its responsibility for the Westminster area, was all the more poignant since it included not only the districts of St James's, Whitehall and Westminster but also the Palace of Westminster, the seat of national law and government, whose reconstruction he had projected for two decades. In 1794 the House of Lords had commissioned him to design alterations to their facilities, and he had expanded this into a project for a grand Neoclassical structure on the Thames. War intervened, and when work at the Houses of Parliament went forward in 1800 it fell to George III's favourite, the Surveyor-General James Wyatt. Wyatt rejected Soane's Neoclassical approach in favour of a Gothic scheme that capitalised on the growing appreciation of Westminster's medieval

FIGURE 176

monuments. Portions were completed in the same rather gutless, castellated style as he was then using for the King's new palace at Kew. The ranges at Westminster were widely derided, and the project was abandoned before Wyatt's death in 1813. Having continually revised his Neoclassical designs and exhibited them at the Royal Academy, Soane assumed the position of Attached Architect with high hopes.

Through the 1820s he completed a series of important public works at the Palace and elsewhere, including a new Royal Entrance to the House of Lords, the reconstruction of the Law Courts alongside Westminster Hall and new offices for the Board of Trade and Privy Council on Whitehall. In these spaces, he synthesised established elements of his architecture, in particular canopied, top-lit forms and the modulation of spatial transitions, with a keen understanding of picturesque aesthetics and an appreciation of a broader range of structural and decorative effects, including Gothic, Renaissance and even Hindu forms. The visual complexity and ornamental richness of Soane's late public works distinguished them from his sparer, earlier work. Their mannered, syncretic forms reflected his desire to formulate an architectural language expressive of the modern, global character of the British Empire, in much the same way as the panoply of classical forms had expressed the diversity of the Roman Empire. This formal variety was unified by Neoclassical principles of symmetry and decorum and by the predominance of classical forms and motifs, especially on their exteriors where they imbued his works with a clearly legible civic authority.

This cosmopolitan impulse conflicted with the patriotic and antiquarian enthusiasm for Gothic, particularly in work at Westminster, and for archaeological correctness in strict Neoclassical design: all of Soane's completed works met with criticism in Parliament and the press. The ornate, almost garish Royal Entrance (see cats 190–191) was lambasted among 'modern additions of mongrel architecture' in the Commons in 1824. The Law Courts (see cats 197–209) occasioned the sharpest criticism for both their aesthetic idiosyncrasies and their functional inadequacies when completed in 1826, and the ostentatious character of his Privy Council Chamber (see cat. 188) also came under attack from the Council itself in 1827.

Determined to answer his critics and restore his professional reputation, Soane produced two versions of

Figure 178

Diagram of Soane's
Processional Route
through Westminster as
outlined in 'Designs for
Public Improvements in
London and Westminster'
(1827–28)

A Brief Statement of the Proceedings respecting the New Law Courts at Westminster and the New Entrance for His Majesty in the House of Lords, the first unpublished in early 1827, and the published edition in 1828. That spring, however, George IV expressed interest in his designs for a Royal Palace exhibited at the Royal Academy, and this motivated him to conceive of a new publication that would be dedicated to the King and be less defensive and more celebratory in tone. Entitled 'Designs for Public Improvements in London and Westminster' and first produced in unpublished form in September 1827, this sought to affirm his identity as a civic architect of national stature. An enlarged 'second impression', also unpublished, of January 1828 even more explicitly cultivated royal favour by casting Soane's civic architecture as a framework for a Processional Route for the King from Windsor to the House of Lords.

This concept accorded with George IV's interests and needs. He had been an important patron of architecture as Prince of Wales and as Regent – sponsoring Nash's Regent's Park and Regent's Street developments – and had continued to conceive of projects on a grand scale upon his accession to the throne in 1820, in particular Nash's palatial reconstruction of Buckingham House begun in 1825 and the extensive remodelling of Windsor Castle begun by Jeffry Wyatville the year before. As King, he cultivated royal ceremonial and pageantry as a means of redressing his enduring unpopularity. The most spectacular example of this was his extraordinarily lavish Coronation of 19 July 1821, which was modelled on that of James II (1685). Yet ultimately more significant was his aggrandisement of the annual State Opening and Prorogation of Parliament in which the

monarch processed in state to inaugurate or close the parliamentary session from the Throne in the House of Lords. He had redirected the procession from its bucolic path across St James's Park to the more urban and public route down Whitehall and Parliament Street, and commissioned Soane to reconstruct the Royal Entrance to the House of Lords in 1822. Soane's Processional Route clearly originated in George IV's avowed concern to raise the monarch's public profile in these annual rituals of governance.

As represented by the first twenty-four plates in 'Designs for Public Improvements in London and Westminster', Soane's route combined his recently completed public works with projected designs to present his Neoclassical vision of the imperial capital. Coming from the chivalric fantasies of Wyatville's Windsor, the King would pass through the classicising *cordon sanitaire* of Soane's 'Western Entrance to the Metropolis' at Kensington Gore (see cat. 182) – a configuration of triumphal arches – and down the King's Private Road along Hyde Park to a single triumphal arch at Hyde Park Corner. Crossing Piccadilly, the King's carriage would enter into the courtyard of a magnificent Royal Palace projected for Constitution Hill (see cat. 183). This was akin to the designs that had attracted the King's attention at the Royal Academy exhibition, which Soane had made in an attempt to thwart Nash's usurpation of the work at Buckingham House, officially in Soane's district. The King's arrival at the palace provided an interlude in the processional itinerary and a vantage point, as Soane wrote, for him to survey the monumental landscape of his capital.

Having refreshed and refitted his entourage, the King would continue down the Mall to Horse Guards Parade and pass by both a 'Monopteral Temple' honouring the Duke of York, the recently deceased Commander-in-Chief, and a 'Sepulchral Church' (see cat. 184). These were clearly two separate projects but are conflated in the text, and only the latter is illustrated. This temple-cum-mausoleum constituted a drastic consolidation of his designs for a National Monument of 1818 and contained two levels: lower catacombs for war heroes and an upper sanctuary. Continuing this militaristic ethos, the procession would pass through a triumphal arch at the western end of a monumentally

1 Western entrance to the metropolis
2 Piccadilly entrance to Hyde Park
3 Royal Palace
4 Sepulchral Church
5 Downing Street
6 Westminster Abbey
7 Law Courts
8 Houses of Parliament

FIGURE 178

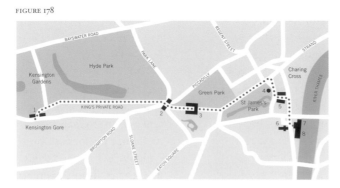

Figure 179

Sketch for a presentation
perspective showing the
processional Entrance to
the House of Lords in
section and set in clouds,
drawn by Joseph Michael
Gandy, 1824 (SM 71/2/76)

FIGURE 179

reconstructed Downing Street (see cat. 185). This was
to be terminated by two arches – the western dedicated
to naval victories, especially Trafalgar, and the eastern
commemorating military valour and Waterloo in
particular – and lined by large colonnaded blocks. That
to the north was to include Soane's recently completed
Board of Trade and Privy Council Offices (see cats
186–188), while the symmetrical southern range was to
house a variety of departments, including the Colonial
Office and diplomatic corps. Equestrian statues of
George III and George IV were to top the western and
eastern arches, respectively, and the latter was to point
southward, directing the royal procession down
Parliament Street to the Palace of Westminster.

Here the procession would slow and move past the
north front of Soane's new Law Courts, which he
illustrated in its original neo-Palladian guise rather than

the Gothic form in which he was forced to rebuild it.
Passing the east end of Henry VII's chapel,
Westminster's most glorious Gothic monument,
the King's carriage would enter Old Palace Yard and
confront the sham castellated entrance front of the
Houses of Parliament that Wyatt had begun and Soane
had continued in constructing his new Royal Entrance
at its southern corner (see fig. 176). Sheltered beneath
its *porte cochère*, the obese, gout-ridden King would
descend from his carriage and pass through the curved
'Cloister' to enter the Neoclassical splendour of Soane's
Royal Entrance suite (see fig. 179 and cats 190–192).
Attended by the officers of state and admired by the
ranks of invited spectators, George IV would be able
to indulge his fondest monarchical reveries within this
symbolically charged, light-suffused realm and for a
moment transport the nation along with him.

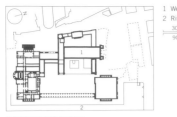

1 Westminster Hall
2 River Thames
300 feet
90 metres

The House of Lords, Palace of Westminster: The First Project, 1794

180 Design perspective of the new House of Lords facing the river, 1794
Diploma work, deposited 1802
Watercolour: 70.2 × 125.4 cm
The Royal Academy of Arts, London

Soane deposited this perspective of his project for reconstructing the House of Lords – his most significant public commission to date – with the Royal Academy as his diploma drawing on his election as a full academician in 1802. Depicting a water stair to the Thames in the foreground, it represents the principal south elevation of his design as submitted to the Treasury in November 1794. By the time of his election, however, Pitt's government had abandoned the project in the face of the escalating war on the Continent and unrest at home. The Royal Entrance is within the central, pedimented pavilion beneath Britannia in a *chariga*, while the Lords' Chamber lies behind the riverfront dome. The project as a whole represents a return to the academic Neoclassicism of Soane's student days to cultivate a character of Antique civic magnificence for the seat of Britain's empire. ss

181 Design perspective of the Scala Regia, drawn by Joseph Michael Gandy, August 1800
Watercolour: 1050 × 830 mm, in a Soane frame
SM P283

The Scala Regia, a staged, barrel-vaulted stair, lined with statues of monarchs, had been part of Soane's design for the Royal Entrance in his project for the House of Lords of 1794. Gandy made this perspective in August 1800, however, as part of Soane's effort to redesign his project to compete with James Wyatt's proposals. Gandy's dramatic lighting effects and distortions of scale create an aura of Romantic grandeur, but the architecture is more traditionally composed than the earlier design and encrusted with archaeologically correct ornament, principally the giant Corinthian order with its full entablature. The addition of side aisles, where spectators might view the King's procession, demonstrates Soane's growing appreciation for the spectacular nature of the Royal Entrance. Yet in competition with Wyatt, he sacrificed the integrity of his reductive Neoclassicism for the fashionable appeal of decorative enrichment. ss

CATALOGUE 181

256

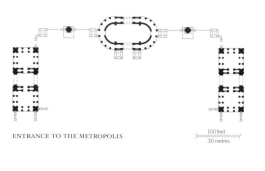

ENTRANCE TO THE METROPOLIS

100 feet
30 metres

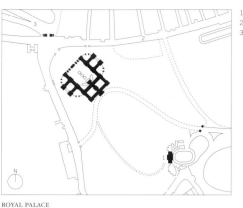

1 Buckingham Palace
2 Piccadilly
3 Hyde Park

ROYAL PALACE

The Processional Route, 1828

182 Design for a 'Grand National Entrance into the Metropolis, intended to combine the Classical Simplicity of Grecian Architecture, the Magnificence of the Roman Architecture, and the fanciful intricacy and playful effects of the Gothic Architecture', drawn by Joseph Michael Gandy, 1826
Perspective, with inset plan on an Antique fragment in the foreground
Pen and watercolour: 930 × 1500 mm, in a Soane frame
SM P83

Soane designed several versions of his proposed 'Western Entrance into the Metropolis', which was to be situated at Kensington Gore, and published two more sober designs as part of his Processional Route. Although he had erected new gateways and lodges at Cumberland Gate and Constitution Hill during his brief tenure as Deputy Surveyor of Woods and Forests in 1797, these much more monumental designs were inspired by the ambitions for erecting a 'national monument' in the aftermath of Waterloo. Soane stated that the 'general idea' derived from the Athenian Propylaea, which is apparent in the three designs' essential tripartite composition with a central element indicating the principal avenue of approach into the city. This design is distinct in the almost Baroque exuberance of its architecture and suggests a more direct precedent in Neoclassical ephemeral architecture, such as that of the Roman Festa della Chinea. Gandy's perspective also dramatises its processional character as a troop of soldiers departs the metropolis. ss

183 Design perspective of the portico, with the carriage entrance on an inclined plane, for a Royal Palace on Constitution Hill, drawn by Joseph Michael Gandy, 1827
Watercolour: 845 × 1415 mm, in a Soane frame
SM P260

Soane made two designs for a Royal Palace in response to Nash's commission to reconstruct Buckingham House, which was officially in Soane's Office of Works' district. Both called for entirely new, monumental Neoclassical establishments on Constitution Hill opposite the south-east corner of Hyde Park; one was modelled on Vignola's Villa Farnese at Caprarola and the other on Blenheim Palace. Soane represented the latter, more emphatically patriotic design as part of his Processional Route. This perspective by Gandy shows the central entrance portico-cum-porte cochère within its immense forecourt and suggests both the ease of access for the infirm King and the richness of its Neoclassical ornament, which may well be exaggerated in Gandy's translation. ss

CATALOGUE 182

CATALOGUE 183

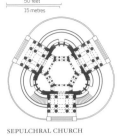

SEPULCHRAL CHURCH

TRIUMPHAL ARCH, DOWNING STREET

Sepulchral Church for the Duke of York, St James's Park, London, 1827

184 Design perspective, drawn by Joseph Michael Gandy, 1827
Watercolour: 81×1030 mm, in a Soane frame
SM P275

Another manifestation of Soane's enthusiasm for the notion of a 'national monument', this design (see fig. 50) was derived from his unexecuted design for a family chapel at Tyringham of 1800 and was termed a 'sepulchral church' in 'Designs for Public Improvements in London and Westminster'. It became conflated with his contemporary projects for a monument to the Duke of York, the former Commander-in-Chief, who died in 1827. The three Paestum Doric porticoes and the rearing equestrian statues representing death in battle imbue this temple-cum-mausoleum with a martial air, while the elegant caryatids framing the window openings and the sarcophagi atop the pediments speak of the human toll of war, which is enacted in Gandy's rendering by the approaching military funeral cortège. ss

Triumphal Arches in Downing Street connecting the Board of Trade and Privy Council Offices on the right to the State Paper Office and Colonial Office on the left, c. 1827

185 Design perspective showing the Triumphal Arches connecting the two blocks of offices; on either side are sections through the first Triumphal Arch, framed by curtains; below are cut-out plans and an elevation of the Board of Trade and Privy Council Offices pasted to the main sheet, drawn by Joseph Michael Gandy
Pen and watercolour: 725×1300 mm
SM 15/5/5

The Processional Route passed from the Sepulchral Church along the eastern edge of St James's Park to enter Downing Street, which is shown in this design as a monumental *via triumphalis*. This perspective shows the entrance to the street from Whitehall. The two Arches commemorated the defeat of the Armada and the victory of Trafalgar, and the defeat of Napoleon at Waterloo. Equestrian statues of George III and George IV surmount the western and eastern Arches respectively, presenting these monarchs as the motive force behind Britain's military superiority. Furthermore these Arches are monumental links connecting the Board of Trade and Privy Council Offices on the north, which Soane had begun designing in 1823 (see cats 186–188), with a symmetrical secretariat to house the Colonial Office and the State Paper Office to the south. These proposals were not realised but the Neoclassical grandeur of this urban scheme coincides with John Nash's large-scale works, particularly Chester Terrace of 1825. ss

CATALOGUE 185 (DETAIL OPPOSITE)

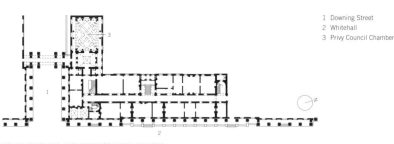

BOARD OF TRADE AND PRIVY COUNCIL OFFICES

The Board of Trade and Privy Council Offices, Downing Street and Whitehall, 1823–1826

186 Model of an early design,
June 1824
Painted pine:
295×878×355 mm
SM MR31

The design of the new offices for the Board of Trade and Privy Council was dogged by difficulties, caused principally by the interference of the Chancellor of the Exchequer, Frederick John Robinson, referred to by Soane as 'an amateur of Grecian architecture' (*Memoirs*, p. 58).

On 5 June 1824 Soane's design featuring a continuous insulated colonnade of the Tivoli Corinthian order was approved, but Robinson wanted Soane to replace the Tivoli order (see cat. 20) with the more ornate 'Jupiter Stator' form of the Corinthian capital (see cat. 22). Uneasy with the illusionary nature of the proposed insulated colonnade he also requested three-quarter-engaged columns, and commissioned this model so that he could judge their effect more easily (see fig. 47). MR, SS

187 Design perspective, drawn by Joseph Michael Gandy
Pen and watercolour.
741×1282 mm
Exh. 1828, Royal Academy, no. 990
SM 15/5/2

This perspective shows the building as if it were complete, with the pavement and road in the process of being laid. It also shows the final design in which the five southern bays are articulated as a projecting pavilion, although the colonnades are shown as having Soane's insulated columns rather than the three-quarter-engaged columns which Robinson had requested (see cat. 186). Soane probably wanted to present his preferred design to a wider audience.

Gandy conveys the Antique grandeur of the design by displaying the different elements of the Jupiter Stator order in the foreground combined with the tools of builders: a mason's square, a mallet and a piece of scaffolding. MR

CATALOGUE 187 (DETAIL OPPOSITE)

CATALOGUE 188

ENTRANCE, SCALA REGIA AND APPROACH
TO THE HOUSE OF LORDS

1 Entrance
2 Vestibule
3 Scala Regia
4 Royal Gallery
5 Painted Chamber
6 House of Lords

CATALOGUE 192

188 View of the interior of the Privy
Council Chamber, drawn by
Joseph Michael Gandy, 1827
Watercolour: 951×723 mm
Exh. 1827, Royal Academy,
no. 905
SM 15/5/1

The Privy Council Chamber is
one of the most sublime and
strange manifestations of
Soane's later style. It was
located in the Privy Council
Offices which extended
westward along Downing
Street. Begun in late 1825,
they were complete by 1827.
Soane provided a setting of
some magnificence. The room
itself rose through two floors
with a pair of Siena marble
Ionic columns supporting an
entablature on each side of the
room. Suspended between the
skylights, like a canvas canopy,
the ceiling is the most extreme
version of Soane's favourite
starfish vault (see cats 62, 65),
creating an effect of soaring
space.

The members of the Privy
Council received the design
with mixed feelings and Soane
was asked to remove the
columns and prepare estimates
for a flat ceiling. In the end
his decoration was allowed to
remain, although only for little
more than a decade before
Charles Barry drastically
remodelled the Chamber and
the entire building in the
1840s. MR

189 Model of the proposed
Processional Route
Scale 1: 1250
Timber, acrylic and
chemiwood: 3×2.8×1.08 m
Made in 1999 by Lucy Marston,
Matthew Driscoll, Malcolm
Dugdale, Paul Houston, Azher
Mahmood, Dan Peer, John
Pengelly, Crain Storey, Ben
Williamson and Philip Wykes
at Kent Institute of Art and
Design (tutor: George Rome
Innes)

The House of Lords, Palace of Westminster: The 1820s Project

190 View of the New Vestibule,
drawn by Joseph Michael
Gandy, c. 1823
Pencil, pen and watercolour:
362×253 mm
SM Vol. 61, 28

One of a series of Gandy's
detailed views of the
completed Royal Entrance,
this shows Soane's
reconstruction of Wyatt's
existing vestibule and a
glimpse of the Gothic entrance
'cloister' beyond. This
contrasts with the vestibule's
rich Neoclassical plasterwork
decoration; the overdoor
cornices were borrowed from
the Bank but what had been
fleur-de-lis were here
transformed into feathers
in reference to the Prince
of Wales's insignia. The
iconography is explicitly royal
and imperial: the royal coat of
arms and a bust of George IV
filled the arched openings
above, while roundels
allegorising 'the Rise and Fall
of Rome' were mounted below.
The latter were salvaged from
the fire of 1834 and survive at
the Palace of Westminster. ss

191 View of the Scala Regia,
drawn by Joseph Michael
Gandy
Pen and watercolour:
1325×925 mm, framed
Exh. 1823, Royal Academy,
no. 974
SM XP16

This is the primary view of
Soane's Scala Regia built in
1822–23. In the foreground is
the lobby he created within
the last bay of Wyatt's existing
arcade. The dramatic top-
lighting and combination of
Gothic and Neoclassical forms
signify the transition from one
stylistic zone to the other and
create the sublime affects of
scale and light that he had long
admired in the Gothic while

maintaining a more rigorously
Neoclassical vocabulary. To
Bolton, the Scala Regia was
perhaps, 'the best of all Soane
designs, and even if it was
possibly somewhat gaudy in
detail, in character with the taste
of the last of the four Georges,
it is undoubtedly a fine and
characteristic composition'
(Bolton 1924, p. 112). SS, MR

192 View of the Royal Gallery,
leading to the House of Lords,
drawn by Joseph Michael Gandy
Pen and watercolour:
1030×770 mm, in a Soane frame
Exh. 1824, Royal Academy,
no. 965
SM P285

The Royal Gallery and its
Anteroom formed the final
phase of Soane's Royal Entrance
suite and were constructed with
great rapidity in the autumn and
winter of 1823–24. That spring,
however, his works at the Palace
of Westminster came under
attack in Parliament and the
press. In particular, an
anonymous attack entitled
'The Sixth or Bœotian Order
of Architecture', in *Knight's
Quarterly Magazine*, derided the
Royal Entrance for 'the quantity
and singularity of the ornament
distributed over it' (vol. II,
London, 1824, p. 457). In
response, it seems, Soane
exhibited this perspective by
Gandy at that spring's Royal
Gallery exhibition. This shows
it stripped of furnishings and its
most novel ornamentation.
While the unrolled plan in the
foreground might imply ongoing
construction, this may be
understood as Soane's attempt
to focus attention on the
architectural qualities rather
than the decorative excesses of
the space. ss

CATALOGUE 191

David Watkin

Freemasons' Hall

Figure 180

Freemasons' Hall, London:
sketch for a design
perspective of the kitchen
below the Hall, with its
arcaded side walls and
exposed, timber-trussed
roof, drawn by Joseph
Michael Gandy, 1828
(SM 52/5/44)

Figure 181 (opposite)

Perspective view of the
Council Chamber by night,
drawn by Joseph Michael
Gandy (detail of cat. 195)

FIGURE 180

Freemasons' Hall
1   Council Chamber
2   The Ark
3   Great Queen Street

Initiated as a Freemason on 1 December 1813, Soane was installed later in the month by his friend HRH the Duke of Sussex as Grand Superintendent of Works, a post Soane held until his death. We have four plans made by him in 1826 for a new Freemasons' Hall in Great Queen Street, but the final designs were not realised until 1828. An extraordinary intermediary design of June 1828 shows a neo-Tudor interior with an unmistakably Soanean manner, boasting a roof of notched timber beams surmounted by groin vaults and shallow domes, and lit with mullioned windows containing diamond-paned glass. The walls are lined with the kind of simplified linenfold panelling which featured in Soane's Law Courts at Westminster Hall of 1822–25 (see cats 201–202). The room thus belongs to that late phase in his career when he seemed to be moving towards a style appropriate to historic or national institutions, a synthesis of Classic and Gothic.

The Tudor flavour was largely dropped in the executed design which was, nonetheless, one of the most personal and richly ornamented interiors of his career. It formed the upper part of a substantial new building with a kitchen and scullery on the ground floor, and a new staircase on the west side. It was characteristic of him to devote almost as much care to the design of the kitchen (whose strikingly exposed, timber-trussed roof [fig. 180] was of a Palladian type introduced to England by Inigo Jones) as to the hall.

By this time in his career, coloured light was central to Soane's understanding of the effects which architecture should create. Thus the four side windows were glazed with richly coloured and patterned glass, including a yellow diaper on an orange ground, while the compartments in the central lantern above the 'sarcophagus lid' contained the signs of the zodiac in yellow ground glass alternating with rosettes. The painted glass in the four clerestory windows contained representations of five columns, a Masonic reference to the five orders of antiquity.

Silhouetted against the golden light filtering from the lantern above, a canopy hovered above the room like an outspread bat's wing. With its high canted sides, this had a steep profile which is Gothic or Baroque in flavour. Soane was evidently anxious to create, in classical terms, a daring and sublime Gothic aesthetic effect akin to the Tudoresque flavour of the design of June 1828. The hall became a piece of speaking architecture, rich with symbolical and natural ornament as in Gothic churches. Its ornamental complexity helps explain why it took so long to complete: the foundation stone was laid in the summer of 1828 but the room was not ready until early in 1831.

The destruction in 1863 of an interior of such startling intensity was a tragedy, for, as we can now see, it was probably a more complete physical expression of Masonic metaphor than anything achieved by Soane's contemporaries. Responding warmly to the Masonic love of ceremony and fraternal affection, he felt at home in the world of the eighteenth-century Enlightenment as expressed in the ideals of continental Freemasonry.

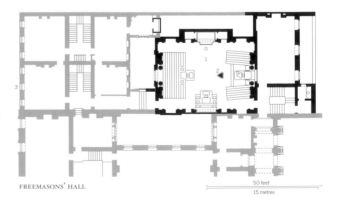

FREEMASONS' HALL

50 feet

15 metres

193 Design for the Ark of the Masonic Covenant, drawn by George Underwood, Soane's pupil, 1813–14
Pen and coloured washes: 1228 × 795 mm
SM 14/4/6

Following his initiation as a Freemason in 1813, Soane was immediately invited to design an Ark of the Masonic Covenant to be used in December at the union of the two Fraternities, known as the Grand Lodge, founded in 1717, and the Antient Grand Lodge, founded as its rival in 1751.

Soane's ark bore no resemblance to the conventional Biblical ark, a modest portable object, whose image featured in the arms of the two Lodges which were to be united. Those images reflected the directions given to Moses to make an ark to contain God's Testimony, made of shittim wood (acacia) and flanked by two cherubim. Soane's totally different mahogany ark, four feet three inches high, and three feet four inches wide, was triangular with a column at each corner, Doric, Ionic, Corinthian, symbolising wisdom, strength and beauty. DW

194 Design perspective of the interior of the Council Chamber by day, drawn by Joseph Michael Gandy, 1828
Pen and watercolour: 930 × 1300 mm, in a Soane frame
SM P89

A preliminary sketch for this perspective is dated *Dec 3 1828*; propped up in the foreground is Gandy's formal perspective of the kitchen.

195 Perspective view of the Council Chamber by night, drawn by Joseph Michael Gandy, 1831
Pen and watercolour: 840 × 1400 mm, in a Soane frame
SM P268

As is customary with Soane's profoundly three-dimensional interior spaces, the vaulted ceiling provided the key to the whole design. The bays containing the windows and chimneypieces were linked across the room by broad segmental arches, ornamented with coffering. By inserting a window immediately over a chimneypiece Soane reversed normal functional procedure, for the area devoted to the window was that customarily reserved for the flue.
He further stressed the constructional daring by resting the coffered vaults not on solid walls but on the heads of the windows, thus suggesting that solid masonry was supported on glass. The most memorable feature of this uncanny room, also challenging expectations of constructional propriety, was the pendant dome in the form of an unsupported canopy, resembling Soane's favourite 'sarcophagus lid' motif. DW

196 John Wood (1801–1870) after Sir Thomas Lawrence
Portrait of Sir John Soane
Dated: *1829*
Oil on canvas: 181.5 × 120.5 cm
Drawings Collection, The British Architectural Library, Royal Institute of British Architects, London

According to its label this copy of the Lawrence portrait which hangs in the Dining Room at 13 Lincoln's Inn Fields was presented by Sir John Soane to the Institute of British Architects, the early RIBA. It shows Soane as a successful gentleman without any of the trappings of the architectural profession, in contrast to the early Hunneman portrait (cat. 1). HD

CATALOGUE 193

CATALOGUE 195

The Law Courts

Figure 182
The exterior of the Law
Courts, viewed from
Parliament Square,
c. 1880. Taken only a year
or two before the
demolition of Soane's
masterpiece in 1883, this
photograph shows part of
Soane's building (the tower
in the foreground) and,
further down the street,
Vardy's neo-Palladian block
built between 1755 and
1769 (National Monuments
Record, Howarth-Loomes
Collection)

Figure 183 (opposite)
The interior of the Court of
Chancery, drawn by Joseph
Michael Gandy, c. 1825
(detail of cat. 201)

The Law Courts at Westminster of 1822–25 are the most historically significant and architecturally compelling of Soane's late public works, but at their completion they were perceived to be a signal failure. His challenge was to preserve the historic association of the Royal Courts of Justice with Westminster Hall by constructing seven courtrooms on a constrained, adjacent site.

The superior courts of common law and equity were established in Westminster Hall by the late thirteenth century. The two principal courts, King's Bench and Chancery, sat in partitions on the southern dais, while the Court of Common Pleas occupied the north-west corner and the Court of Exchequer a substantial brick structure extending from the Hall's north-west tower. In the mid-eighteenth century William Kent reconstructed the King's Bench and Chancery partitions in a fanciful Gothic style and designed a self-contained Common Pleas structure west of the Hall that was to serve as a model for Soane. Kent's top-lit courtroom was fitted between a pair of the Hall's buttresses and communicated with it through a portal opened in its west wall. His intention to replicate this formula for the other courts was not pursued. In the first decade of the nineteenth century, James Wyatt proposed a similar project during his tenure as Surveyor-General, but this was also abandoned.

FIGURE 182

The impetus for Soane's commission was circumstantial. In addition to its judicial function, Westminster Hall accommodated ceremonies of state; early in 1820 Kent's partitions were cleared to begin preparations for George IV's Coronation Banquet. Queen Caroline's return from the Continent that June and her subsequent trial in the House of Lords postponed the coronation for a year. Soon after her return Lord Liverpool passed through the Hall and, admiring its unencumbered expanse, determined to reconstruct the Courts of King's Bench and Chancery west of the Hall. Soane was charged with this limited commission in July 1820.

Over the next two years, however, he expanded the project to comprise the reconstruction of the entire judicial complex and the concomitant demolition of all the existing structures except for John Vardy's three-storey neo-Palladian 'Stone Building', which occupied the south and west sides of the site. Soane extended this northward to make it symmetrical and continued a neo-Palladian composition – derived from the Basilica at Vicenza – around to the north front of Westminster Hall.

Behind these façades, Soane produced a masterpiece of interstitial planning. With the Hall serving as a magnificent, historically sanctified public entrance, the courtrooms were placed between its western buttresses and accessed via portals cut through its western wall. The Chancery Courts were located at the south end of the site and the common-law jurisdictions north of them, with the Court of King's Bench given the largest zone overlooking New Palace Yard. A continuous, sky-lit public corridor ran between the Hall and the courtrooms, while the judges' chambers and clerical offices west of the courtrooms were linked by a service corridor that connected to private entrances from St Margaret's Street. The courtrooms were principally top-lit, but small light courts were also interspersed throughout the complex.

The dramatic, filtered top-lighting is the most distinctive characteristic of the Law Courts as depicted in Joseph Michael Gandy's renderings of the completed spaces and combines with the varied forms, contrasting textures and angular viewpoints to create a picturesque ensemble. Yet contemporary observers commented most on the idiosyncratic, extravagant character of the architecture with its repetition of Soanean forms, such as hanging arches and pendentive canopies, and the combination of Gothic forms and classical detailing.

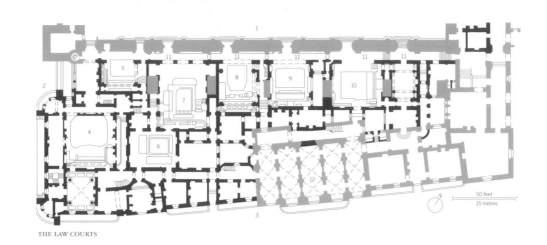

THE LAW COURTS

Figure 184

The Basilica, Vicenza, by
Andrea Palladio, 1449–60,
visited by Soane on his
Grand Tour, 1778–90, and a
source for his Palladian
scheme for the Law Courts

Figure 185

Thomas and George
Martyr's plan model of the
Law Courts, 1827 (cat. 209)

Figure 186 (opposite)

Presentation model of
the north range of the Law
Courts, the neo-Palladian
design, 1826 (detail of
cat. 207)

One critic declared that the courtrooms 'have more the air of fairy halls than of seats of justice'. Rather than having lost sight of the principles of decorum, however, it seems that Soane was attempting to formulate an architecture that expressed the empirical nature of systems of jurisprudence that were based on the interpretation of precedent rather than statute. The Greco-Gothic character of the architecture represented a synthesis of the site's Gothic identity with Soane's commitment to Neoclassicism in civic architecture.

Construction began in the autumn of 1822 and was nearing completion in March 1824 when controversy erupted. Led by Henry Bankes of Dorset, an independent-minded cadre of MPs strenuously protested against the appearance of the neo-Palladian north façade as an offence to national taste, especially in juxtaposition with the restored north front of Westminster Hall. Bankes obtained a Select Committee ruling and succeeded in forcing the demolition of the partially built façade, dictating the form of the Gothic façade of the New Palace Yard elevation. Soane disowned this design and spent the next decade attempting to convince the government to reconstruct it, even offering to pay for it himself.

The reforms of Lord Brougham's Lord Chancellorship of 1830–34 initiated an unprecedented expansion of the judiciary that rendered Soane's complex obsolete by mid-century. In 1882, after six hundred years at the Palace of Westminster, the Royal Courts of Justice left for George Edmund Street's new complex on the Strand; the next year Soane's was demolished.

FIGURE 185

FIGURE 184

MODEL·PLAN·OF·THE·LAW·COURTS, WESTMINSTER. 1821–1826.

197 Design models for a lantern
198 and dome, *c.* 1823
Mahogany: 155 × 268 × 268 mm
and 130 × 186 × 192 mm
SM MR1353, MR1454

Soane had a series of small
study models made to help him
develop the design of the
various lanterns in the Courts.
These models do not
necessarily relate to the
completed building, although
they have traditionally been
associated with the Court of
Common Pleas. They show
Soane experimenting with the
form of vaulting and apertures
in the lanterns, which were
instrumental in creating the
picturesque effects he desired.
Both models are made of
mahogany, one of the more
expensive woods that Soane
specified when greater
definition of detail was
required. SA

199 Model of the ceiling of the
Court of King's Bench, *c.* 1823
Painted softwood and plaster:
956 × 820 × 200 mm
SM M1456

This is one of the largest design
studies for a complete ceiling
in the Law Courts, showing the
flat part of the ceiling and the
transition to the lantern, the
major source of natural light.
The ceiling is depicted almost
as executed. SA

200 Model of a pendant ornament
for the ceiling of the Court of
Equity, *c.* 1823
Softwood and plaster:
185 × 255 × 255 mm
SM M1455

This study model for one of
the units of hanging arches on
the ceiling of the Court of
Equity is one more of the series
of studies that Soane had made
for him to assess various ideas
for the decoration of the
interiors of the Law Courts. SA

201 Interior view of the Court of
Chancery, drawn by Joseph
Michael Gandy, *c.* 1825
Pencil, pen and ink,
watercolour and bodycolour:
1015 × 742 mm
SM 16/1/3

As the seat of the Kingdom's
chief law officer, the Lord
Chancellor's Court received
lavish treatment in Soane's
representation of the Law
Courts. This large-scale
drawing presents a dramatic,
idealised view of the tribunal.
The lantern's circular opening
burns with solar intensity and
evokes the enlightening,
awesome authority of the Lord
Chancellor. Gandy contrasts
this with the quotidian detritus
left in the court by the
barristers, including books,
papers – some tied in red tape –
and an umbrella, as if
proceedings had just been
interrupted. SS, SA

202 Two interior views of the Court
203 of King's Bench, drawn by
Joseph Michael Gandy, 1826
Pencil and watercolour:
321 × 235 mm, 328 × 245 mm
SM Vol. 61, 43 and 46

Offering glimpses within the
Court of King's Bench, these
watercolours were part of
Gandy's series of views of the
completed courts made during
the late summer judicial recess
of 1826. The view across the
courtroom distorts its
proportions and emphasises
the illumination provided by
the central lantern and the
skylight over the south gallery,
perhaps to counter criticism
from the legal community that
it was too small and dark.
Intended for legal personnel
and students, the south gallery
had two mirrored bookcases
set within the remarkable
arcaded partition along its
rear wall. Light from the
continuous arched skylight
played off its surfaces as well as
the freely adapted Neoclassical
ornament. SS

CATALOGUE 201

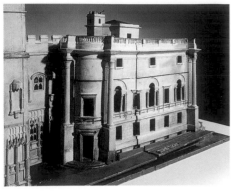

CATALOGUE 207   CATALOGUE 208

204 The Court of Exchequer,
viewed from the entrance
from Westminster Hall,
drawn by Joseph Michael
Gandy, 1826
Pencil and watercolour:
287×256 mm
SM Vol. 61, 57

Gandy dramatised the
immediacy of the public
approach to the Court of
Exchequer in this view through
its arcaded east wall from the
corridor alongside Westminster
Hall. This was the broadest of
all the courtrooms – taking in
the full distance between this
pair of buttresses – and this is
emphasised by the exaggerated
size of its box lantern. ss

205 View of the public corridor
outside the Lord Chancellor's
Court, drawn by Joseph
Michael Gandy, 1826
Pencil and watercolour:
458×282 mm
SM Vol. 61, 71

This view shows the southern
end of the public corridor
outside the Lord Chancellor's
Court where it rose to the
passage to the House of
Commons. Its extraordinary
ceiling articulated the
interdependence between
the Courts and Westminster
Hall: the series of triangular
skylights illuminates the gap
between the structures while
silhouetting the transverse
beams connecting them.
The bracketed hanging arches
suggest arcaded corbel tables or
even perhaps the hammerbeam
roof of Westminster Hall. ss

206 View of the lantern of the
Court of Common Pleas,
drawn by Joseph Michael
Gandy, 1826
Pencil and watercolour:
454×281 mm
SM Vol. 61, 63

The lanterns were the most
distinctive features of the
courtrooms' picturesque
architecture and Gandy made
detailed views of all of them.
In the Court of Common Pleas
light was concentrated and
filtered through a pair of back-
to-back canopied diaphragms,
whose pendentives, like those
of the canopy in Soane's own
Breakfast Room, were pierced
by small oculi. ss

207 The presentation models of
208 the north range of the
Law Courts, 1826
Painted softwood:
500×1200×430 mm,
430×800×404 mm
SM MR32, MR30

These models were important
visual aids in Soane's campaign
to reconstruct the north range
of the Law Courts that
Bankes's Committee had
demolished. Constructed
simultaneously with the
drafting of *A Brief Statement of
the Proceedings respecting the New
Law Courts at Westminster...* in
the autumn of 1826, the models
represent his original neo-
Palladian design and a design
for transposing its elements
into Gothic equivalents.
A third, less well-made, model
shows the Committee's façade.
The neo-Palladian model also
presents the interior spaces of
the Court of King's Bench and
may be viewed in section to
convey the consequences of
the Committee's actions.
In February 1827 Soane invited
members of the legal
profession to view the models,
but their support failed to
convince the Treasury to act. ss

209 Thomas and George Martyr
Plan model of the Law Courts
and Westminster Hall, 1827
Mahogany and limewood:
65×870×670 mm
SM MR41

Soane had this plan model of
the entire judicial complex,
including Westminster Hall,
made in early 1827 in order to
clarify the spatial relationships
between the courts for the
legal professionals viewing
the façade models. The model
also shows his proposal for a
shallow wing east of the Hall
and was altered in January 1829
to show his latest design for the
north front. ss

CATALOGUE 205

Imaginative Compositions

Margaret Richardson

Figure 187

Giovanni Paolo Panini, *Views of Ancient Rome with the Artist Finishing a Copy of the Aldobrandini Wedding ('Roma Antica')*, oil on canvas, painted *c.* 1755 for the Duc de Choiseul along with an equally celebrated pendant, '*Roma Moderna*', providing an impressive summary of more recent architectural and sculptural achievements in Rome (Staatsgalerie Stuttgart)

Figure 188

Soane's ticket for Nelson's funeral at St Paul's Cathedral on 9 Jan 1806, which he attended with his fellow architect James Spiller (see cat. 211) (SM Archive Newscuttings Vol. 1805ff)

Figure 189 (opposite)

A draughtsman, perhaps Soane or Gandy, seated at a table, dwarfed by the magnificence of Soane's works (detail of cat. 210)

The imaginative compositions produced by Gandy for Soane in 1818 and 1820 are two of the most elaborate and inventive architectural perspectives ever made, both in their technical handling of perspective and light and in their imaginative presentation of Soane's architecture.

In the first, *Public and Private Buildings Executed by Sir John Soane between 1780 and 1815*, Gandy evokes the conceit and grandeur of Panini's '*Roma antica*' of 1755 (Staatsgalerie, Stuttgart), in which views of ancient Rome are displayed in paintings skied high on the walls of an immense Classical temple. He also underlines Soane's passion for collecting by presenting the architect's buildings in the form of models, paintings and architectural sculpture lit by an oil lamp as if on display in some vast Soanean gallery. Two years later Gandy painted the companion piece *Architectural Visions of Early Fancy…*, in which Soane's unbuilt projects are set in a picturesque landscape.

When first painted, the two watercolours hung in Soane's Library–Dining Room in Lincoln's Inn Fields, facing each other above the sideboard and chimneypiece, the perfect site as this was Soane's principal entertaining room where he often received clients and friends. John Britton commented upon *Public and Private Buildings* (Britton 1827, p. 34) as being 'a very interesting drawing … the idea of thus bringing together, in an abridged form, the principal features of the various works of a single architect, is both ingenious and interesting'.

FIGURE 187

By 1830 the paintings were relocated within the moveable planes on the south side of the Picture Room, where they hang to this day. As drawings they were extremely influential in later years: they may well be the source for C. R. Cockerell's famous watercolour *A Tribute to the Memory of Sir Christopher Wren* (1838), a work which depicted all of Wren's major works including many of the City churches, and may even have inspired a similar composite view of A.W. N. Pugin's buildings which formed the frontispiece to his *Apology for the Revival of Christian Architecture in England* (1843).

FIGURE 188

PLANS. ELEVATIONS AND SECTIONS
OF BUILDINGS

ERECTED IN THE COUNTIES OF
Norfolk
Suffolk
Yorkshire
Wiltshire
Warwickshire
Staffordshire
Somersetshire
et cetera

By   JOHN SOANE
Architect to the Bank of England
Member of the Academies
At Palma and Florence

LONDON

Published by Messrs TAYLOR at
the Architectural Library
Holborn

1 Bank of England, corridor to the Rotunda
2 National Debt Redemption Office, Pitt Cenotaph
3 Elizabeth Johnstone tomb, St Mary Abbot's churchyard, Kensington
4 Kelshall Rectory
5 Hamels Park, dairy
6 Design for a villa
7 Butterton farmhouse
8 Tyringham, stables
9 Lees Court, stables
10 Saxlingham Rectory
11 Castello d'acqua, Wimpole Hall
12 Unidentified
13 Bentley Priory, lodge
14 Bank of England
15 Wardour Castle Chapel
16 Dulwich Picture Gallery Mausoleum
17 Macartney House, Greenwich
18 13 Lincoln's Inn Fields, the Dome

19 Bank of England, the Rotunda
20 Unidentified
21 Bank of England, Lothbury Court
22 Yellow Drawing Room, Wimpole Hall
23 Bank of England
24 Bank of England, west side of Governor's Court
25 Gothic Library, Stowe
26 Bank of England
27 Unidentified
28 Buckingham House, Pall Mall, staircase
29 Bank of England
30 Bagshot Park, lodge
31 Pitzhanger Manor
32 Pitzhanger Manor, plan
33 Bank of England, Lothbury Façade
34 Wimpole Hall, lodge
35 Evelyn Monument, Felbridge
36 Chillington Hall
37 Baronscourt

38 Simeon Monument, Reading
39 Unidentified
40 New Bank Buildings
41 Buckingham House, Pall Mall
42 Dulwich Picture Gallery
43 Norwich, County Gaol
44 Chelsea Hospital Infirmary
45 Bentley Priory, music room
46 Bank of England, Princes Street Vestibule
47 13 Lincoln's Inn Fields, Loggia
48 Stowe, detail of a canopy and chimneypiece in the Gothic Library
49 Soane Tomb, St Pancras churchyard, London
50 Bank of England, Governor's Court
51 Port Eliot, family pew
52 2 New Bank Buildings, Princes Street
53 Unidentified
54 Claude Bosanquet Monument, St Stephen's Coleman Street

55 Bank of England, barracks
56 Cumberland Gate, Hyde Park
57 Blackfriars Bridge, Norwich
58 Bank of England, Consols Office
59 Samuel Bosanquet Monument, Leytonstone
60 Pitzhanger Manor, gateway
61 Hamels Park, lodge
62 Pitzhanger Manor, back parlour
63 Langley Park, lodges
64 Tyringham
65 Bank of England, detail of the Rotunda
66 Pitzhanger Manor, gatepier finial
67 Bank of England, detail
68 Bentley Priory, entrance hall
69 Bank of England
70 Bank of England, Consols Office stove
71 Unidentified
72 12, 13 and 14 Lincoln's Inn Fields, rear elevation

210 Joseph Michael Gandy
(1771–1843)
Public and Private Buildings Executed by Sir John Soane between 1780 and 1815, 1818
Lettered within a *tabula ansata*:
A SELECTION/OF PARTS OF BUILDINGS/PUBLIC AND PRIVATE/ERECTED/FROM THE DESIGNS OF JOHN SOANE ESQ. RA. FSA./IN THE METROPOLIS AND OTHER PLACES IN THE/UNITED KINGDOM/ BETWEEN THE YEARS/ MDCCLXXX AND MDCCCXV./QUONIAM DIU VIXIS E DENEGATUR ALI QUID FACIAMUS QUO POSSIMUS/OSTENDERE NOS VIXISSE
Pencil, pen and ink, watercolour and bodycolour:
725 × 1293 mm, in a Soane frame
Exh. 1818, Royal Academy,
no. 915
SM P87

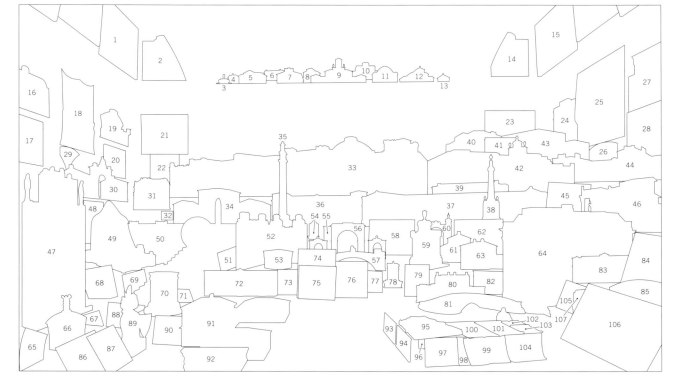

This painting was exhibited at the Royal Academy in 1818 under Gandy's name, the only one of all the paintings Gandy had executed illustrating Soane's works for which he was credited in the Academy catalogues. It shows over one hundred of Soane's buildings, all of them executed before 1815, the year of his wife's death. The buildings, depicted either as models or paintings, are assembled in a fictive room, crowned with one of Soane's great domes.

The space is lit by an oil lamp behind a reflector, allowing Gandy to display his virtuosity in the handling of light. In the centre of the composition is the Bank of England – Soane's greatest achievement. To its right is Dulwich Picture Gallery. At the extreme left is the façade of Soane's home, 13 Lincoln's Inn Fields. Beside this and draped funereally in black, is the tomb Soane designed for his wife.

In the right foreground is a table, covered in plans, and a model of the Bank. Seated at the table is a draughtsman who may be Soane, romantically dwarfed by the achievement of his genius, or perhaps Gandy himself. SA, HE, MR

CATALOGUE 210

211 *Architectural Visions of Early Fancy....*, drawn by Joseph Michael Gandy, 1820
Inscr. (on the face of a rock) *ARCHITECTURAL/Visions of early fancy,/IN the gay morning of youth/And dreams in the even.g/ of life.*
Pencil, pen and ink, watercolour and bodycolour: 735×1305 mm, in a Soane frame
Exh. 1820, Royal Academy, no. 894
SM P81

This painting brings together Soane's unbuilt works and places them in a dramatic mountainous landscape under a cloud-swept sky. The buildings are a melancholy mix of the Neoclassical dreams of his student years and early career, together with the inevitable professional disappointments.

On the left is the Triumphal Bridge, which won him the Royal Academy gold medal in 1776 and led to his Royal Travelling Scholarship. On the far left is the James King mausoleum and on the central mountain a proposal for a mausoleum for the Earl of Chatham. In the centre is a design made by Soane in Italy in 1779 for the British Senate House. In the foreground is a triumphal arch intended for Hyde Park Corner, and above the Senate House is his 1794 design for a new House of Lords. The melancholy mood is deepened by the inclusion of the funeral procession of Nelson, winding its way up the hill to the left.

This drawing was exhibited at the Royal Academy in 1820. Two years earlier Gandy had exhibited a drawing showing Soane's idea for a new palace for the Duke of Wellington. Set on top of Primrose Hill, with a cemetery and Antique ruins in the foreground, it was clearly the precursor of this painting. SA, HE, MR

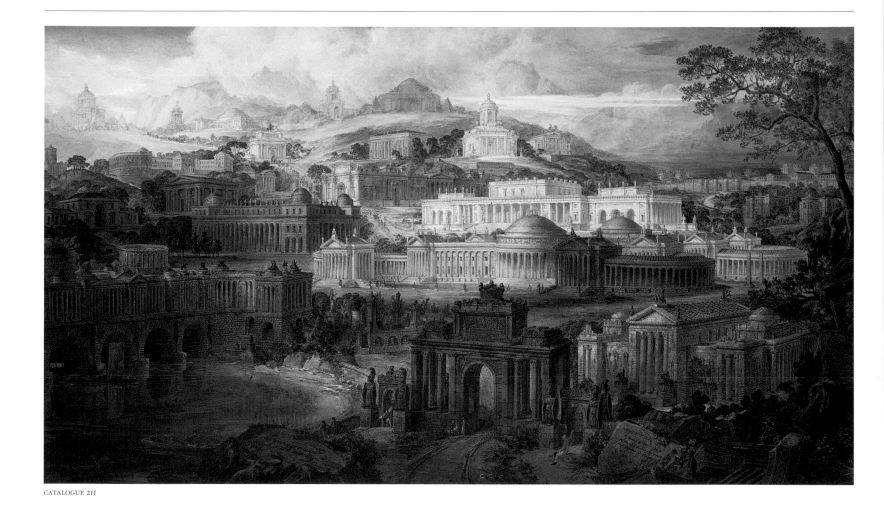

CATALOGUE 211

Chronology

Susan Palmer

1753 10 September: birth of John Soan, the youngest child of John Soan, a bricklayer from Goring-on-Thames, near Reading

1768 The young Soan meets James Peacock and, through him, enters the office of George Dance the Younger

1771 25 October: enters the Royal Academy Schools as a student of architecture

1772 Appointed to a junior post in the office of Henry Holland at a salary of £60 per annum. December: wins Royal Academy silver medal for a measured drawing of the Banqueting House, Whitehall, and exhibits for the first time at the Royal Academy

1774 Competes (unsuccessfully) for the Royal Academy gold medal

1776 December: wins the Royal Academy gold medal (subject, a Triumphal Bridge); the medal is presented by Sir Joshua Reynolds

1777 By March, Soan is living at 7 Hamilton Street, Piccadilly. His Triumphal Bridge designs are submitted by Sir William Chambers to George III, who expresses his approbation. December: General Assembly of the Royal Academy votes to recommend to the King that Soan be appointed travelling student to Italy for three years

1778 Publication of *Designs in Architecture*. 18 March: leaves for Italy in the company of Robert Brettingham and arrives in Rome on 2 May having travelled via Paris. September or October: meets Frederick Hervey, Bishop of Derry. Before 9 November: meets Piranesi, probably by letter of introduction from Sir William Chambers

1779 Takes various trips from Rome visiting Bologna, Florence, Sicily, Malta, Milan, Naples, Padua, Parma, Venice, Verona and Vicenza

1780 Invited to become architect to Frederick Hervey, Bishop of Derry (who had succeeded to the title of fourth Earl of

Bristol on 23 December 1779), at Downhill, Ireland. 10 January: elected to the Florentine Accademia del Disegno. 19 April: leaves Rome for England travelling via Switzerland and Germany and arriving at the end of June. Then to Ireland, arriving at Downhill on 27 July. 2 September: leaves Downhill, the commission having been cancelled. September and October: in Scotland and County Durham for various commissions. November: returns to London and rents rooms at 10 Cavendish Street

1781 13 March: elected to honorary membership of the Parma Academy. June: rents rooms at 53 Margaret Street. Commenced London practice

1784 21 August: marries Elizabeth (Eliza) Smith, niece of George Wyatt, a wealthy builder. Begins to spell his name with an 'e'. 1 September: takes his first pupil, John Sanders, for five years

1786 29 April: birth of John Soane junior. The family moves to 77 Welbeck Street, whose lease Soane had purchased, on 30 November

1788 16 October: appointed architect to the Bank of England. Publication of *Plans ... of Buildings executed in the Counties of Norfolk, Suffolk...*

1789 28 September: birth of George Soane

1790 23 February: death of Eliza Soane's uncle, George Wyatt, who leaves his niece a considerable sum of money in the form of property. Soane establishes a separate office at Albion Place, Blackfriars, in property inherited from Wyatt. October: Soane is appointed Clerk of Works to St James's Palace, the Houses of Parliament and other public buildings in Westminster (resigns 1793) and is elected to the Society for the Encouragement of Arts, Manufactures and Commerce (now the Royal Society of Arts)

1791 April: Soane moves his office to Great Scotland Yard, Whitehall

1792 June: purchases 12 Lincoln's Inn Fields, and begins demolition immediately, prior to complete rebuilding for his own occupation

1793 Publication of *Sketches in Architecture*

1794 18 January: Soane and his family move into 12 Lincoln's Inn Fields. Soane's office is transferred to the back of the premises

1795 Elected an Associate of the Royal Academy and a Fellow of the Society of Antiquaries. Appointed Deputy Surveyor of His Majesty's Woods and Forests (resigned 1799)

1798 Becomes a magistrate. 16 July: pays for a certificate for armorial bearings

1800 September: Pitzhanger Manor, Ealing, purchased by Soane, and rebuilt (1800–02) as a country retreat intended for the artistic education of his two sons

1802 10 February: elected a full Royal Academician. 11 February: elected to the Vestry of the Parish of St Giles-in-the-Fields

1806 28 March: elected Professor of Architecture at the Royal Academy

1807 2 March: appointed Clerk of Works to Chelsea Hospital. Purchases 13 Lincoln's Inn Fields

1808 On the site of the stables at the back of 13 Lincoln's Inn Fields, Soane begins to build an extension to his office and a domed double-height tribune for the display of plaster casts (completed 1809), which in its final form becomes the present Dome area of the Museum

1809 27 March: delivers his first lecture at the Royal Academy

1810 July: Pitzhanger Manor is sold and the contents taken to Lincoln's Inn Fields. Soane becomes a Justice of the Peace for the County of Middlesex and one of the licensing magistrates for the Holborn Division (resigns 1836)

1812 17 July: commencement of demolition of 13 Lincoln's Inn Fields; rebuilt 1812–13

1813 12 October: Soane and his wife move into 13 Lincoln's Inn Fields, No. 12 being let to the previous occupant of No. 13. Soane appointed Grand Superintendent of Works to the United Fraternity of Freemasons

1814 Meets Tsar Alexander I of Russia at the Bank of England. Soane presents him with drawings and receives a diamond ring. 15 August–5 September: visits Paris. Soane appointed Attached Architect to the Office of Works, together with John Nash and Robert Smirke

1815 10 and 24 September: George Soane writes two anonymous articles for *The Champion*, reviling his father's architecture. 22 November: death of Eliza Soane. She is buried in St Giles-in-the-Fields parish burial ground at St Pancras. A tomb is erected there to Soane's design in 1816

1816 Mrs Sarah (Sally) Conduitt became Soane's housekeeper

1819 21 August–23 September: visits Paris with a pupil, Henry Parke, and Mr and Mrs Conduitt

1821 Elected a Fellow of the Royal Society

1823 Soane purchases 14 Lincoln's Inn Fields. 21 October: death of John Soane junior

1824 14 Lincoln's Inn Fields is rebuilt to be let. On the rear portion of the site Soane builds an extension to his Museum in the form of the Picture Room and the Monk's Parlour below

1825 Becomes a member of the Athenaeum a year after its foundation

1827 Publication of John Britton's *The Union of Architecture, Sculpture and Painting*, a description of Soane's house and museum dedicated to George IV

1828 Publication of *Designs for Public and Private Buildings*

1830 Publication of the first edition of *Description of the Residence of John Soane, Architect*

1831 21 September: knighted by William IV, on the completion of the New State Paper Office, after seventeen years as Attached Architect to the Office of Works. Becomes a member of the Garrick Club, founded that same year

1832 Publication of a second edition of the *Description...*, with more plates but unchanged text

1833 20 April: the *Act for the setting up and preserving of Sir John Soane's Museum* received Royal Assent. The Act stipulates that on Soane's death, 13 Lincoln's Inn Fields and its contents are to be vested in trustees to be opened as a museum for the benefit of the public, and 12 Lincoln's Inn Fields is to be let to provide an income to support the museum. 13 Lincoln's Inn Fields is to be preserved as nearly as possible in the arrangement left by Soane. Publication of *Plans, Elevations and Perspective Views of Pitzhanger Manor House...* 16 October: retires as Architect to the Bank of England, at the age of eighty, after 45 years

1835 24 March: at a private ceremony at 13 Lincoln's Inn Fields, followed by a 'Soane Festival' at the Freemasons' Hall in the evening, Soane is presented with a gold medal by the Architects of England, paid for by 350 subscribers, in recognition of his services to architecture. *Memoirs of the Professional Life of an Architect* privately printed. 150 copies of a revised and enlarged *Description...* printed and privately circulated, 1835–56

1837 20 January: death of Soane; he is buried a few days later in the family tomb at St Pancras. Under the terms of his will, George Bailey, a former pupil and his chief clerk, is appointed first curator of the museum, and Sally Conduitt, Soane's housekeeper, the first Inspectress

Chronological List of Soane's Building Projects

Stephen Astley

This list comprises the principal architectural works of Sir John Soane. It does not include student projects such as the Triumphal Bridge, nor does it list the many buildings Soane surveyed for leases or for legal cases. Also excluded are the smaller works which were simply repairs to existing buildings.

The date under which a project first appears is the date when Soane started work on the commission. Subsequent building campaigns on the same site are listed in the first entry. Each entry is arranged in the following way: location | client | nature of works | outcome. Entries are arranged alphabetically within years. To save space the following abbreviations have been used:
alts = alterations;
dem = demolished;
exec = executed;
exts = extensions;
ints = interiors;
unex = unexecuted;
? = not known.

In cases where the archives left by Soane are inconclusive, or where physical evidence has been demolished or rebuilt, the extent of Soane's contribution (or even if the work was executed at all), is sometimes not clear. Sometimes Soane's designs were executed by a local builder and so what was built is a local interpretation of Soane's drawings.

It should also be stressed that this list is not the final word on the subject. New discoveries are still being made, especially where Soane's work has survived subsequent remodelling. Sadly, Soane's work is still being demolished, such as in 1997 at Colomberie House, St Helier, C.I., or remodelled, as at Cricket St Thomas, Somerset (1998–99). Vigilance is clearly needed.

This list owes much to pioneering work by Dorothy Stroud and Sir Howard Colvin and also to the continuing work of my colleagues at the Soane Museum. I am especially grateful to Ptolemy Dean who read this list when it was in draft form and made many helpful suggestions. His book *Sir John Soane and the Country Estate*, London, 1999, provides an illustrated gazetteer of Soane's country-house practice.

1779 Kingston Hall (Kingston Lacy), Dorset | Henry Bankes the Younger | alts | unex

1780 Allanbank, Berwicks | John Stuart, later 4th Baronet | designs for alts to house; designs for new village | unex

Castle Eden, Co. Durham | Rowland Burdon, MP | alts etc. including new porch | remodelled

Downhill, Co. Londonderry | 4th Earl of Bristol, Bishop of Derry | alts | unex

London, Battersea | Commissioners for Prisons | competition design for new prison | unex

1781 Hamels Park, Herts | Hon. Philip Yorke, later 3rd Earl of Hardwicke | alts to house; gateway, lodges, dairy (1783), offices and gardener's cottage; 1784: crescent of houses | dairy dem, house remodelled 1830–40; offices, lodges and cottage extant; 1784: crescent unex

London, Adams Place, Southwark | Francis Adams | new shops and tenements | dem

London, Grove Lane, Walthamstow, house (possibly Clevelands) | James Neave | alts and exts; if Clevelands then dem 1960

London, 7 New Cavendish Street (later 63) | Hon. Philip Yorke, later 3rd Earl of Hardwicke | alts and decorations | house survives much altered

London, Petersham Lodge, Richmond | Thomas Pitt, later 1st Baron Camelford | repairs and alts | dem

London, 148 Piccadilly | Hon. William Tollemache | completion and decorations of house | dem 1972

Spencerswood, Berks | William Sotheby | design for a house; later design for a library | probably unex

Unlocated | Lady Rivers | four designs for garden buildings | ?

1782 Belvedere, Kent | Sir Sampson Gideon | designs for garden buildings | unex

Coombe House, nr. Kingston, London | Hon. Wilbraham Tollemache | repairs and alts; later acquired by Lord Hawkesbury (future 2nd Earl of Liverpool) for whom Soane did further alts 1801–09 | dem 1933

London, Berkeley Square, house | Hon. Mrs Perry | alts to house | probably exec and dem

1783 Bath, Powis Place, house | Francis Adams | advised on house | any works probably unex

Burn Hall, Co. Durham | George Smith | new house and cow barn | house unex; cow barn extant, now monastery

Burnham Westgate Hall, Norfolk | Thomas Pitt, later 1st Baron Camelford | alts to house and stables; new farm buildings and a prospect tower | exec; house and stables extant; prospect tower unex

Dunmow, Essex | Michael Pepper | designs for a villa | probably unex

Letton Hall, Norfolk | Brampton Gurdon Dillingham | new house and domestic offices | extant but remodelled

London, Rectory Manor, Walthamstow | William Cooke | alts including new kitchen and possibly new gateway | dem c. 1897

London, 42 Wimpole Street | John Stuart of Allanbank | alts and decorations | exec

Malvern Hall, Warwicks | Henry Greswold Lewis | alts including new wings and offices; 1798: designs for barn (936 Warwick Road, Solihull) | remodelled 1899; offices probably unex; house and barn extant

Marlesford, Suffolk | George Smith | cow house | exec and burnt down 1942

Norwich, Norfolk, Blackfriars Bridge | Norwich City Corporation | new bridge | survives but altered c. 1931

Tyttenhanger, Herts | Hon. Mrs Yorke | repairs to house; 1789 further repairs | exec

1784 Binfield, Berks, unlocated site | Dr Teighe | designs for farmhouse | exec but unidentified

Cockley Cley, Norfolk | J. R. Dashwood | house and offices | house unex and rebuilt 1870–71

Costessey, Norfolk | Sir William Jerningham Bart. | designs for stables and dove house | stables burnt 1996; ruins remain; dove house possibly unex

Earsham, Norfolk | William Wyndham | kitchen wing and detached music room or greenhouse | extant

Herringfleet, Suffolk | John Leathes | alts | probably unex

Langley Park, Norfolk | Sir Thomas Proctor-Beauchamp Bart. | entrance gateways and lodges; 1788: repairs to roof of house | extant; house remodelled

London, Park Street, house | Hon. Philip Yorke | repairs to house | ?

London, 48 Park Street (?) | Hon. James Hamilton, later 9th Earl and 1st Marquis of Abercorn | repairs and decorations | dem c. 1900

London, St Mary Abbot's churchyard, Kensington | The Earl of Bellamont | tomb for Miss Elizabeth Johnstone | extant

London, St Mary's Church, Walthamstow | William Cooke | unspecified works | unidentified

London, 18 Savile Row | Lady Banks | alts to drawing room | dem

Saxlingham Rectory, Saxlingham, Norfolk | Revd John Gooch | Design for new rectory | extant with later exts

Tendring Hall, Suffolk | Admiral Sir Joshua Rowley Bart. | new house and offices | dem 1955, except for porch and walled garden

Taverham Hall, Norfolk | M. S. Branthwayte | internal alts | rebuilt 1858; walled garden extant

1785 Benacre Hall, Suffolk | Sir Thomas Gooch | design for lodges | unex

Blundeston House, Suffolk | Nathaniel Rix | new house | extant but mutilated

Chillington, Staffs | Thomas Giffard | alts to house, new chapel and bridge | house extant; chapel and bridge unex

Felbridge, Surrey | James Evelyn | monument in grounds of house to Mr Evelyn's parents | extant but moved in 1927 to Lemmington Hall, Northumberland

Hingham, Norfolk, St Andrew's Church | Revd P. Woodhouse | alts to chancel, and new reredos | reredos now removed

Little Green, West Sussex | Thomas Peckham Phipps | alts and stables; new house | unex (?), house remodelled 1912

London, Hereford Street | 1st Baron Camelford | conversion of two houses to premises for Dilettanti Society | unex

Nayland, Suffolk, St James Church | Mr Alston | internal alts including pews | exec by local builder

Norwich, Norfolk | Hellesdon Bridge | Norwich City Corporation | unex (?)

Piercefield, Gwent | George Smith | additions, and new façade | executed; now derelict

Shottisham Hall (now Shotesham Hall), Norfolk | Robert Fellowes | new house and domestic offices | extant

Solihull, Warwicks | W. Moland | design for a bridge | unex

1786 Beauport, Surrey | General Murray | alts; new greenhouse and obelisk; 1794: further alts for James Bland Burgess | exec (?); remodelled 1923

Boconnoc, Cornwall | 1st Baron Camelford | alts to house and stables; new top on obelisk in park | survives with some alts

Castle Hill, Devon | 1st Earl Fortescue | alts to house and offices | house burnt 1934 and rebuilt; offices survive

Cricket St Thomas, Somerset, Cricket Lodge | 1st Viscount Bridport | alts and new kitchen wing; offices and estate buildings; 1801–07: further alts to house; 1814: monument in St Thomas's Church | some work survives but much altered in 19th century, 1906 and 1998–99; monument extant but moved

Great Horksley House, Essex | Mrs Gibbs | alts | unidentified

Hockerill, Herts | Ralph Winter | small house, offices and cow house | exec but unlocated

Holwood House, Kent | Rt. Hon. William Pitt | alts and additions; 1795: further works | dem 1823; cellars survive

Lees Court, Kent | Hon. Lewis Thomas Watson | alts to house, new stables and domestic offices | all extant; house remodelled 1910

London, 16 Bedford Square | Thomas Wildman | alts | probably exec

London, Forest House, Leytonstone | Samuel Bosanquet | alts to house | dem

London, 37 Pall Mall | Royal Exchange Assurance | new building or remodelling of existing | exec but now?

London, St Stephen's Church, Coleman Street | Samuel Bosanquet | monument to Claude Bosanquet | destroyed 1940

Mulgrave Hall (now Castle), Yorks | 2nd Baron Mulgrave | additions and alts; stables | remodelled 1804 but some Soane work survives; stables extant but altered

Nackington, Kent | Richard Milles | alts to house | dem c. 1922

Ossington Hall, Notts | John Dennison | alts and additions to house; prospect tower, temple and lodges | all probably unex, except for lodges which are extant but remodelled; house dem 1963

Ryston Hall, Norfolk | Edward Roger Pratt | remodelled including new wings; lodge | extant; lodge unex

Tofts, Norfolk | Payne Galwey | alts to house and new keeper's lodge | dem 1950s

Unlocated house | William Dinwody | additions to house | ?

Worlingham Hall, Suffolk | Robert Sparrow | designs for house | unex

1787 Fonthill, Wilts | William Beckford | picture gallery and other works | unex; house dem 1807

Lyndford Hall, Norfolk | George Nelthorpe | alts and additions to house | unex (?); house rebuilt 1856–61

Skelton Hall, Yorks | John Hall (later Wharton) | rebuilding of house, alts to house, new kitchen wing, lodges and stables | rebuilding unex; all else exec and extant, except lodges which are possibly unex and now dem

1788 Bemerton, Wilts, Rectory | Dr William Coxe | alts | probably exec

Bentley Priory, Middlesex | Hon. James Hamilton, later 9th Earl and 1st Marquis Abercorn | extension and remodelling of house | although much altered some Soane work survives

Bury St Edmunds, Suffolk, 81 Guildhall Street | James Oakes | extension | extant

Gawdy Hall, Norfolk | Revd Gervase Holmes | alts to house | dem 1939

Halsnead, Lancs | Richard Willis | new façade and portico | house dem 1932

Hetherset, Norfolk | J. F. Iselin | alternative designs for house | unex

Honing Hall, Norfolk | Thomas Cubitt | alts | extant

Kelshall Rectory, Herts | Revd Thomas Waddington | alts to rectory | extant

London, Bank of England | The Governor and Court | minor repair works. 1791–92: Bank Stock Office; 1793–97: Four and Five Per Cent (later Consols Dividend) Office; 1794–95: Rotunda; 1796–1800: Bullion Gateway and Lothbury Court; 1798–99: Consols Transfer Office; 1802–06: Accountants' Office; 1803–05: Governor's Court; 1803–05:

Lothbury Wall and Tivoli Corner; 1803–08: Princes Street Vestibule; 1806–08: Bullion Office; 1816–26: Threadneedle Street Façade and Bartholomew Lane Façade; 1818–23: New Four Per Cent (later Colonial) Office and Old Four Per Cent (later Dividend) Office; many subsequent works to 1830 | dem apart from c. 75% of external wall

London, Pembroke Lodge, Richmond Park | Countess of Pembroke | alts and additions; 1796: further works | some Soane work survives

London, Queen Anne Street West, house | William Martin | alts and decorations | exec

London, St James's Church, Piccadilly | Vestry of St James's Parish | alts and improvements | probably unex

London, 21 St James's Square | Mrs Sturt | alts and additions | house rebuilt in last century

Norwich Hospital, Norfolk | through Robert Fellowes | advised on alts | exec

Shadwell Lodge, Norfolk | Robert Buxton | alts to house | remodelled c. 1856

Unlocated house in Norfolk, probably Melton Constable | Jacob Astley | alts and additions | probably exec but unidentified

Wardour Castle, Wilts | 8th Baron Arundell of Wardour | enlargement of chapel | extant

Wokefield, Berks | Mrs Brocas | alts to house and new gateway | house remodelled c. 1845; gateway dem

1789 Chilton Lodge, Berks | William Morland | new house | dem 1800

Fairford House, Glos | J. R. Barker | alts to house and outbuildings | dem 1957

Gunthorpe Hall, Norfolk | Charles Collyer | new house | extant but remodelled late 19th century

London, Westhill, Wandsworth | D. H. Rucker | alts to house | probably unex

Norwich Castle, County Gaol, Norwich, Norfolk | Norfolk Magistrates | remodelled and new wing | dem 1825

Simonds' Brewery, Reading, Berks | William Blackall Simonds | new residence, offices, brewhouse and stables; 1803: office building; 1804: house in Castle Street | dem 1900; Castle Street house probably unex

Stanmore, Middlesex, Old Church of St John the Evangelist | at Lord Abercorn's request | new gallery | church now a ruin but Soane work can be identified

Sydney Lodge, Hamble, Hants | Hon. Mrs Yorke | new house and offices; 1820: alts | extant but offices remodelled; 1820 alts unex

Tawstock Court, Devon | Sir Bourchier Wrey Bart. | alts to exterior and new staircase | altered but much extant

Wreatham Hall, Norfolk | William Colhoun | designs for new house | probably unex

1790 Castle Forbes, Co. Longford, Ireland | Lady Granard | dower house | unex (?)

Colne Park, Essex | Philip Hills | memorial column for M. R. Hills | extant

London, 23 or 24 Bruton Street | Sir William Milner | alts and extensions | (?)

London, Buckingham House, 91 Pall Mall | 1st Marquis of Buckingham | remodelled; 1813: further alts | dem 1908

London, Leicester Square | designs for Royal Opera House | unex

London, 103 Pall Mall | Mr Crooke | design for a shop front | dem 1836

Norwich, Surrey Street, house | John Patteson | alts and additions | extant

Steephill, Isle of Wight | Hon. Wilbraham Tollemache | alts | rebuilt in 1830s

Wimpole Hall, Cambs | 3rd Earl of Hardwicke | alts to house; domestic offices and estate building; 1820 alts to parish church | extant apart from Arrington Lodge, the castello d'acqua, hen house and all but one estate house, which are dem; 1820: alts to church unex

Wood Eaton Manor, Oxon | John Weyland | new porch and kitchen wing | extant

Wycombe Abbey, Bucks | 3rd Earl of Shelburne | alts and new stables | alts unex; stables possibly exec, dem 1962

1791 Baronscourt, Co. Tyrone | 1st Marquis of Abercorn | major alts and extensions | centre burnt 1796, rebuilt 1837–41; little by Soane survives

Cambridge | Vice Chancellor, University of Cambridge | Senate House, new Museum, etc. | unex

London, 23 Hill Street | 1st Earl Fortescue | alts and decorations | destroyed WW2

London, House of Commons | Office of Works | supervised new plumbing, heating and ventilation | burnt 1834

London, 19 Old Cavendish Street | Edward Foxhall | shop front | dem

London, 56 Pall Mall | Ransom, Moreland and Hammersley | alts, decorations and extension | dem

London, 147 Piccadilly | Charles-Alexandre de Calonné | new chimneypiece | dem

London, St James's Place, house | Robert Smith, later 1st Baron Carrington | alts | exec and probably dem

London, Whichcotes (?), Hendon | John Cornwall | repairs and decorations | if Whichcotes, dem

Moggerhanger, Beds | Godfrey Thornton | alts to house, unex; various schemes including kitchens, lodge, stables and offices to 1809 when remodelled for son, Stephen Thornton | extant

Netheravon House, Wilts | Michael Hicks Beach | alts and new lodges | remodelled; lodges dem this century

Unlocated country house | Hon. Henry Fane | new porch | probably exec

Williamstrip Park, Glos | Michael Hicks Beach | alts and new stables | remodelled 1946: stables extant but altered

Wiston Hall, Suffolk | Samuel Beachcroft | additions | alts in 1860s but Soane work survives

1792 Arrington, Cambs, The Hardwicke Arms Inn | 3rd Earl of Hardwicke | alts | exec

Berry Hill House, Bucks | Lady Wynn | extension to house | exec but dem

Buckland, Berks | Sir John Throckmorton | alts including new library | unex

Cambridge, Caius College | The Syndics | restoration and alts to hall | executed, remodelled 19th century and recently partially reinstated

Cambridge, St John's College | The Syndics | repairs to college | dem

Cambridge, Senate House Yard | The Vice Chancellor | improvements | railings survive

London, Cloak Lane, house | J. F. Iselin | repairs and alts | dem

London, 27 Fenchurch Street | Charles Thellusson | repairs and decorations | dem

London, 14 Hereford Street (?) | Joseph Smith | repairs and decorations | exec

London, 12 Lincoln's Inn Fields | the architect | new house and office | house extant; office, superseded by first picture room, rebuilt 1889–90

London, 17 Mark Lane | Samuel Boddington | alts to counting house | executed and dem

London, 15 Philpot Lane | P. I. Thelluson | repairs and decorations | dem

London, St James's Palace | Office of Works | new Guard Room | dem

London, 1 Upper Grosvenor Street | Mrs Brocas | repairs and decorations; 1819 further works | dem 1957

London, Wandsworth Common, unlocated house | Benjamin Cole | alts to house | ?

Norwich, Norfolk, unlocated house | Alderman Crowe | designs for house | ?

Sulby Hall, Northants | René Payne | remodelling of house; 1793: alts to farmhouse at Dunton; 1794: new stables; 1798: bridge; 1824: further alts | exec; house remodelled c. 1830 and dem c. 1953; stables extant

Tyringham, Bucks | William Praed | house, stables, gateway, bridge, garden structures and chapel | extant apart from unex chapel; house altered internally and dome added

Unlocated | Sir Frederick Eden | alternative designs for a villa | ?

Winchester, Hants, The King's House | Commissioners of HM Treasury | repairs and alts | exec, but burnt 1894

Wydiall, Herts | Mr Ellis | designs for new cottages | probably unex

1793 Barselton House, Herts | Hon. Mrs York | minor alts | exec

Dunton Bassett, Leics | René Payne | new cottage | exec but unlocated

London, 6–7 Old Palace Yard | G. Rose and H. Compton, Clerks of the Parliament | alts | extant

London, Paddington, Grand Junction Canal | ?Bishop of London's Estate | decorative arch | probably unex

London, 104 Pall Mall | Lady Louisa Manners | alts and repairs | dem c. 1837

Sheerness, Kent | The Levant Merchants | Lazaretto | unex

Unlocated | Richard Crichton | design for house | unex

Wimbourne, Dorset, St Giles' House | 5th Earl of Shaftsbury | alts to house and offices | probably unex

1794 Cairness House, Aberdeenshire | Charles Gordon | new portico | exec but not quite to Soane's design

Cuffnels, Hants | George Rose | decorations, refacing, new orangery | dem 1957

London, Houses of Parliament | Office of Works | New House of Lords | unex

London, 51 Lincoln's Inn Fields | John Pearce | alts | dem 1904

Pitshill, Sussex | William Mitford | alts | exec in modified form by local builder (?); remodelled 1830s–40s

Reading, Berks, London Place | W. B. Simonds | terrace of houses | probably unex

Sunbury House, Middlesex | Roger Boehm | alts | dem

Sunderland, Co. Durham | Rowland Burdon | advised on Wear bridge | exec but to another's design

Unlocated | Edward Darrell | design for chimneypiece | ?

Unlocated | R. Gervas Kerr | design for portico | ?

1795 Bagdon (or Savernake Lodge), Wilts | 1st Earl of Ailesbury | conversion of lodge to house | survives in modified form

Dunninald House, Angus | David Scott | alternative designs for house | unex

Hinton St George, Som | 4th Earl Poulett | alts and new lodge | unex

Little Green, Surrey | T. P. Phipps | designs for alts and new house | unex

London, 57 and 58 Lincoln's Inn Fields | Estate of Lord Mansfield | division into two houses | exec; some Soane work survives including porch

London, 25 (later 70) Portland Place | Sir Alan, later 1st Lord Gardner | alts; 1810 further alts | dem

London, 21 St James's Square | 5th Duke of Leeds | completion of house | dem 1934

London, 56 South Audley Street | Miss Anguish | repairs and decorations | exec but later rebuilt

London, 429 Strand | Westminster Insurance on Lives | alts | probably exec

London, 12 Stratton Street | Col. Thomas Graham, later Baron Lynedoch | new house | dem this century

Richmond Park, Surrey | Office of Works | lodge and gateway | probably unex

Southgate, Middlesex | Samuel Boddington | alts | exec and dem

Southgate, Middlesex | John Grey | new gardener's house and lodge | exec and dem

Unlocated | Mr Henderson | cottage | ?

Winchester, Hants, Hyde Close | Revd Mr Richards | new Academy | extant but altered

1796 London, 22 Bedford Square | Hon. John Eliot | decorations | exec

London, 12 Downing Street | Hon. John Eliot | repairs and decorations | exec but later remodelled

London, St Botolph, Aldgate | Vestry Committee | survey of steeple and alts | ?

London, Park Lane, house | 2nd Earl of Mornington | alts | dem

Reading, Berks, Greyfriars Rectory | Lancelot Austwick | new rectory | dem 1959 apart from flanking walls and railings

Tortworth Court, Glos | 3rd Baron Ducie | alternative designs for lodges, and prospect tower | unex

1797 Cardigan House, Richmond Hill, Surrey | Duke of Clarence | extension | house dem 1970

London, Constitution Hill | Office of Woods and Forests | lodge and gateway | dem

London, 44 (later 49) Grosvenor Square | Countess of Pembroke | alts | 1801 and 1805 further alts for Robert Knight | dem 1925

London, Hyde Park, Cumberland Gate and lodge | Office of Woods and Forests | dem

London, Strand | ? | house and shop on south side by Strand Lane | unex

North Mymms Park, Herts | 5th Duke of Leeds | alts, greenhouse, dairy and lodges | house remodelled 1893; rest remodelled

Unlocated | ?Miss Backwell | design for almshouses | probably unex

Weston, Hants | W. Moffat | alts to house | house dem

1798 Bagshot Park, Surrey | Prince William, Duke of Clarence (later William IV) | alts and new lodge | house and lodges rebuilt 1877

Betchworth Castle, Surrey | Henry Peters | alts to castle; new domestic offices | castle ruinous, lodge and dairy dem; stables (1799) converted to housing

Buchanan Street, Glasgow | Robert Dennistoun | new house | dem

London, Fountain Court | W. A. Jackson | repairs; 1802: new building | dem in last century

London, 34 Gower Street | Mrs Peters | alts to house and stables | dem

London, Heathfield Lodge, Acton | John Winter | alts to house; two tenements | house and one tenement dem 1969

London, Wandsworth, Clapham Common | Thomas Abbot Green | alts | exec

Methven, Perthshire | Col. Graham, later Baron Lynedoch | farmhouse and offices | offices extant but derelict

Richmond Park, Surrey, Thatched House Lodge | Office of Woods and Forests | alts | extant

Stanmore, Middlesex, 'Thieves Hole' | Mrs Brewer | alts | probably unex

1799 Aynhoe Park, Northants | Richard Cartwright | alts and additions | extant

Cosgrove Hall, Bucks | Mr Mansel | new house and offices | probably unex

Down Ampney House, Glos | Hon. John Eliot | alts | executed by local builder; extant

Dublin, Bank of Ireland | The Court of Directors | new bank | unex

London, 7 Austin Friars | Commercial Commissioners | repairs and decorations | exec

London, Clapham, house | Mrs Adams | alts | probably unex

London, Frederick's Place | J. W. and I. Whitmore | alts | extant

London, 24 George Street | Dr Pemberton | alts | house dem this century

London, 22 (later 25) Grosvenor Square | 1st Marquis of Abercorn | alts and repairs | dem 1957

London, 6 and 7 Kings Arms Yard | Thornton, Bayley and Armyard | repairs and decorations | exec

London, Lincoln's Inn Fields | Trustees of the Fields | terrace of houses | unex

London, 12 Mansfield Street | Charles Mills | alts | dem

London, 22 St James's Square, | Samuel Thornton | alts; 1805 and 1811: further work | dem 1847

1800 Albury Park, Surrey | Samuel Thornton | alts; new bridge, church window and stables | remodelled 1842 but some ints survive; stables dem; bridge and church window probably unex

Bath, Seymour Street | Christopher Barnard | new eating room | houses bombed in WW2

London, 67 (?) Grosvenor Square | Duchess of Leeds | decorations | exec

London, 54 Old Broad Street | Stephen Thornton | alts | dem

London, 50 Park Street | Henry Peters | repairs | dem

London, Pitzhanger Manor, Ealing | the architect | house remodelled; 'ruins' in garden | house extant; gateway, cottage, bridge and garden layout extant; ruins and kitchen dem

Micklefield Hall, Bucks | Elisha Briscoe | alts | extant but house remodelled in the early 20th century

Moat House, or Moor House, Rickmansworth, Herts | T. H. Earle | alts and additions | probably unex

Wall Hall, Herts | G. W. Thellusson | new entrance and rooms | unex

1801 Aldenham House, Herts | Lady Dalling | repairs and decorations | exec but remodelled in 1870s

Bramley, Hants, Church of St James | Mrs Brocas | new chapel | extant

London, Bartholomew Lane | Down, Thornton and Free | alts and decorations | dem

London, Chelsea | Gen. Wilford | alts to house | unknown if exec; house dem 1854

London, 189 Fleet Street | W. M. Praed | new banking house | dem 1923

London, 22 New Norfolk Street (now Dunraven Street) | J. Hammet | alts | exec but house remodelled

London, 54 Park Street | Kenelm Digby | alts and repairs | exec

Norwood Hall, Middlesex | John Robins | new house | house extant but remodelled early 20th century

South Hill Park, Berks | George Canning | alts | exec but house remodelled 1853

1802 London, Fountain Court, Aldermanbury | W. A. Jackson, Peters and Co. | new premises | dem

London, Macartney House, Greenwich | Hon. G. F. Lyttleton | alts and additions | much work survives

Port Eliot, Cornwall | Edward, 1st Baron Eliot, then Hon. John Eliot, 2nd Baron and later Earl of St Germans | remodelled house; new stables, bridge, pew in church | house remodelled in 19th century but much remains; stables extant; bridge unex; pew extant but altered

Uxbridge, Middlesex, Crown and Treaty Inn | conversion by James Spiller; Soane was consultant

Wakefield, All Saints Church | ? | report on spire | report submitted

1803 Little Hill Court, Herts | Mrs Saunders | internal alts | unlocated; possibly unex

London, Breadalbane House, Park Lane | 4th Earl of Breadalbane | alts | dem 1876

London, 19 Curzon Street | Sir John Sebright Bart. | alts | extant

London, Hampstead | Daniel Bayley | alts to house | ?

London, 14 Upper Grosvenor Street | Thomas Raikes | alts | dem 1908

1804 Beechwood, Herts | Sir John Sebright Bart | alts | unex

London, Cedar Court, Roehampton, | John Thomson | alts and extension | dem 1910

London, Palmer's Green, house | Thomas Lewis | alts and decorations | exec and dem

Ramsey Abbey, Cambs | W. H. Fellowes | house remodelled; new stables | house extant but remodelled 1838; lodges, if exec, dem

Reading, Market Place | Edward Simeon | monument | extant but has public WC abutting

1805 Astrop Park, Northants | Revd W. S. Willes | additions and alts; lodge | remodelled 19th century and wings dem 1961; internal alts survive; lodge dem

Banbury, Oxon | James King | two designs for house | unex

Combe House, Devon | Reymundo Putt | alts; 1811: new house | alts and house unex

London, 6 Audley Square | Richard Benyon | repairs | exec

London, St Giles-in-the-Fields | Parish Council | new lobby and porch | unex

London, 33 St James's Square | 2nd Baron Eliot | alts; 1817: further alts | remodelled; only traces of Soane left

Stowe, Bucks | 1st Marquis of Buckingham | library and vestibule; 1818: alts to family apartments | library and vestibule extant; 1818 alts unex

1806 Englefield House, Berks | Richard Benyon | unidentified repairs | exec but house remodelled 1823 and 1850

London, 4 Fredericks Place | Thomas Lewis | alts | exec

London, Leytonstone, St Mary's churchyard | Bosanquet family | monument to Samuel Bosanquet | reduced 1957, only base survives

1807 Belfast, Northern Ireland | Management Committee | new Academical Institution | executed in simplified form and extant

London, 38 Charlotte (now Hallam) Street | Sir Francis Bourgeois | mausoleum | dem c. 1812

London, 4 Dean (now Deanery) Street | Robert Knight | alts to house | dem

London, 34 (later 39) Grosvenor Street | Mrs Benyon | alts | dem 1962

London, Royal Hospital, Chelsea | The Governor and Board | repairs; 1810: Infirmary; 1814: stables; 1815: alts to Clerk of Works's house; 1815: bakehouse; 1817: gardener's house and gatehouse; 1818: secretary's office; 1821: surgeon's house; 1829: Chelsea Gate; 1834: garden shelter | Infirmary bombed and dem 1941; Clerk of Works's house dem 1856; much else survives

London, Princes Street | Bank of England | New Bank Buildings (5 residences) | dem 1891

Oxford, Brasenose College | The Seniority of the College | alts; new building on High Street | alts exec but remodelled 1980s; new building unex

Whitley Abbey, Warwickshire | 1st Viscount Hood | alts and extensions | dem 1953

1808 Hagley, Worcs, Church of St John Baptist | 2nd Baron Lyttleton | memorial urn | truncated 1858

London, 13 Lincoln's Inn Fields | the architect | rebuilding of rear premises; 1812: house rebuilt | both extant

London, Southwark Cathedral | Newland family | monument to Abraham Newland | extant

Taymouth Castle, Perthshire | 4th Earl of Breadalbane | alts | unex

1809 Butterton Hall, Staffs | Thomas Swinnerton | alts | unex

London, Fife House, Whitehall | 2nd Earl of Liverpool | alts and further work over several years | dem 1869

Mells Park, Somerset | Col. Thomas Horner | alts to house and offices; 1815: further alts | house dem 1917; offices extant but remodelled

1810 Colomberie House, St Helier, Jersey, C.I. | Clement Hemery | alts | dem 1998; some elements saved and stored

Norwich | Norwich City Corporation | lamp standard | unex

Unlocated | Sir John Coxe Hippisley | new cottage; 1812: new seat designs | ?

1811 Everton House, Beds | William Astell | alts | dem 20th century

Lampton (?) | ? | new villa and bungalow | ?

London, Chiswick, Church of St Nicholas | Mrs de Loutherbourg | tomb for Philippe Jacques de Loutherbourg | extant

London, Dulwich Picture Gallery and Mausoleum | The Master and Wardens of Dulwich College | picture gallery and mausoleum | extant; damaged 1944 and rebuilt; being extended 1999

London, 22 (later 18) Park Lane | John Robins | new house | bombed and dem 1942

Walmer, Kent, St Mary's (Old) Church | request of 2nd Earl of Liverpool | enlargement | unex

Walmer, Kent, Walmer Cottage | Captain Lee | extension | executed but remodelled

Unlocated | Captain Mason | new house | ?

1813 Isle of Wight | Sir John Coxe Hippisley | alts to unlocated house | ?

London, Freemasons' Hall, Great Queen Street | Grand Master's Lodge | repairs; 1821: new gallery; 1828: new Council Chamber and kitchen | dem 1863

Petworth House, Sussex | 3rd Earl of Egremont | portico; 1816: prospect tower | both unex

Ringwould House, Kent | Revd John Monins | new house | extant

1814 Putteridgebury, Herts | John Sowerby | alts and new stables | house exec but remodelled 1910; stables partly extant

1815 Butterton Grange Farm House, Staffs | Thomas Swinnerton | new house and stables | extant

Camolin Park, Co. Wexford, Ireland | Viscount Valentia | alts and extension | unex

Sudeley Castle, Glos | 2nd Marquis of Buckingham | alts; 1819: further alts | both unex

1816 London, 13 (later 14) Grosvenor Square | 2nd Lord Berwick | alts | dem

London, St Giles's Burial Ground, St Pancras Gardens | the architect | Soane family tomb | extant

London, Westminster | National Monument; 5 designs to 1818 | unex

London, Whitehall, Carrington House | 1st Baron Carrington | stable block; 1818: alts | dem 1886

London, St Albans Street, St James's | 1st Earl of St Germans | stabling | dem

1817 London, Lambeth, St Mary's Church | Mrs Storace | memorial to Anna Storace | extant

London, Snaresbrook | Jeremiah Harman | new verandah | ?

1818 Canada | William Halton, Provincial Agent | Government House for Upper Canada | unex

London, Old Jewry | Commissioners for the Reduction of the National Debt | National Debt Redemption and Life Annuities Office | dem c. 1900

London, 3 St James's Square | 4th Earl of Hardwicke | extension | dem 1930

London, 62 Threadneedle Street | Grote, Prescott and Grote | alts to bank | exec

London, Upper Clapton, house | Thomas Bros | alts and repairs | executed and ?dem

Marden Hill, Herts | C. G. Thornton | alts and new porch | extant

1820 London, Marylebone, Holy Trinity Church | Commissioners for Church Building | new church | 1926 and 1955 alts but largely extant

London, 16 Montague Place | Henry Hase | alts | exec

London, 14 New Burlington Street | Admiral Sir Joseph Yorke | alts | unex

London, Palace of Westminster | Office of Works | repairs; 1822: Royal Entrance and Gallery, Library and Committee Rooms | partly fire-damaged 1834; dem 1851

London, 156–170 Regent Street | John Robins and others | block of shops and house | dem

Wotton House, Bucks | 2nd Marquis of Buckingham | remodelled after fire | extant with some alts

1821 Fan Grove, Berks | Vice Admiral Sir Henry Hotham | alts | probably unex

London, Portugal Street | Commissioners for the Insolvent Debtors' Court | New Debtors' Court and Offices | dem 1911

Wootton Manor, Somerset | Sir Alexander Hood | additions | unex

1822 London, St Peter's Church, Walworth | Commissioners for Church Buildings | new church | extant

London, Westminster | Office of Works | The Law Courts | dem 1883

Pell Wall, Staffs | Purney Sillitoe | new house, offices, coach house, gardener's house and walled kitchen garden, brick lodge and Gothic lodge | 1861 remodelled and enlarged; 1986 burnt; shell under restoration; lodges extant but extended; coach house and gardener's house extant

1823 London, 14 Lincoln's Inn Fields | the architect | rebuilding of rear premises; 1824: house rebuilt | extant

London, Whitehall | Office of Works | Board of Trade and Privy Council Offices | remodelled 1846; some ints survive

1824 London, Old Foreign Office | Office of Works | alts | some work survives

1825 London, 10, 11 and 12 Downing Street | Office of Works | alts including new dining room and anteroom at No. 10, and new dining room (originally breakfast room) at No. 11 | extant

1826 Birmingham, branch bank | Bank of England | repairs and alts | 1829: further alts; dem in 19th century

Bristol, branch bank | Bank of England | repairs and alts | 1827: further alts; bombed in WW2 and dem

Exeter, branch bank | Bank of England | repairs and alts | minor alts; bombed in last war and dem

Gloucester, branch bank | Bank of England | repairs and alts | exec and ?extant

Hull, branch bank | Bank of England | repairs and alts | minor alts; remodelled in 19th century

Leeds, branch bank | Bank of England | repairs and alts | 1827: proposed alts unex

Liverpool, branch bank | Bank of England | repairs and alts | proposed extension: 1834; unex, ?dem

London, Bethnal Green, St John's Church | Commissioners for Church Building | new church | remodelled 1870 and 1888

Manchester, branch bank | Bank of England | repairs and alts | exec; 1830: further work; dem 1835

Newcastle, branch bank | Bank of England | repairs and alts | minor alts; dem

Norwich, branch bank | Bank of England | repairs and alts | minor alts; dem

Swansea, Bank of England | repairs and alts | 1830: further alts; dem 1859

1827 London, Horse Guards Parade | Monument to Duke of York (Sepulchral Church) and Triumphal Arches in Downing Street | unex

1828 London, The Banqueting House, Whitehall | Office of Works | repair and restoration | extant

1829 Hardenhuish, Wilts | Thomas Clutterbuck | alts and extension | extant

London, Westminster | Office of Works | New State Paper Office | dem 1862

1830 London, 30 Belgrave Place | Sir Francis Chantry | ante-room and alts to façade | exec and dem in 19th century

1831 London | Wellington Memorial | unex proposal

Bibliography

Stephen Astley

A Chronological List of Publications by Sir John Soane

Designs in architecture; consisting of plans, elevations, and sections, for temples, baths, cassines, pavilions..., London, 1778; 2nd ed., London, 1789; 3rd ed., London, 1790; 4th ed., London, 1797

Plans, Elevations and Sections of Buildings executed in the Counties of Norfolk, Suffolk, Yorkshire, Staffordshire, Warwickshire, Hertfordshire...&c by Sir John Soane, London, 1788

Sketches in Architecture containing plans and elevations of cottages, villas and other useful buildings with characteristic scenery, London, 1793

A Statement of Facts respecting the Designs of a New House of Lords, London, 1799

A Letter to the Earl Spencer, K.G. &c. &c. &c. from John Soane, architect, privately printed, London, 1799

'On the Causes of the Present Inferior State of Architecture in England', *The Artist*, no. 14, 13 June 1807, pp. 1–8

'An Appeal to the Public: Occasioned by the Suspension of the Architectural Lectures in the Royal Academy. To which is subjoined an Account of a Critical Work, Published a Few Years Ago, entitled "The Exhibition; or, a Second Anticipation:" With Observations on Modern Anglo-Grecian Architecture; and Remarks on the Mischievous Tendancy of the Present Speculative System of Building, &c. In Letters to a Friend. Illustrated with Engravings', unpublished, 1812

'Designs for Public Improvements in London and Westminster', unpublished, 1827

A Brief Statement of the Proceedings respecting the New Law Courts at Westminster, the Board of Trade, and the New Privy Council Offices etc, London, 1828

'Description of Three Designs for the Two Houses of Parliament, made in 1779, 1794 and 1796', 1835

Description of the House and Museum on the North Side of Lincoln's Inn Fields, London 1830, 1832, 1835–36

Designs for Public and Private Buildings, London, 1828; 2nd ed. with extra illustrations, 1832

Plans, Elevations, and Perspective Views of Pitzhanger Manor-House, and of the ruins of an edifice of Roman architecture, situated on the border of Ealing Green, London, 1832

Plans, Elevations et vues en perspective, du Domaine de Pitzhanger, privately printed, London, 1833

Memoirs of the Professional Life of an Architect between the years 1768 and 1835 written by Himself, privately printed, London, 1835

Memoirs relating to Mr John Soane, Junior, Mrs John Soane, and Captain Chamier: also a brief description of Pitzhanger Manor-House and Domains...from 1800 to 1835..., privately printed, London, 1835

Observations respecting a Royal Palace, National Gallery, British Senate House etc. extracted from the Professor of Architecture's Fifth and Sixth Lectures, London, n.d.

Details respecting the Conduct and Connexions of George Soane....and also of Frederick Soane, privately printed, London, n.d. (but after 9 June 1835)

Description de la Maison et du Musée situés au nord de la Place de Lincoln's Inn Fields, à Londres, demeure du Chevalier Soane, London, 1835

General Bibliography

ABRAMSON 1993, Daniel M. Abramson, 'Money's Architecture: the Building of the Bank of England, 1731–1833', Ph.D. thesis, Harvard University, 1993

ABRAMSON 1994, Daniel M. Abramson, 'C. R. Cockerell's "Architectural Progress of the Bank of England"', *Architectural History*, vol. 37, 1994, pp. 112–129

ANGELL 1848, S. Angell, 'Sketch of the Professional Life of George Dance, Architect R.A.', *Builder*, vol. V, 1848, pp. 333–334

BALLANTYNE 1994, Andrew Ballantyne, 'First Principles and Ancient Errors: Soane at Dulwich', *Architectural History*, vol. 37, 1994, pp. 96–111

BINGHAM 1993, Neil Bingham, 'Architecture at the Royal Academy Schools, 1768 to 1836', in Neil Bingham, ed., *The Education of the Architect: Proceedings of the 22nd Annual Symposium of the Society of Architectural Historians of Great Britain*, London, 1993

BIRNSTINGL 1925, H. J. Birnstingl, *Sir John Soane*, London, 1925

BOLTON 1923, Arthur T. Bolton, *Architectural Education a Century Ago. Being an account of the office of Sir John Soane, R.A., with special reference to the career of George Basevi*, London, n.d. (?1923)

BOLTON 1924, Arthur T. Bolton, *The Works of Sir John Soane, F.R.S., F.S.A., R.A. (1753–1837)*, London, 1924

BOLTON 1927, Arthur T. Bolton, *The Portrait of Sir John Soane, R.A.*, London, 1927

BOLTON 1929, Arthur T. Bolton, ed., *Lectures on Architecture by Sir John Soane...As delivered to the Students of the Royal Academy from 1809 to 1836 in Two Courses of Six Lectures each*, London, 1929

BOLTON 1933, Arthur T. Bolton, *A short Account of the Evolution of the Tivoli Corner of The Bank of England, designed by Sir John Soane, R.A. 1804–5. Issued by the Trustees of Sir John Soane's Museum as a protest against any alteration of the Design and as a record*, London, 1933

BOWDLER AND WOODWARD 1999, Roger Bowdler and Christopher Woodward, 'An Ornamental Stucture and Very Likely to Be Damaged...: Sir John Soane's Tomb in St Pancras Gardens', *Architectural History*, vol. 42, 1999

BRITTON 1827, John Britton, *The Union of Architecture, Sculpture and Painting; exemplified by a series of illustrations, with Descriptive Accounts of the House and Galleries of John Soane*, London, 1827

BRITTON 1834, John Britton, *A Brief Memoir of Sir John Soane*, London, 1834

BRITTON AND PUGIN 1828, John Britton and A. C. Pugin, *Illustrations of the Public Buildings of London*, London, 1828

BUILDINGS 1995, *Buildings in Progress: Soane's Views of Construction*, exh. cat., Sir John Soane's Museum, London, 1995

BUZAS 1994, Stefan Buzas, *Sir John Soane's Museum, London*, Tübingen/Berlin, 1994

CARR 1973, Gerald L. Carr, 'Soane's Specimen Church Designs of 1818', *Architectural History*, vol. 16, 1973, pp. 37–53

CARR 1976, Gerald L. Carr, *The Commissioners' Churches of London 1818–1837*, University of Michigan, Ph.D. thesis, 1976

CRUICKSHANK 1989, Dan Cruickshank, 'Soane and the Meaning of Colour', *Architectural Review*, vol. 185, January 1989, pp. 46–52

CRUICKSHANK 1998, Dan Cruickshank, 'Complex Classicism: Wren and Soane at the Royal Hospital, Chelsea', *Architect's Journal*, 26 November 1998, pp. 26–42

DARLEY 1999, Gillian Darley, *John Soane: An Accidental Romantic*, London and New Haven, 1999

DAVIES 1985, Colin Davies, 'Dulwich Picture Gallery', *Architect's Journal*, vol. 181, no. 17, 1985, pp. 44–65

DEAN 1950, Captain C. G. Dean, *The Royal Hospital, Chelsea*, London, 1950

DEAN 1999, Ptolemy Dean, *Sir John Soane and the Country Estate*, London, 1999

DONALDSON 1837, Thomas Leverton Donaldson, *A Review of the Professional Life of Sir John Soane*, London, 1837

DOREY 1991, Helen Dorey, 'Sir John Soane's Acquisition of the Sarcophagus of Seti I', *Georgian Group Journal*, 1991, pp. 26–35

DU PREY 1972 (1), Pierre de la Ruffinière du Prey, *John Soane's Education 1753–80*, Princeton University Ph.D. thesis, 1972; New York 1977

DU PREY 1972 (2), Pierre de la Ruffinière du Prey, 'Soane and Hardwick in Rome: a Neo-Classical Partnership', *Architectural History*, vol. 15, 1972, pp. 51–67

DU PREY 1979 (1), Pierre de la Ruffinière du Prey, 'John Soane, Philip Yorke, and Their Quest for Primitive Architecture', *National Trust Studies*, London, 1979, pp. 28–38

DU PREY 1979 (2), Pierre de la Ruffinière du Prey, 'Eighteenth Century English Sources for a History of Swiss Wooden Bridges', *Zeitschrift für schweizerische Archäologie und Kunstgeschichte*, vol. 36, 1979, pp. 51–63

DU PREY 1982, Pierre de la Ruffinière du Prey, *John Soane: The Making of an Architect*, Chicago and London, 1982

DU PREY 1985, Pierre de la Ruffinière du Prey, *Catalogues of Architectural Drawings at the V&A: Sir John Soane*, London, 1985

FEINBERG 1984, Susan G. Feinberg, 'The Genesis of Sir John Soane's Museum Idea: 1801–1810', *Journal of the Society of Architectural Historians*, vol. 43, October 1984, pp. 225–237

FEINBERG MILLENSON 1987, Susan G. Feinberg Millenson, *Sir John Soane's Museum*, Ann Arbor, 1987

FINDLAY 1985, D. Findlay, *All Hallows, London Wall: A History and Description*, London, 1985

GANDY 1982, *Joseph Michael Gandy*, exh. cat., Architectural Association, London, 1982

GARNIER 1999, Richard Garnier, 'Downing Square in the 1770s and 1780s', *The Georgian Group Journal*, vol. IX, 1999, pp. 139–157

HARRIS 1990, Eileen Harris, 'Sir John Soane's Library: "O, Books! Ye Monuments of Mind"', *Apollo*, vol. 81, April 1990, pp. 242–247

HARRIS 1992, John Harris, 'Soane's Classical Triumph: A Lost Westminster Triumph Revealed', *Apollo*, vol. 135, May 1992, pp. 288–290

HEWLINGS 1995, Richard Hewlings, '11 Downing Street: Sir John Soane's Work for John Eliot', *Transactions of the Ancient Monuments Society*, 1995, 51

JACKSON 1992, Anthony Jackson, 'The Façade of Sir John Soane's Museum: A Study in Contextualism', *Journal of the Society of Architectural Historians*, vol. 51, December 1992, pp. 417–429

KALMAN 1971, K. H. Kalman, *The Architecture of George Dance the Younger*, Ph.D. thesis, Princeton University, 1971

KELLY 1989, Alison Kelly, 'Soane's Use of Coade Stone', *Apollo*, April 1989

LEARY 1990, Emmeline Leary, *Pitzhanger Manor: An Introduction*, London, 1990, and subsequent eds

LEEDS 1828, W. H. Leeds, 'An Essay on the Architectural Character of the Bank of England', in Britton and Pugin 1828

LORCH 1982, Richard Lorch, 'The Architectural Order of Sir John Soane's House', *International Architect*, vol. 2, no. 9, 1982, pp. 43–48

LUKACHER 1983, Brian Lukacher, 'Phantasmagoria and Emenations: Lighting Effects in the Architectural Fantasies of Joseph Michael Gandy', *AA Files*, vol. 4, 1983, pp. 40–48

LUKACHER 1987 (1), Brian Lukacher, 'John Soane and His Draughtsman Joseph Michael Gandy', *Daidalos*, vol. 25, September 1987, pp. 51–64

LUKACHER 1987 (2), Brian Lukacher, *Joseph Michael Gandy: The Poetical Representation and Mythography of Architecture*, Ph.D. thesis, University of Delaware, 1987; Ann Arbor, 1993

LUKACHER 1994, Brian Lukacher, 'Joseph Gandy and the Mythography of Architecture', *Journal of the Society of Architectural Historians (USA)*, vol. 53, September 1994, pp. 280–299

MATHEOU 1994, Demitrios Matheou, 'Restoring Soane's Last House Exactly as He Intended', *Architect's Journal*, 4 August 1994, pp. 14–15

MCCARTHY 1985, Michael McCarthy, 'Soane's "Saxon" Room at Stowe', *Journal of the Society of Architectural Historians*, XLIV, May 1985, pp. 129–146

MCCARTHY 1991, Michael McCarthy, 'Thomas Pitt, Piranesi and John Soane: English Architects in Italy in the 1770s', *Apollo*, vol. 34, December 1991, pp. 380–386

MIDDLETON 1996, Robin Middleton, 'The History of John Soane's "Designs for Public and Private Buildings"', *Burlington Magazine*, August 1996, pp. 506–516

MIDDLETON AND WATKIN 1980, Robin Middleton and David Watkin, *Neoclassical and Nineteenth Century Architecture*, New York, 1980

MORGAN 1964, H. C. Morgan, *A History of the Organization of the Royal Academy Schools from the Beginning of the Academy to 1836*, Ph.D. Thesis, University of Leeds, 1964

MOSLEY 1999, James Mosley, *The Nymph and the Grot: The Revival of the Sanserif Letter*, London, 1999

PALMER 1990, Susan Palmer, 'The Papers of Sir John Soane', *Apollo*, vol. 81, April 1990, pp. 248–251

PALMER 1998, Susan Palmer, *The Soanes at Home: Domestic Life at Lincoln's Inn Fields*, London, 1998

RICHARDSON 1989, Margaret Richardson, 'Model Architecture', *Country Life*, 21 September 1989

RICHARDSON 1990, Margaret Richardson, 'Soane's Use of Drawings', *Apollo*, vol. 81, April 1990, pp. 234–241

RICHARDSON 1991, Margaret Richardson, 'John Soane: The Business of Architecture', in *Georgian Architectural Practice*, The Georgian Group Symposium 1991, London, 1991

RICHARDSON 1992, Margaret Richardson, 'Soane in Chelsea', *The Chelsea Society Report*, 1992, pp. 45–51

RICHARDSON 1993, Margaret Richardson, 'Learning in the Soane Office', in Neil Bingham, ed., *The Education of the Architect: Proceedings of the 22nd Annual Symposium of the Society of Architectural Historians of Great Britain*, London, 1993

ROBINSON 1989, John Martin Robinson, 'Scraping the Ceiling', *Country Life*, 20 April 1989, pp. 192–193

ROYAL ACADEMY 1768–1784, Royal Academy of Arts, 'Minutes of Council Meetings', vol. 1, 1768–1784

ROYAL ACADEMY 1768–1796, Royal Academy of Arts, 'Minutes of General Assembly Meetings', vol. 1, 1768–1796

ROYAL ACADEMY 1769–1795 (1), Royal Academy of Arts, 'Royal Academy Cash Book', 1769–1795

ROYAL ACADEMY 1769–1795 (2), Royal Academy of Arts, 'Account of the Income and Expenditure of the Royal Academy, 1769–1795', compiled by George Dance and William Tyler

ROYAL ACADEMY 1796, Royal Academy of Arts, *Abstract of the Instrument of Institution of the Royal Academy of Arts in London Established December 10, 1786*, London, 1796

ROYAL ACADEMY 1962, Royal Academy of Arts, 'Students Admitted to the Royal Academy from 1769 [to 1829]' (transcript published by S. C. Hutchinson in *The Walpole Society*, vol. XXXVIII, 1962, pp. 123–191)

SANDBY 1790, Thomas Sandby, Autograph (?) Draft of Royal Academy Lectures, late 1790s, British Architectural Library MS (SaT/1/1)

SAVAGE 1988, Nicholas Savage, 'The Academicians' Library: A Selection, not a Collection', *Apollo*, vol. 128, October 1988, pp. 258–263, 297

SAVE 1987, Sophie Andreae and Ken Powell, eds, 'Pell Wall Hall: Soane's Shell Must Survive', *SAVE Britain's Heritage*, London, 1987

SAWYER 1996, Sean Sawyer, 'Sir John Soane's Symbolic Westminster: The Apotheosis of George IV', *Architectural History*, 39, 1996, pp. 54–76

SCHUMANN-BACIA 1989, Eva Schumann-Bacia, *Die Bank von England und ihr Architekt John Soane*, Zurich and Munich, 1989; *John Soane and The Bank of England*, London, 1991

SOANE 1815, George Soane (published anonymously), 'The Present Low State of the Arts in England and more particularly of Architecture', *The Champion*, 10 and 24 September 1815

SOANE 1983, *John Soane*, Academy Editions Monograph, London 1983

SOANE 1989, 'Sir John Soane and Pitshanger Manor', *RSA Journal*, vol. CXXXVII, no. 5392, March 1989

SOANE 1995, *Soane: Connoisseur & Collector; A Selection of Drawings from Sir John Soane's Collection*, exh. cat., Sir John Soane's Museum, London, 1995

SOANE 1996, *Soane Revisited: A Journey of Rediscovery of the Buildings of Sir John Soane*, exh. cat., Sir John Soane's Museum, London 1996

SOUDEN 1991, David Souden, *Wimpole Hall, Cambridgeshire*, London, 1991, and subsequent eds

STEELE AND YERBURY 1930, H. R. Steele and F. R. Yerbury, *The Old Bank of England*, London, 1930

STILLMAN 1988, Damie Stillman, *English Neo-classical Architecture*, 2 vols, London, 1988

STROUD 1957 (1), Dorothy Stroud, 'The Early Work of Soane', *Architectural Review*, February 1957, pp. 121–122

STROUD 1957 (2), Dorothy Stroud, 'Soane's Designs for a Triumphal Bridge', *Architectural Review*, April 1957, pp. 260–262

STROUD 1961, Dorothy Stroud, *The Architecture of Sir John Soane*, London, 1961

STROUD 1966, Dorothy Stroud, *Henry Holland: His Life and Architecture*, London, 1966

STROUD 1982, Dorothy Stroud, 'Sir John Soane and the Rebuilding of Pitzhanger Manor', in Helen Searing, ed., *In Search of Modern Architecture: A Tribute to Henry-Russell Hitchcock*, New York, 1982, pp. 38–51

STROUD 1971, Dorothy Stroud, *George Dance: Architect 1741–1825*, London, 1971

STROUD 1984, Dorothy Stroud, *Sir John Soane, Architect*, London 1984; revised ed., 1996

SUMMERSON 1936, John Summerson, 'The Strange Case of J. M. Gandy', *Architect and Building News*, 10 January 1936, pp. 38–44

SUMMERSON 1937, John Summerson, 'Sir John Soane', *The Times*, 20 January 1937

SUMMERSON 1947, John Summerson, 'The Subtle Magic of Sir John Soane', *Listener*, 11 September 1947, pp. 427–428

SUMMERSON 1949, John Summerson, 'Change, Decay and the Soane Museum', *Architectural Association Journal*, October 1949, pp. 50–53

SUMMERSON 1951, John Summerson, 'Soane: The Case History of a Personal Style', *RIBA Journal*, 3rd series, LVIII, 1951, pp. 83–91

SUMMERSON 1952, John Summerson, *Sir John Soane*, London, 1952

SUMMERSON 1978, John Summerson, 'Sir John Soane and the Furniture of Death', *Architectural Review*, March 1978, pp. 147–158

SUMMERSON 1982, John Summerson, 'The Union of the Arts', *Lotus International*, 35, 1982, II

SUMMERSON 1983, John Summerson, *Architecture in Britain, 1530–1830*, Harmondsworth, 1983

SUMMERSON 1984, John Summerson, 'The Evolution of Soane's Bank Stock Office in the Bank of England', *Architectural History*, vol. 27, 1984

SUMMERSON 1990, John Summerson, *The Unromantic Castle and Other Essays*, London, 1990

TALIOTIS 1994, Xenia Taliotis, 'Saving Soane's Swansong', *Heritage Today*, September 1994, pp. 32–33

TAYLOR 1802, Josiah Taylor, *A Catalogue of the Library in the Royal Academy, London*, London, 1802

THORNTON 1985, Peter Thornton, 'Lit Up with Gorgeous Hues', *Country Life*, 19 December 1985

THORNTON 1987, Peter Thornton, 'An Architectural Kaleidoscope: Sir John Soane's Museum in London', *The Magazine Antiques*, New York, January 1987

THORNTON 1990, Peter Thornton, 'The Soane as It Was', *Apollo*, vol. 81, April 1990, pp. 228–232

THORNTON AND DOREY 1992, Peter Thornton and Helen Dorey, *A Miscellany of Objects from Sir John Soane's Museum*, London, 1992

VISIONS 1999, *Visions of Ruin: Architectural Fantasies and Designs for Garden Follies*, exh. cat., Sir John Soane's Museum, London, 1999

WATERFIELD 1987, Giles Waterfield, ed., *Soane and After: The Architecture of Dulwich Picture Gallery*, exh. cat., Dulwich Picture Gallery, London, 1987

WATERFIELD 1996, Giles Waterfield, ed., *Soane and Death*, exh. cat., Dulwich Picture Gallery, London, 1996

WATKIN 1995, David Watkin, 'Freemasonry and Sir John Soane', *Journal of the Society of Architectural Historians*, 54: 4, December 1995, pp. 402–417

WATKIN 1996 (1), David Watkin, *Sir John Soane: Enlightenment Thought and the Royal Academy Lectures*, Cambridge, 1996

WATKIN 1996 (2), David Watkin, *Sir John Soane & Enlightenment Thought: The Annual Soane Lecture, 1996*, London, 1996

WEDGWOOD 1992, Alexandra Wedgwood, Soane's Law Courts at Westminster, *AA Files* 24, Autumn 1992

WIGHTWICK 1853–55, George Wightwick, 'The Life of an Architect – My Sojourn at Bath – The Late Sir John Soane', *Bentley's Miscellany*, vol. 34, 1853, pp. 108–114; 1855, pp. 402–409

WILTON-ELY 1969, John Wilton-Ely, 'The Architectural Models of Sir John Soane: A Catalogue', *Architectural History*, vol. 12, 1969

WOODWARD 1999, Christopher Woodward, 'Dancing Soane: The Yellow Drawing Room at Wimpole Hall', *Apollo*, April 1999, pp. 8–13

WORSLEY 1988, Giles Worsley, 'Pell Wall Hall, Staffordshire', *Country Life*, 7 April 1988

The following sources are of particular relevance to the sections under which they are listed

Beginnings and Early Training
Angell 1848; du Prey 1972 (1), 1977 and 1982; Findlay; Kalman 1971; Stroud 1966; Stroud 1971

A Royal Academy Student in Architecture
Bingham 1993; du Prey 1972 (1), 1977 and 1982; Morgan 1964; Royal Academy 1768–1796; Royal Academy 1768–1784; Royal Academy 1769–1795 (1) and (2); Royal Academy 1796; Royal Academy 1962; Sandby 1790; Savage 1988; Stroud 1957; Taylor 1802; Watkin 1996 (1)

The Grand Tour
du Prey 1972, 1977 and 1982; McCarthy 1991

Early Practice
Stroud 1957; du Prey 1972 (1), 1977, 1979 and 1982

Wimpole Hall
du Prey 1982; Souden 1991; Woodward 1999

Tyringham
Richardson 1990

Pitzhanger Manor
Leary 1990; Robinson 1989; Soane 1989; Stroud 1982

12–14 Lincoln's Inn Fields
Buzas 1994; Dorey 1991; Lorch 1982; Feinberg 1984; Feinberg Millenson 1987; Jackson 1992; Palmer 1998; Richardson 1989; Soane, *Description*; Summerson 1949 and 1982; Thornton 1985, 1987 and 1990; Thornton and Dorey 1992; Visions 1999

Dulwich Picture Gallery
Ballantyne 1994; Davies 1985; Soane 1983 and 1987

The Royal Hospital, Chelsea
Cruickshank 1998; Dean 1950; Richardson 1992; Soane 1815; Watkin 1996 (1)

The Soane Family Tomb
Bowdler and Woodward 1999

Pell Wall
Matheou 1994; Save 1987; Soane, *Designs*; Taliotis 1994; Worsley 1988

The Bank of England
Abramson 1993 and 1994; Bolton 1933; Leeds 1828; Schumann-Bacia 1989; Steele and Yerbury 1930; Summerson 1984

The Processional Route
Garnier 1999; Hewlings 1995; Sawyer 1996; Soane, *A Brief Statement* and *Designs*

Freemasons' Hall
Watkin 1995

The Law Courts
Harris 1992; Wedgwood 1992

Imaginary Compositions
Lukacher 1983 and 1987 (1)

Glossary

Stephen Astley

acroteria Pedestals or plinths, empty or with statue or vase, placed on the three angles of a **pediment** to stand out against the skyline

aedicule A frame, usually inside a building, often consisting of **columns** and **pediment**, sometimes to hold doors or niches, but occasionally complete in itself

antae Pilasters that do not conform to the **order** of a building, usually placed on a corner or projection

anthemion One of the principal motifs of classical ornament, resembling a flattened honeysuckle flower and leaf

apse A recess, semicircular in plan, originally terminating the chancel of a church but used generally for any such recess, including polygonal examples

architrave Used with two distinct meanings: the lowest part of the entablature of any of the orders; the moulded frame that surrounds a door or window

articulation The expression on elevation or plan of the separate visual and logically discrete elements of a building

astylar Term to describe a classical building in which there is no controlling **order**, and so no **columns** or **pilasters**

barrel vault An uninterrupted vault of semicircular section

bombé Term to describe a façade whose centre projects forward on a round or semicircular plan

bucrania Carved ox or bull skulls used in decoration, deriving originally from the animals' sacrificial role

caducei Winged staffs entwined with snakes, a symbol carried by Mercury, the messenger of the gods, which came to be a symbol of Commerce at, for example, the Bank of England

capital The uppermost part of a **column** or **pilaster**

caryatid A sculpted female figure used in classical architecture instead of a **column**

chariga A sculpted composition of a chariot and horses often used to ornament the roof of a building or to crown an arch

clerestory The upper storey of a nave, with windows above the aisle roof to light the interior

coffer An ornamental panel sunk into a ceiling or **soffit**, usually square but sometimes polygonal

column A vertical supporting member which in classical architecture is composed of base, shaft and **capital**. If a column is built into a wall so that at least half its section projects it is known as an **engaged column**; if it is free-standing in front of a building it can be called **insulated**. If much less projects or it is in low relief it is called a **pilaster**

concatenation In Palladian architecture, the theory by which large façades are divided into discrete units, each with its own roof, projecting or recessed from the line of the façade

corbel A projection from a wall, often decoratively carved, and used as a support, for example, for an arch

Corinthian *see* **order**

cornice Term to describe both the upper main part of an **entablature** and any moulded projection at the top of an internal wall

cortile A courtyard

dentils Small spaced blocks running along the lower edge of a **cornice**

diaper A repeat pattern, usually using a lozenge framework

Doric *see* **order**

enfilade A suite of rooms whose doorways align, thereby offering a long vista

engaged column *see* **column**

entablature In classical architecture, the horizontal element composed of **architrave**, **frieze** and **cornice**, supported by **columns**

exedra A large recess often containing seats, either roofed or open

finial The crowning ornament of a spire, gable, **pediment** or roof

frieze The part of the **entablature** between the **architrave** and the **cornice**, and more generally, a running decorative band or moulding

glyph A vertical groove on the rectangular blocks on a **Doric frieze**, used in threes, hence **triglyphs**

groin-vault A type of vault named after the arched diagonals formed by the intersection of two **barrel vaults**

hypocaust A form of underfloor heating, pioneered by the Ancient Romans, achieved by ducting hot air under floors and through hollow passages in walls

Ionic *see* **order**

impost A block or band set within a wall from which an arch springs

insulated column *see* **column**

key-fret A decorative running motif derived from classical architecture

linenfold panelling A decorative motif representing folded cloth applied to wooden panelling especially in the sixteenth and seventeenth centuries

loggia A covered space open through arches or a colonnade on one or more sides, either attached to a building, or free-standing (usually in gardens)

lunette A semicircular panel or window

Mannerism A style of architecture originating in Italy in c. 1520, characterised by the deliberate breaking of established rules of classical architectural composition

mansard A term, derived from the name of the seventeenth-century French architect André Mansard, to describe a roof of double pitch in which the lower part of the roof has the steeper pitch

metope The space, plain or decorated, between the **triglyphs** in a **Doric frieze**

mullion A major vertical division in a window opening

neo-Palladianism The revival of the **Palladian** style in Great Britain between 1715–55 as a national style that is still influential today

oculus A round window, usually in the top of a dome

opus reticulatum In antiquity, the scoring of a plaster or cement covering on a wall with intersecting diagonal lines to resemble a net

order The basis of classical architecture, the orders are composed of a column, with or without base or **capital**, supporting an **entablature** composed of an **architrave**, **frieze** and **cornice**. The Greek orders are **Doric**, **Ionic** and **Corinthian**. The Romans added Tuscan and Composite. **Doric** was seen as the toughest, most masculine order; it is simple, pure and sometimes the columns are without a base. The **Ionic** order, more feminine than the **Doric**, has **volutes** or spiral, scrolling mouldings on the **capital**. The **capital** of the **Corinthian order**, decorated with layers of carving of acanthus leaves, is richer, lighter and more elegant than the **Doric** and **Ionic**

Palladianism A style of architecture, promulgated between 1615 and the 1660s by a small circle around the English Court, derived from the architecture and writings of Andrea Palladio (1508–1580) whose *Quattro Libri dell' Architettura* was published in Venice in 1570 and in many later editions. See also **neo-Palladianism**

pediment A triangular gable, usually of low pitch, placed above the **entablature** to finish a roof

pendentive A concave panel in the form of an inverted near triangle below a dome and between its supporting arches

pilaster A column in very low relief attached to a wall, and projecting much less than an **engaged column**

podium A pedestal or base upon which a building or structure sits

post-and-lintel A method of construction based on vertical elements supporting a horizontal beam

propylaeum The entrance to a temple, such as that of the Acropolis at Athens

rustication Masonry in which the courses or individual stones are distinguished by deeply recessed joints

segmental arch An arch whose shape is that of a segment of a circle, the centre of which is below the springing line

socle A plain block of stone which supports a column, vase or statue

soffit The undersurface of an architectural element such as an arch, lintel, cornice, balcony or door-head

strigilation Parallel, curved incisions derived from sarcophagus decoration

tribune A space penetrating the ground and upper floors of a building, usually **articulated** by arcades

triglyphs In the **Doric order**, one of the rectangular blocks between the **metopes**, having vertical grooves or **glyphs**

truss A frame made of several elements placed at intervals along a roof to support and space the elements running along the roof's length and to provide a structure for its covering

volute A spiral scroll, the distinguishing form of the **Ionic capital**, but also used in the **Corinthian order** and on brackets

Index

Photographic Acknowledgements

All works of art are reproduced by kind permission of the owners. Every effort has been made to trace copyright holders and any omission is greatly regretted by the publishers.

All photographs of items owned by the Trustees of Sir John Soane's Museum are by Geremy Butler unless otherwise stated.

Specific acknowledgements are as follows:

Barcelona: Duccio Malagamba, figs 65, 68

Copenhagen: Ole Woldbye, fig. 135; cats 51, 70

Florence: Photo © Scala, figs 41, 184

London: Richard Bryant/Arcaid, figs 17, 130, 131, 140, 141, 143

London: Paul Raftery/Arcaid, fig. 35

London: Photo © Bank of England, figs 51, 121, 128, 129, 130, 131, 152

London: Photo © Place de Stalingrad/Giraudon/ Bridgeman Art Library, fig. 49

London: Martin Charles, figs 70, 87, 134, 138, 145, 147, 185, 186; cats 2, 50, 71, 78, 86, 88, 89, 93, 126, 131, 135, 145, 146, 207

London: A. C. Cooper Ltd, cat. 172

London: Paul Barker/*Country Life* 1999, figs 81, 82, 88, 98, 109, 110, 111, 112, 113, 114, 115, 122, 123, 124, 126, 127, 128, 129, 153, 154

London: Prudence Cuming Associates Ltd, fig. 15

London: © Peter Durant, fig. 69

London: Photo © B. E. C. Howarth-Loomes, fig. 141

London: Photo © National Gallery, fig. 63

London: © National Trust Photographic Library/Andreas von Einsiedel, figs 118, 119, 120

London: © National Trust Photographic Library/Rupert Truman, fig. 117

Mainz: Dieter Leisdner, fig. 62

University of Michigan: G. H. Forsyth, fig. 21

Middlesex, John Wibberley: figs 159, 160

New York: Michael Graves and Associates, fig. 60

New York: © 1999 The Museum of Modern Art, New York, fig. 33

New York: Ezra Stoller © Esto, figs 58, 59

Tokyo: Tomio Ohashi, fig. 61

Opposite:
The Monk's Parlour,
13 Lincoln's Inn Fields,
as shown in the
Illustrated London News, 25 June 1864,
detail

Royal Academy Trust

Major Benefactors

The Trustees of the Royal Academy Trust would like to thank all those who have been exceedingly generous over a number of years in support of the galleries, the exhibitions, the conservation of the Permanent Collection, the Library, the Royal Academy Schools and the education programme:

H M The Queen
The 29th May 1961 Charitable Trust
The Annie Laurie Aitken Charitable Trust
American Associates of the Royal Academy Trust
The Honorable and Mrs Walter H Annenberg
Barclays Bank
B.A.T. Industries plc
Brenda M Benwell-Lejeune
John Frye Bourne
British Telecom
The Brown Foundation Inc
The Trustees of the Clore Foundation
The John S Cohen Foundation
Sir Harry and Lady Djanogly
The Dulverton Trust
Alfred Dunhill Limited
The John Ellerman Foundation
Esso UK plc
Esmée Fairbairn Charitable Trust
Mr and Mrs Eugene V Fife
Walter Fitch III
Mrs Henry Ford II
The Foundation for Sport and the Arts
Friends of the Royal Academy
The Getty Grant Program
Glaxo Holdings plc
Diane and Guilford Glazer
Jack and Grete Goldhill
Maurice and Laurence Goldman
The Horace W Goldsmith Foundation
Dr Armand Hammer
Mr and Mrs Jocelin Harris
The Philip and Pauline Harris Charitable Trust
The Hayward Foundation
Drue Heinz Trust
Henry J & Drue Heinz Foundation

Heritage Lottery Fund
IBM United Kingdom Limited
The Idlewild Trust
The JP Jacobs Charitable Trust
The Japan Foundation
Mr and Mrs Donald P Kahn
The Kresge Foundation
The Lankelly Foundation
Mr John S Latsis
Mrs Katherine L Lawrence
The Leverhulme Trust
Lex Service plc
The Linbury Trust
Mr & Mrs Sydney Lipworth
John Madejski
Her Majesty's Government
The Manifold Trust
Mr and Mrs John L Marion
Marks and Spencer
Mr and Mrs Jack C Massey
Ronald and the Honourable Rita McAulay
McKinsey and Company Inc
Paul Mellon KBE
The Mercers' Company
The Monument Trust
The Henry Moore Foundation
The Moorgate Trust Fund
Museums and Galleries Improvement Fund
National Westminster Bank
Stavros S Niarchos
The Otemae College
The Peacock Trust
The Pennycress Trust
PF Charitable Trust
The Pilgrim Trust
The Edith and Ferdinand Porjes Trust
Rio Tinto plc
John A Roberts FRIBA
The Ronson Foundation
The Rose Foundation
Rothmans International plc
Mrs Arthur M Sackler
Mrs Jean Sainsbury
The Saison Foundation
The Basil Samuel Charitable Trust
Mrs Louisa S Sarofim
Sea Containers Ltd
Shell UK Limited
Miss Dasha Shenkman
William and Maureen Shenkman
The Archie Sherman Charitable Trust
The Starr Foundation
Alfred Taubman
Mr and Mrs Vernon Taylor Jr

Sir Anthony and Lady Tennant
Eugene & Clare Thaw Charitable Trust
Ware and Edythe Travelstead
The Trusthouse Charitable Foundation
The Douglas Turner Trust
Unilever plc
The Weldon UK Charitable Trust
The Welton Foundation
Garry H Weston
The Honourable and Mrs John C Whitehead
Mr and Mrs Frederick B Whittemore
The Maurice Wohl Charitable Foundation
The Wolfson Foundation
and others who wish to remain anonymous

Benefactors

The Trustees of the Royal Academy Trust would like to thank all those who have recently supported the galleries, the exhibitions, the conservation of the Permanent Collection, the Library, the Royal Academy Schools or the education programme:

Miss B A Battersby
Mr Tom Bendhem
The Charlotte Bonham-Carter Charitable Trust
Mr Keith Bromley
The Dorothy Burns Charity
The John Coates Charitable Trust
The John S Cohen Foundation
The Ernest Cook Trust
Crabtree & Evelyn
Mr and Mrs Keith Dawson
The Dorner family and friends in memory of Lotte Dorner
The D'Oyly Carte Charitable Trust
The John Ellerman Foundation
The Gilbert & Eileen Edgar Foundation
Miss Jayne Edwardes
The Elephant Trust
Mr M E Flintoff
The Worshipful Company of Goldsmiths
Mrs Sue Hammerson

Philip and Pauline Harris Charitable Trust
Mr and Mrs David Haynes
The Hayward Foundation
Mr Tony Howitt
The Idlewild Trust
The Leche Trust
The Leverhulme Trust
Lex Service PLC
Pamela Littman JP
John Lyon's Charity
Sir Edwin and Lady Manton
The Richard and Margaret Merrell Foundation
The Millichope Foundation
The Worshipful Company of Painter-Stainers
The Austin and Hope Pilkington Trust
The Radcliffe Trust
Mr Charles Saatchi
The Schneer Foundation Inc
Mr Paul Smith CBE
Sotheby's
The South Square Trust
Joseph Strong Frazer Trust
Time Out Magazine
The Celia Walker Art Foundation
The Welton Foundation
and others who wish to remain anonymous

Exhibition Patrons Group

The Exhibition Patrons Group was established in May 1997 to encourage the regular and committed support of individuals who believe in the Royal Academy's mission to promote the widest possible understanding and enjoyment of the visual arts. The Royal Academy is delighted to thank the following for generously supporting the exhibition programme with donations of £1,000 and more:

President
Mr Garry Weston

Co-Chairmen
Sir Trevor Chinn CVO
The Hon Mrs Anne Collins
The Lady Lever of Manchester

Members
The 29th May 1961 Charitable Trust
Mrs Annabel Agace

Mr and Mrs V Alaghband
Mr and the Hon Mrs Michael Alen-Buckley
Mr John Asprey
Lord and Lady Attenborough
Mr Stephen Bampfylde
The Duke of Beaufort
Tom Bendhem
Mr and Mrs Thomas J Berger
Mrs Vanessa Bernstein
Sir Victor and Lady Blank
Mr and Mrs George Bloch
Mr Peter Boizot MBE
Mr and Mrs Mark Booth
Alain and Marie Boublil
Mrs Adrian Bowden
Mr Peter Bowring CBE
Ivor Braka
The Britto Foundation
Lady Brown
Jeremy Brown
Mr and Mrs John Burns
Marlene and Neville Burston
Mr Raymond M Burton CBE
Jim and Margaret Butler
Mr and Mrs P H G Cadbury
Mrs Lily Cantor
Jean and Eric Cass
Mrs Rivka Chenevix-Trench
John Chiene
Sir Trevor and Lady Chinn
C H K Charities Limited
Mrs Denise Cohen
The Hon Mrs Anne Collins
Mr and Mrs G L Collins
Neville and Carole Conrad Charitable Trust
David J and Jennifer A Cooke
Corona Extra Beer
Mr Arnold M Crook
Mr and Mrs Andrew Dalton
Ian and Morny Davison
The Marquise de Cérenville
Peter and Kate De Haan
The de Laszlo Foundation
Mr and Mrs Patrick Doherty
Sir Philip Dowson PRA and Lady Dowson
John Drummond, FCSD, HON, DES, RCA
Mr and Mrs Maurice Dwek
EFG Private Bank Limited
Mrs Alyce Faye Eichelberger Cleese
Amelia Chilcott Fawcett
Mary Fedden RA
Mrs Juliet Fenton
Mr and Mrs Bryan Ferry
Mrs Donatella Flick
Dr Gert-Rudolf Flick

Mr and Mrs Gerald Fogel
Mr and Mrs George
 Fokschaner
Mrs Helena Frost
A Fulton Company Limited
Mr and Mrs Richard Gapper
The Robert Gavron Charitable
 Trust
Jacqueline and Michael Gee
Jacqueline and Jonathan
 Gestetner
Sir Paul and Lady Girolami
M. and Mme Michel Goldet
Sir Nicholas and Lady
 Goodison's Charitable
 Settlement
David and Maggi Gordon
Lady Gosling
Mrs Mary K Graves
Mrs Michael Green
Mr Robert Alan Green
Mrs Maro Hadjipateras
Mrs Sue Hammerson
Mr and Mrs Jocelin Harris
Michael and Morven Heller
Mr and Mrs Alan Hobart
Anne Holmes-Drewry
Mr and Mrs Allan Hughes
Jasper Jacob Associates
Mr and Mrs Ian Jay
Mr and Mrs Harold Joels
Mr and Mrs David Josefowitz
Mrs Gabrielle Jungels-Winkler
Mr and Mrs Donald P Kahn
Mr and Mrs Joseph Karaviotis
Mr and Mrs James Kirkman
Mr and Mrs Henry L R Kravis
The Kreitman Foundation
Mrs Thomas Kressner
Mr and Mrs Irvine Laidlaw
The Kirby Laing Foundation
Mrs Panagiotis Lemos
Mr George Lengvari
The Lady Lever of Manchester
Mr and Mrs John Lewis
Sir Sydney Lipworth QC and
 Lady Lipworth
Mr Jonathon E Lyons
Fiona Mactaggart
Sir John and Lady Mactaggart
Mr and Mrs Michael (RA) and
 José Manser
Mr and Mrs M Margulies
Marsh Christian Trust
R C Martin
Mrs Jack Maxwell
Sir Kit and Lady McMahon
The Mercers' Company
Lt Col L S Michael OBE
Nancy Miller Jong

Mr and Mrs Peter Morgan
Mr Thomas F Mosimann III
Mr Harry Moss
Jim Moyes
Mr and Mrs Carl Anton Muller
Paul and Alison Myners
John Nickson and Simon Rew
Mr Michael Palin
Lord and Lady Palumbo
Mrs Chrysanthy Pateras
Lynda Pearson
The Pennycress Trust
The P F Charitable Trust
Miss Karen Phillipps
Mr Godfrey Pilkington
George and Carolyn Pincus
The Quercus Trust
Barbara Rae RA
John and Anne Raisman
The Rayne Foundation
Mrs Jean Redman-Brown
Mr T H Reitman
Mr and Mrs Robert E Rhea
Sir John and Lady Riddell
Mr and Mrs John Ritblat
Mr John A Roberts FRIBA
Mr and Mrs Ian Rosenberg
Alastair and Sarah Ross
 Goobey
Mr and Mrs Cyril Sainsbury
Mrs Coral Samuel CBE
Mr and Mrs Victor Sandelson
Mr Adrian Sassoon
Ms Pierrette Schlettwein
Dr Lewis Sevitt
The Cyril Shack Trust
Mr and Mrs D M Shalit
Mrs Stella Shawzin
Mr and Mrs Clive Sherling
Mrs Lois Sieff OBE
Silhouette Eyewear
Mr and Mrs Richard Simmons
Mr Peter Simon
Mrs Roama Spears
James and Alyson Spooner
Mr and Mrs Nicholas Stanley
Mrs Jack Steinberg
Mr and Mrs David Stileman
Swan Trust
Mr and Mrs David Swift
Mr and The Hon Mrs Richard
 Szpiro
Sir Anthony and Lady Tennant
Eugene V and Clare E Thaw
 Charitable Trust
Mr and Mrs Julian Treger
Mrs Claire Vyner
The Walter Guinness
 Charitable Trust
John B Watton

Edna and Willard Weiss
Mrs Gerald Westbury
Mrs Linda M Williams
Roger and Jennifer Wingate
Mr and Mrs Rainer Zietz
Mr and Mrs Michael Zilkha
*and others who wish to remain
anonymous*

Benjamin West Group Donors

The Benjamin West Group
was founded in March 1998
for American citizens living
temporarily or permanently
in Britain. The group takes its
name from Benjamin West,
a founder Member of the
Royal Academy and the first
American artist to become an
Academician who also served
as President from 1790 to 1805
and from 1806 to his death in
1820.

 The Royal Academy is
delighted to thank the
following members of the
group who have also generously
contributed donations of
£1,000 and more to support
the conservation of works
touring the United States
in the exhibition 'The Royal
Academy in the Age of Queen
Victoria 1837–1901: Paintings
and Sculpture from the
Permanent Collection'.

Patron
The Hon Raymond G H Seitz

Chairman
The Hon Barbara S Thomas

Donors
Mr Paul Abecassis
Mrs Wendy Becker Payton
Bernadette J Berger
Mr and Mrs Charles
 Brocklebank
Mr and Mrs Paul Collins
Mrs Joan Curci
Miss Elizabeth Gage
Mr and Mrs John Gore
Mrs Robin Hambro
Lady Harvie-Watt
Mr and Mrs Peter Holstein
Mr and Mrs Richard Kaufman
Mr and Mrs Philip Mengel
Mr and Mrs Donald Moore
Mr Neil Osborn and Ms Holly
 Smith

Sir William and Lady Purves
Mrs Robert Rose
Albert and Marjorie Scardino
Mrs Sylvia B Scheuer
Mr and Mrs Paul Shang
Barbara and Allen Thomas
Mr Fred M Vinton

American Associates of the Royal Academy Trust

Benefactors
American Express
Mrs Russell B Aitken
Chase Manhattan Bank
Mr Walter Fitch III
Mrs Henry Ford II
The Honorable Amalia L de
 Fortabat
Glaxo Wellcome
The Horace W Goldsmith
 Foundation
Mr and Mrs Lewis P Grinnan Jr
Mrs Henry J Heinz II
Mr and Mrs Donald Kahn
Mr and Mrs Jon B Lovelace
Mr and Mrs John L Marion
Mrs Jack C Massey
Mr and Mrs Michael Meehan
 II
Mr Charles J Meyers
Mrs Nancy B Negley
Mrs Arthur M Sackler
Mrs Louisa S Sarofim
The Starr Foundation
The Honorable John C
 Whitehead
Mr and Mrs Frederick B
 Whittemore
Mrs William W Wood Prince

Sponsors
The Honorable and Mrs
 Walter H Annenberg
Mr and Mrs Samuel R Blount
Mrs Jan Cowles
Mrs Donald Findlay
Mr D Francis Finlay
Mrs Roswell L Gilpatric
Mr James Kemper
Ms Stephanie Krieger
Mrs Linda Noe Laine
Mrs Janice H Levin
Mrs Jean Chisholm Lindsey
Mr and Mrs Vernon Taylor Jr
Prince Charitable Trusts
Mrs Sylvia Scheuer
US Trust Company of New
 York

Patrons
Mr and Mrs John W Annan
Mr and Mrs Robert J Arnold
Mr and Mrs Stephen D
 Bechtel Jr
Mrs Helen Benedict
Mr and Mrs James Benson
Mrs Bette Berry
Mr Donald A Best
Ms Jan F Blaustein
Mr and Mrs Henry W Breyer
 III
Mrs Mildred C Brinn
Mrs Caroline Chapin
Mr William L Clark
Ms Dorothea F Darlington
Ms Anne S Davidson
Mrs Charles H Dyson
Mrs John W Embry
Mrs Patricia Zoch Ferguson
Mrs A Barlow Ferguson
Mrs Robert Ferst
Mr Ralph A Fields
Mr Richard E Ford
Mr and Mrs Lawrence S
 Friedland
Mr and Mrs Ralph W Golby
Mrs Betty N Gordon
Mrs Melville Wakeman Hall
Mr and Mrs Gurnee F Hart
Mr and Mrs Gustave M Hauser
The Honorable Marife
 Hernandez
Mr Robert J Irwin
Ms Betty Wold Johnson and
 Mr Douglas Bushnell
Ms Barbara R Jordan
The Honorable and Mrs
 Eugene Johnston
Mr William W Karatz
Mr and Mrs Stephen M Kellen
Mrs Katherine K Lawrence
Mr and Mrs William M Lese
Dr and Mrs Peter Linden
Mrs John P McGrath
Mrs Mark Millard
Mr Achim Moeller
Mrs Robin Heller Moss
Mr Paul D Myers
Ms Diane A Nixon
Mr and Mrs Jeffrey Pettit
Mr Robert S Pirie
Dr and Mrs Meyer P Potamkin
The Honorable and Mrs
 Charles H Price II
Mrs Signe E Ruddock
Mrs Frances G Scaife
Mrs Frederick M Stafford
Mr and Mrs Robert L
 Sterling Jr

Mrs Kenneth Straus
Mr Arthur O Sulzberger and
  Ms Alison S Cowles
Mrs Frederick Supper
Mr and Mrs A Alfred
  Taubman
Ms Britt Tidelius
Mrs Susan E Van de
  Bovenkamp
Mrs Bruce E Wallis
Mrs Sara E White
Mrs Joseph R Wier
Mrs Mary Louise Whitmarsh
Mr Robert W Wilson
Mr and Mrs Kenneth
  Woodcock
*and others who wish to remain
anonymous*

Friends of the Royal Academy

Patron Friends
Mrs Denise Adeane
Mr Paul Baines
Mr P F J Bennett
Mr and Mrs Sidney Corob
Mr Michael Godbee
Mrs M C Godwin
Mr David Ker
Mr Andrew D Law
Dr Abraham Marcus
Mr Thomas Mosimann
Mr and Mrs David Peacock
Mr Nigel J Stapleton
Mr Robin Symes
Mrs K L Troughton
Mrs Cynthia H Walton
Mrs Roger Waters
The Hon Mrs Simon
  Weinstock
Miss Elizabeth White
Mrs I Wolstenholme

Supporting Friends
Mr Richard B Allan
Mr Peter Allinson
Mr Ian Anstruther
Mr John R Asprey
Mrs Yvonne Barlow
Mr J M Bartos
Mrs Wendy Becker-Payton
Mrs Susan Besser
Mrs C W T Blackwell
Mr Christopher Boddington
Mr Peter Boizot MBE DL
Mrs J M Bracegirdle
Mr Cornelius Broere
Mrs Gertraud Brutsche
Mrs Anne Cadbury OBE JP
  DL
Mr W L Carey-Evans

Miss E M Cassin
Mr R A Cernis
Mr S Chapman
Mr W J Chapman
Mr and Mrs John Cleese
Mrs Ruth Cohen
Mrs D H Costopoulos
Mr and Mrs Chris Cotton
Mrs Saeda H Dalloul
Mr John Denham
Miss N J Dhanani
The Marquess of Douro
Mr Kenneth Edwards
Mr and Mrs John R Farmer
Mr Ian S Ferguson
Mrs R H Goddard
Mr Gavin Graham
Mrs Richard Grogan
Miss Julia Hazandras
Malcolm P Herring Esq
Mr R J Hoare
Mr Charles Howard
Mrs O Hudson
Mrs Manya Igel
Mr S Isern-Feliu
Mrs Ilse Jackson
Mrs Jane Jason
Mr Harold Joels
Mr and Mrs S D Kahan
Mrs P Keely
Mr and Mrs J Kessler
Mr D H Killick
Mr N R Killick
Mr Peter W Kininmonth
Mrs Joan Lavender
Mr and Mrs David Leathers
Mr Owen Luder CBE, PRIBA,
  FRSA
Mr Donald A Main
Ms Rebecca Marek
The Hon Simon Marks
Mrs Janet Marsh
Mr J B H Martin
Mrs Gillian M S McIntosh
Mr J Moores
Mrs A Morgan
Miss Kim Nicholson
Mrs E M Oppenheim
  Sandelson
Mr Brian Oury
Mrs J Pappworth
Mrs M C S Philip
Mrs Anne Phillips
Mr Ralph Picken
Mr William Plapinger
Mr Benjamin Pritchett-
  Brown
Mr Clive Richards
Mr F Peter Robinson
Mr D S Rocklin

Mrs A Rodman
Mr and Mrs O Roux
The Hon Sir Steven Runciman
  CH
Dr Susan Saga
Sir Robert and Lady Sainsbury
Mr G Salmanowitz
Mr Anthony Salz
Mr and Mrs Julian Schild
Dr I B Schulenburg
Mrs Bernard L Schwartz
Mrs Lisa Schwartz
Mrs D Scott
Mr Mark Shelmerdine
R J Simmons Esq CBE
Mr John H M Sims
Miss L M Slattery
Dr and Mrs M L Slotover
Mrs P Spanoghe
Professor Philip Stott
Mr James Stuart
Mr J A Tackaberry
Mr G C A Thorn
Mrs Andrew Trollope
Mr and Mrs Vignoles
Mrs Catherine I Vlasto
Mr and Mrs Ludovic de
  Walden
Miss J Waterous
Mrs Claire Weldon
Mr Frank S Wenstrom
Mrs Ann S Wilberding
Mr David Wilson
Mr W M Wood
Mr R M Woodhouse
Ms Karen S Yamada
Dr Alain Youell
Mrs Pia Zombanakis
*and others who wish to remain
anonymous*

Corporate Membership of the Royal Academy of Arts

Launched in 1988, the Royal Academy's Corporate Membership Scheme has proved highly successful. With 115 members it is now the largest membership scheme in Europe. Corporate membership offers company benefits to staff and clients and access to the Academy's facilities and resources. Each member pays an annual subscription to be a Member (£6,000) or Patron (£20,000). Participating companies recognise the importance of promoting the visual arts. Their support is vital to the continuing success of the Academy.

Corporate Membership Scheme

Corporate Patrons
Arthur Andersen
Bloomberg LP
B.P. Amoco p.l.c.
Debenhams plc
The Economist Group
GE Group
Glaxo Wellcome plc
Merrill Lynch Mercury
Morgan Stanley International
Rover Group Ltd

Honorary Corporate Patrons
Ernst & Young

Corporate Members
Alliance & Leicester plc
Apax Partners & Co. Ltd.
Athenaeum Hotel
Aukett Associates
AXA Sun Life plc
Bacon and Woodrow
Bank of America
Bankers Trust
Banque Nationale de Paris
Barclays plc
Bear, Stearns International
  Ltd
BG plc
BICC plc
BMP DDB Limited
Bovis Europe
BT plc
British Airways plc
British Alcan Aluminium plc
British American Tobacco plc

The Brunswick Group
Bunzl plc
CB Hillier Parker
CJA (Management
  Recruitment Consultants)
  Limited
Christie's
Chase Manhattan Bank
Chubb Insurance Company of
  Europe
Clayton Dubilier and Rice
  Limited
Clifford Chance
Colefax and Fowler Group
Cookson Group plc
Credit Agricole Indosuez
Credit Suisse First Boston
The Daily Telegraph plc
Deutsche Bank AG
Diageo plc
De Beers
E D & F Man Limited
  Charitable Trust
Esprit Telecom
Eversheds
Foreign & Colonial
  Management plc
Gartmore Investment
  Management plc
Granada Group PLC
HSBC plc
Hay Management Consultants
  Limited
H J Heinz Company Limited
ICI
John Lewis Partnership
King Sturge and Co.
Kleinwort Benson Charitable
  Trust
Korn/Ferry International
KPMG
Kvaerner Construction Ltd
Land Securities PLC
Lex Service PLC
Linklaters & Paines
Marks & Spencer
Marsh Ltd
McKinsey & Co.
Mitchell Madison Group
MoMart Ltd
Newton Investment
  Management Ltd
Ove Arup Partnership
Paribas
Pearson plc
The Peninsular and Oriental
  Steam Navigation Company
Pentland Group plc
PricewaterhouseCoopers
Provident Financial plc

Robert Fleming & Co. Ltd
Rothmans UK Holdings
  Limited
The Royal Bank of Scotland
Sainsbury's PLC
Salomon Smith Barney
Schroders plc
Sea Containers Ltd.
SG
Slaughter and May
SmithKline Beecham
The Smith & Williamson
  Group
Sotheby's
Sun Life and Provincial
  Holdings plc
TI Group plc
Trowers & Hamlins
Unilever UK Limited
United Airlines
Wilde Sapte

Honorary Corporate Members
All Nippon Airways Co. Ltd
Goldman Sachs International
  Limited
London First
Old Mutual
Reuters Limited
Yakult UK Limited

Corporate Associates
Bass PLC
The General Electric
  Company plc
Macfarlanes

Sponsors of Past Exhibitions

The President and Council
of the Royal Academy thanks
sponsors of past exhibitions
for their support. Sponsors
of major exhibitions during
the last ten years have included
the following:

Alitalia
  Italian Art in the 20th
  Century, 1989
Allied Trust Bank
  Africa: The Art of a
  Continent, 1995*
*Anglo-American Corporation of
South Africa*
  Africa: The Art of a
  Continent, 1995*
A.T. Kearney
  Summer Exhibition, 1999
The Banque Indosuez Group
  Pissarro: The Impressionist
  and the City, 1993
Banque Indosuez and W I Carr
  Gauguin and The School of
  Pont-Aven: Prints and
  Paintings, 1989
BBC Radio One
  The Pop Art Show, 1991
BMW (GB) Limited
  Georges Rouault: The Early
  Years, 1903–1920. 1993
  David Hockney: A Drawing
  Retrospective, 1995*
British Airways
  Africa: The Art of a
  Continent, 1995
BT
  Hokusai, 1991
Cantor Fitzgerald
  From Manet to Gauguin:
  Masterpieces from Swiss
  Private Collections, 1995
The Capital Group Companies
  Drawings from the J Paul
  Getty Museum, 1993
Chilstone Garden Ornaments
  The Palladian Revival: Lord
  Burlington and His House
  and Garden at Chiswick,
  1995
Christie's
  Frederic Leighton 1830–1896,
  1996
  Sensation: Young British
  Artists from The Saatchi
  Collection, 1997

Classic FM
  Goya: Truth and Fantasy,
  The Small Paintings, 1994
  The Glory of Venice: Art in
  the Eighteenth Century, 1994
Corporation of London
  Living Bridges, 1996
*The Dai-Ichi Kangyo Bank
Limited*
  222nd Summer Exhibition,
  1990
The Daily Telegraph
  American Art in the 20th
  Century, 1993
De Beers
  Africa: The Art of a
  Continent, 1995
Deutsche Morgan Grenfell
  Africa: The Art of a
  Continent, 1995
Diageo plc
  230th Summer Exhibition,
  1998
Digital Equipment Corporation
  Monet in the '90s: The Series
  Paintings, 1990
The Drue Heinz Trust
  The Palladian Revival: Lord
  Burlington and His House
  and Garden at Chiswick,
  1995
  Denys Lasdun, 1997
  Tadao Ando: Master of
  Minimalism, 1998
The Dupont Company
  American Art in the 20th
  Century, 1993
The Economist
  Inigo Jones Architect, 1989
Edwardian Hotels
  The Edwardians and After:
  Paintings and Sculpture from
  the Royal Academy's
  Collection, 1900–1950. 1990
Elf
  Alfred Sisley, 1992
Ernst & Young
  Monet in the 20th Century,
  1999
Fiat
  Italian Art in the 20th
  Century, 1989
Financial Times
  Inigo Jones Architect, 1989
Fondation Elf
  Alfred Sisley, 1992
Ford Motor Company Limited
  The Fauve Landscape:
  Matisse, Derain, Braque and
  Their Circle, 1991

Friends of the Royal Academy
  Victorian Fairy Painting, 1997
Gamlestaden
  Royal Treasures of Sweden,
  1550–1700. 1989
*The Jacqueline and Michael Gee
Charitable Trust*
  LIFE? or THEATRE? The
  Work of Charlotte Salomon,
  1999
Générale des Eaux Group
  Living Bridges, 1996
Glaxo Wellcome plc
  Great Impressionist and
  other Master Paintings from
  the Emil G Buhrle
  Collection, Zurich, 1991
  The Unknown Modigliani,
  1994
Goldman Sachs International
  Alberto Giacometti,
  1901–1966. 1996
  Picasso: Painter and Sculptor
  in Clay, 1998
The Guardian
  The Unknown Modigliani,
  1994
Guinness PLC (see Diageo plc)
  Twentieth-Century Modern
  Masters: The Jacques and
  Natasha Gelman Collection,
  1990
  223rd Summer Exhibition,
  1991
  224th Summer Exhibition,
  1992
  225th Summer Exhibition,
  1993
  226th Summer Exhibition,
  1994
  227th Summer Exhibition,
  1995
  228th Summer Exhibition,
  1996
  229th Summer Exhibition,
  1997
Guinness Peat Aviation
  Alexander Calder, 1992
Harpers & Queen
  Georges Rouault: The Early
  Years, 1903–1920. 1993
  Sandra Blow, 1994
  David Hockney: A Drawing
  Retrospective, 1995*
  Roger de Grey, 1996
The Headley Trust
  Denys Lasdun, 1997

The Henry Moore Foundation
  Alexander Calder, 1992
  Africa: The Art of a
  Continent, 1995
The Independent
  The Art of Photography
  1839–1989. 1989
  The Pop Art Show, 1991
  Living Bridges, 1996
Industrial Bank of Japan, Limited
  Hokusai, 1991
Intercraft Designs Limited
  Inigo Jones Architect, 1989
The Kleinwort Benson Group
  Inigo Jones Architect, 1989
Land Securities PLC
  Denys Lasdun, 1997
Logica
  The Art of Photography,
  1839–1989. 1989
The Mail on Sunday
  Royal Academy Summer
  Season, 1992
  Royal Academy Summer
  Season, 1993
Marks & Spencer
  Royal Academy Schools
  Premiums, 1994
  Royal Academy Schools Final
  Year Show, 1994*
Martini & Rossi Ltd
  The Great Age of British
  Watercolours, 1750–1880.
  1993
Paul Mellon KBE
  The Great Age of British
  Watercolours, 1750–1880.
  1993
Mercury Communications
  The Pop Art Show, 1991
Merrill Lynch
  American Art in the 20th
  Century, 1993*
Midland Bank plc
  The Art of Photography
  1839–1989. 1989
  RA Outreach Programme,
  1992–1996
  Lessons in Life, 1994
Minorco
  Africa: The Art of a
  Continent, 1995
*Mitsubishi Estate Company UK
Limited*
  Sir Christopher Wren and
  the Making of St Paul's, 1991
Natwest Group
  Nicolas Poussin 1594–1665.
  1995

301

The Nippon Foundation
Hiroshige: Images of Mist,
Rain, Moon and Snow, 1997
Olivetti
Andrea Mantegna, 1992
Park Tower Realty Corporation
Sir Christopher Wren and
the Making of St Paul's, 1991
Peterborough United Football Club
Art Treasures of England: The
Regional Collections, 1997
*Premiercare (National
Westminster Insurance Services)*
Roger de Grey, 1996*
RA Exhibition Patrons Group
Chagall: Love and the Stage,
1998
Kandinsky, 1999
Redab (UK) Ltd
Wisdom and Compassion:
The Sacred Art of Tibet, 1992
Reed International plc
Sir Christopher Wren and
the Making of St Paul's, 1991
*Republic National Bank of New
York*
Sickert: Paintings, 1992
The Royal Bank of Scotland
Braque: The Late Works,
1997*
Premiums, 1997
Premiums, 1998
Premiums, 1999
Royal Academy Schools Final
Year Show, 1996
Royal Academy Schools Final
Year Show, 1997
Royal Academy Schools Final
Year Show, 1998
The Sara Lee Foundation
Odilon Redon: Dreams and
Visions, 1995
Sea Containers Ltd
The Glory of Venice: Art in
the Eighteenth Century, 1994
Silhouette Eyewear
Egon Schiele and His
Contemporaries: From the
Leopold Collection, Vienna,
1990
Wisdom and Compassion:
The Sacred Art of Tibet, 1992
Sandra Blow, 1994
Africa: The Art of a
Continent, 1995
Société Générale, UK
Gustave Caillebotte: The
Unknown Impressionist,
1996*

Société Générale de Belgique
Impressionism to Symbolism:
The Belgian Avant-Garde
1880–1900. 1994
Spero Communications
Royal Academy Schools Final
Year Show, 1992
Texaco
Selections from the Royal
Academy's Private
Collection, 1991
Thames Water Plc
Thames Water Habitable
Bridge Competition, 1996
The Times
Wisdom and Compassion:
The Sacred Art of Tibet, 1992
Drawings from the J Paul
Getty Museum, 1993
Goya: Truth and Fantasy,
The Small Paintings, 1994
Africa: The Art of a
Continent, 1995
Time Out
Sensation: Young British
Artists from The Saatchi
Collection, 1997
Tractabel
Impressionism to Symbolism:
The Belgian Avant-Garde
1880–1900. 1994
Unilever
Frans Hals, 1990
Union Minière
Impressionism to Symbolism:
The Belgian Avant-Garde
1880–1900. 1994
Vistech International Ltd
Wisdom and Compassion:
The Sacred Art of Tibet, 1992
Yakult UK Ltd
RA Outreach Programme,
1997–2000

* Recipients of a Pairing
Scheme Award, managed
by Arts + Business.
Arts + Business is funded by
the Arts Council of England
and the Department for
Culture, Media and Sport.

Other Sponsors

Sponsors of events,
publications and other
items in the past two years:

Asia House
Atlantic Group plc
Elizabeth Blackadder RA
British Airways Plc
BT Amoco p.l.c.
Corona Beer
Bernard Dunstan RA PPRWA
Green's Restaurant
Mr and Mrs David Haynes
HSBC Holdings plc
Hulton Getty Picture
Collection
John Doyle Construction
Allen Jones RA
KLM UK
The Leading Hotels of the
World
Met Bar
Mikimoto
Morgan Stanley Dean Witter
Old Mutual
Polaroid (UK) Limited
Rothmans UK Holdings Ltd
Royal & Sun Alliance Insurance
Group plc
Salomon Smith Barney
Taittinger
Time Out
ZFL